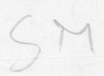

# QUEEN VICTORIA'S RELATIONS

# Queen Victoria's Relations

by

MERIEL BUCHANAN

*With* 10 *half-tone illustrations*

CASSELL & CO LTD

LONDON

CASSELL & CO LTD
37/38 St. Andrew's Hill, Queen Victoria Street,
London, E.C.4.

*and at*

31/34 George IV Bridge, Edinburgh
210 Queen Street, Melbourne
26/30 Clarence Street, Sydney
Haddon Hall, City Road, Auckland, N.Z.
1068 Broadview Avenue, Toronto 6
420 West 45th Street, New York 36
Avenida 9 de Julho 1138, São Paulo
Galeria Güemes, Escritorio 518/520 Florida 165, Buenos Aires
Haroon Chambers, South Napier Road, Karachi
15 Graham Road, Ballard Estate, Bombay 1
17 Central Avenue P.O. Dharamtala, Calcutta
P.O. Box 275, Cape Town
P.O. Box 1386, Salisbury, S. Rhodesia
P.O. Box 959, Accra, Gold Coast
25 rue Henri Barbusse, Paris 5e
Islands Brygge 5, Copenhagen

*First published*, 1954

Set in 12 on 13 pt. Bembo type and
printed in Great Britain by
J. W. Arrowsmith Ltd, Quay Street and Small Street, Bristol
F. 1153

# Foreword

(By Anna Stancioff, *née* Comtesse de Grenaud, Lady-in-Waiting to Princess Clementine, and Mistress of the Robes to Princess Marie Louise, and Queen Eleanor of Bulgaria.)

I FIRST met the author of this most interesting book in 1907, as the shy and lovely daughter of the British Minister at Sofia, Sir George Buchanan, the courteous and cultured diplomatist who was to hold the post of Ambassador at St. Petersburg during the First World War. His wife, Lady Georgina, daughter of Lord Bathurst, was then at the height of her beauty, and the three gracious inmates of the British Legation were much loved in Bulgaria.

Miss Buchanan already gave promise of literary talent and interest in history. She has since written several successful books, and is now giving us a series of remarkable portraits of royal personages she has been associated with during her life. I have had the privilege of meeting most of them myself over a span of years considerably longer than Miss Buchanan's, and this fact allows me to say that Miss Buchanan has evoked with great powers of observation the true character of each of her illustrious sitters.

Queen Marie of Roumania, Princess Alice of Greece, the Arch-Duchess Stephanie, the Empress Frederick, and many more—all so different, and yet all lit by the same light, all sharing the same responsibilities, all belonging to that past world, never to return, and of which Miss Buchanan has re-created for us the forgotten emotion and atmosphere. But she has also emphasized the existence of yet another link between her royal personages—the strongest—that of their greatness in tribulation and distress. Passing abruptly as they did from the secure golden days to the saddest years of the history of mankind, each of them seems to have grown in stature and never to have complained.

The tragic consequences of two shattering world wars; misery, mourning, famine, new instruments of destruction, ill-treatment, new conditions, did not dismay Miss Buchanan's royal friends. Most of the thrones around which they revolved have been swept away; monarchy nowadays in some countries is but a dam which—as fate wills—retains, or lets pass, the flow of events; life is uncertain for the great and for the humble alike; but I feel that the incentive to work for a better future is thereby all the stronger.

It is interesting and profitable to return to the past, and Miss Buchanan helps us to do so by new and varied paths. We are left without nostalgia for the old days, but with deep admiration for Miss Buchanan's heroes and heroines, for their good deeds, carried out with so much abnegation, their unimpaired quality of courage, and their true grandeur in the heaviest trials.

These full and interesting lives should not be forgotten, and we are grateful to the author for presenting us with such excellent portraits for our gallery of hallowed memories.

# Contents

|  |  | page |
|---|---|---|
| PROLOGUE | . . . . . . . . | I |
| THE EMPRESS FREDERICK | . . . . . | 5 |
| THE GRAND DUKE ERNST LUDWIG OF HESSE | . . | 23 |
| PRINCESS ALICE OF HESSE | . . . . . | 47 |
| CROWN PRINCESS STEPHANIE OF AUSTRIA | . . . | 67 |
| THE GRAND DUCHESS ELIZABETH | . . . . | 88 |
| QUEEN MARIE OF ROUMANIA | . . . . . | 113 |
| KING FERDINAND OF BULGARIA | . . . . | 139 |
| PRINCESS ALICE OF GREECE | . . . . . | 165 |
| THE GRAND DUCHESS CYRIL OF RUSSIA | . . . | 193 |
| THE GRAND DUCHESS OLGA NICHOLAIEVNA | . . | 207 |
| BIBLIOGRAPHY | . . . . . . . | 235 |
| INDEX | . . . . . . . . | 237 |

# List of Illustrations

*facing page*

The Princess Royal and Prince Frederick William of
Prussia, at the time of their marriage (*Picture Post
Library*) . . . . . . . . 22

The Grand Duke Ernst Ludwig of Hesse with his daughter Princess Elizabeth (*Picture Post Library*) . . 23

Princess Alice, Grand Duchess of Hesse . . . 23

Princess Stephanie of Belgium and Crown Prince
Rudolf of Austria. (Unpublished photograph, by
courtesy of "Les Admirateurs de Leopold II. Groupe
Dynastique de Belge"). . . . . . 54

The Grand Duchess Serge of Russia . . . . 55

The Grand Duchess Olga Nicholaievna of Russia . 55

Queen Marie of Roumania. (Unpublished photograph
by kind permission of Lady Dering) . . . 150

King Ferdinand of Bulgaria . . . . . 151

Princess Alice of Greece . . . . . . 182

The Grand Duchess Cyril of Russia . . . . 183

# ACKNOWLEDGEMENTS

FOR graciously consenting to read and approve the type-script of the chapter dealing with her life, I wish to express my deepest thanks to Her Royal Highness, Princess Andrew of Greece.

At the same time I wish to express my gratitude to Sir John Murray for giving me permission to quote passages from the *Letters of Queen Victoria* and the *Letters of Princess Alice*. My thanks are also due to Messrs Macmillan, for allowing me to quote extracts from the *Letters of the Empress Frederick*, to Messrs Methuen, the publishers of Count Egon Corti's book *The Downfall of Three Dynasties*, who have allowed me to use some of that material, and to Messrs Hurst & Blackett, who have given me permission to reprint a passage from Walburga, Lady Paget's book *Embassies of Other Days*.

I am most sincerely grateful to Madame Stancioff, for so kindly writing the Foreword to this book, and I wish also to thank those friends who have helped by giving me various information, especially Nadejda Lady Muir, Countess Klein-michel, Baroness Buxhoevenden, Miss Souter, and finally Monsieur Luchie, who took great trouble in obtaining the photograph of Princess Stephanie.

# Prologue

AT a dinner, a little while ago, the son of the house, a boy of fifteen, broke into the conversation about the present political situation, with the sententious remark: "In my opinion the Victorian era is absurdly overrated. It lacked the freedom and vision of the present day. It was hidebound and hypocritical, and frightfully humdrum."

That may be the opinion of some unthinking youth, and of a certain type who in their own minds are firmly convinced that everything that belongs to the past must, *ipso facto*, be evil, and that this "brave new world" in which they have had the luck to be born is unparalleled in its perfection. But those of us who can remember the late Victorian era have still, I think, a wistful regret for those spacious days, which, although they may have had many imperfections, yet possessed a certain grace and dignity, which is quite certainly lacking in the prevailing drabness, the crude manners, and the deafening clamour of this modern age.

Victorian England! Sleepy little villages, with no strident discord of the radio or of television echoing out of the windows, no chain-stores to oust the quaint little shops kept by elderly ladies, where everything could be bought, from stamps, to bull's-eyes, candles, or a reel of cotton; no cinemas to fill the minds of the children with visions of glamorous Hollywood luxury, or the spurious excitement of crime. Old country estates passing on from father to son, their hospitable doors always open, little dreaming that their days were numbered, that they would soon fall under the auctioneer's hammer, be turned into schools or asylums, or occupied by some Government Department caring nothing for their old traditions or the memories which still haunted their panelled rooms.

[ 1 ]

The jingle of hansom cabs in the London streets, the melancholy wail of German bands in the squares. Maids in clean print dresses, and white caps, washing the front-door steps, toiling up endless flights of stairs with brightly polished cans of hot water, or buckets of coal for the bedroom fires. The fragrance of eggs and bacon drifting up from the halls. Family prayers in chilly dining-rooms. Smartly-turned-out carriages in Hyde Park. Church parade on Sundays. Brass bedsteads, oil-lamps and candles, the lack of many luxuries which now seem indispensable, but in spite of this a solid sense of security and comfort which seemed to make each house a stronghold of its own.

And at Balmoral, at Osborne, at Windsor, or in Buckingham Palace, a diminutive lady in black silk dresses, holding in her small, plump hands the destinies of a great empire, a lady whom Disraeli once called "A Mother of Nations", with children, grandchildren, nephews and nieces in every country of Europe, who was "Darling Mama", "Grandmama Queen", or "Dearest Aunt or Cousin" to somebody in every capital. An almost fabulous personality, surrounded by an aura of majesty. A woman whose wishes had to be obeyed, whose little nod of approbation was sought after, whose censure was dreaded. "The most unparalleled Grandmama, as none ever existed," the Emperor William wrote to Sir Frank Lascelles, the British Ambassador in Berlin, when the Queen lay dying. A woman whose passing left, not only in England, but all over the world, a void which nothing, and no one, could ever fill.

It was impossible to come in contact with her without feeling her power. Instinctively all those who were admitted to her presence approached her with quiet footsteps and hushed voices, and although they may sometimes have criticized her, or even perhaps have ridiculed her in their thoughts, they all, when they came face to face with her, were conscious of a feeling of awe.

She could be dictatorial, very often petulant, occasionally

extremely disagreeable, and certainly those, who for one reason or another had been rebuked by her, never forgot the supreme unpleasantness of the moment. But at the same time her thoughtfulness and her consideration for others, especially as she got older, was amazing. She never forgot a name or a face. She always remembered if anyone was in trouble. She always took a keen, personal interest in the welfare of her staff.

During the years my father was accredited to Darmstadt as Chargé d'Affaires he was in frequent communication with the Queen, chiefly owing to the strained relations which existed between her two grandchildren the Grand Duke and Grand Duchess of Hesse, and she would always send for him, when he was in England, in order to discuss the situation. On one occasion, when he was only over for a few days, she sent him a telegram informing him that she wished to see him, but adding that, as she knew he was very busy and had very little time, he was to fix the day when it would be convenient for him to come to Osborne.

Another time, when my father and mother were invited to Windsor, they had to leave me in my grandmother's house, with suspected pneumonia, and several times during the week-end the Queen sent messages of inquiry to London, in order to allay my mother's anxiety, sending me also a big box of flowers from her gardens.

One summer afternoon, when the Grand Duke and Grand Duchess of Hesse were staying at Buckingham Palace, I remember being asked to tea with their little daughter, Princess Elizabeth. The room she had been given as a nursery faced on to the gardens at the back of the palace, and suddenly, in the middle of the game we were playing, she darted out of the open window on to the balcony. "Granny Gran," I heard her call out, and seeing her leaning over the balustrade in a perilous manner, followed her quickly to catch hold of the pink sash round her waist; looking over her shoulder, I saw just below in the garden, a tall Indian leading a cream-coloured pony

[ 3 ]

harnessed to a low kind of bath-chair, and inside the chair a little old lady, with a black shawl round her shoulders, and a black hat tied with ribbons under her chin.

"Granny Gran, I'm here!" Princess Elizabeth called out again, dancing up and down in her excitement. The little old lady looked up, and I caught just a glimpse of her face, and her fleeting smile. "Is that you, my precious? Be careful you don't fall." Her voice with its melodious youthfulness almost startled me, and I gazed after the pony-carriage as it went on its way, with eyes widened with wonder.

Just an ordinary old lady in a bath-chair, huddled in shawls. So the captious might say. But was she so ordinary? Was there not something, on that summer's day so long ago, that communicated itself to my childish mind, leaving me with a vivid, unforgettable memory.

A Mother of Nations. The Grandmother of Europe. A great Queen, and also, in spite of her mistakes, a woman with a wise, far-seeing judgement, a firm, undeviating determination never to see her country lowered or defeated.

"Prince Bismarck", she wrote on a dispatch my father once saw in the Foreign Office, "is treating England as if she were a Second-Rate Power. This makes the *Queen's blood boil*." And in 1879 she wrote to Disraeli, "Never let the Army and Navy down so low, so as to be obliged to go to great expense in a hurry . . . The true economy will be to be always ready. . . It will prevent war."

# The Empress Frederick

IN 1851 the young Prince Frederick William of Prussia had come to London for the Great Exhibition in Hyde Park, had met Queen Victoria and the Prince Consort, and had made the acquaintance of their eldest daughter, the Princess Royal, called Vicky by her family. She was eleven years old at the time, a fresh-faced little girl with sparkling blue-green eyes, completely unselfconscious, and full of a bubbling vitality. The tall, grave young Prussian Prince had been enchanted by her quick mind, her sense of humour, her spontaneous enjoyment of life, and four years later he came again to England, went to stay at Balmoral, and although the Princess Royal was only fifteen, begged permission to propose to her, riding with her over the Scottish moors, and giving her a piece of white heather.

The announcement of the engagement was not received altogether well in Germany. It was regarded with deep suspicion by both France and Russia, and was not popular in England, *The Times* even expressing a doubt that the policies of England and Prussia might at some future date present a painful alternative to the Princess. The Prince Consort was, however, overjoyed that his eldest—and favourite—daughter should be given such golden opportunities, for Prince Frederick William was heir apparent to the throne of Prussia, his father the Crown Prince, acting as Regent for the old king, who was childless and practically insane. The day might well come, Prince Albert thought, when his long-cherished dream would be fulfilled, and Prussia would become the head of a great united German Empire.

During the next two years Prince Albert painstakingly prepared his daughter for her great position, instructing her on the history of Germany, its laws and traditions, guiding her mind with his liberal principles, his exalted ideals of constitutional government. But when, in January 1858, he saw her drive away with her husband in a whirling snowstorm, he was hardly able to contain his grief, realizing how much he was going to miss her, readily agreeing with his wife when she said she could not bear to go near the corridor leading to Vicky's former rooms.

The Queen had been exceedingly annoyed when the Prussian Court had suggested that the marriage should take place in Berlin. She had replied with icy firmness that it was out of the question, and that, whatever had been the custom of Prussian princes in the past, it was not every day that one of them married a daughter of the Queen of England. She had not thought that Prince Frederick William's father had shown any signs of the constitutional ideals Prince Albert said would one day lead an enlightened Germany. She had heard that the Prussian Court was bound by ancient, almost barbarous rules of etiquette. She wondered uneasily how Vicky, with her sense of humour, her quick, impulsive nature, her sometimes regrettable lack of tact, would conform to the formality, the haughty arrogance that had been so manifest among the entourage of the Crown Prince at the wedding.

We do not know what the young English Princess first thought of Berlin, when she arrived on that bitterly cold January day, and drove in a glass coach through the flag-bedecked streets. Did she see in this big, arrogant city, towering over the sandy Brandenburg plain, the "cunningly wrought unimaginative monster", described by Emil Ludwig, "where everything that was not expressly permitted was forbidden"? Did she see in the crowds who filled the streets, her future enemies and detractors, a hard-working, hard-headed race, with no tenderness in their nature, and a rather offensive sense of humour? Or, as she drove down the broad avenue between the lime-trees that had been planted by the Great Elector in the seventeenth century, did she see it all transfigured by love for her fair-haired, blue-eyed husband?

Her first remark when she arrived at the palace, where the royal family waited to welcome her, won for her golden opinions; for when the Queen asked if she was not frozen after her long drive, she answered with one of her quick, radiant smiles, "Completely. All except my heart." But unfortunately this first good impression was only transitory. Accustomed to the cosy warmth of her English homes, the blazing fires, the bright-carpeted passages, the solid comfort that pervaded the rooms, she found the old Berlin Schloss inexpressibly gloomy, and was not slow in expressing her dissatisfaction with the apartments that had been allotted her. They were dark and dingy, and full of icy draughts. She believed they were haunted, for there had been many unexplained sounds and movements. The plumbing left much to be desired, there was no bathroom, and by the time cans of hot water were brought to her room, they were nearly always cold.

And the relentless etiquette, the outdated conventions, the uncompromising rules that governed every hour of the day, roused all her independent spirit to revolt, a revolt she took no pains to conceal, openly expressing her amused contempt. When the old Queen once rebuked her because she had sneezed during an endless Court ceremony, she answered pertly, "But I have a cold, Ma'am." Upon which the Queen explained that it made no difference. It was not permitted to sneeze in the presence of a Sovereign. Looking rather like her mother, Vicky drew herself up, her clear voice ringing through the room as she replied, "We do not have customs like that in our Court at home."

That was her initial mistake, always to speak of England as "home". It profoundly irritated her father-in-law, it aroused the animosity of the Court, and because she said it so often it became generally known, and was freely commented upon. When the engagement of Prince Frederick William was an-

[ 7 ]

nounced, Bismarck, writing to a friend, had expressed his dislike of the "English" in the marriage, and already in Berlin they were beginning to call the Princess "Die Engländerinn" (the Englishwoman) pronouncing it with a sharp hostility as if it were something discreditable.

There can be no doubt that she offended many people by her impulsive thoughtlessness, trained as she had been by her father in political matters and encouraged to air her views, she did not always think before speaking, and was not always discreet in expressing her dislike of Prussian boots, of the lack of baths, the reactionary ideas and arrogant manners of the old nobility. The constant frustrations that confined her, tried her patience to the utmost, and when she and her husband were given the Palace of Unter den Linden to live in, and she asked for certain renovations to be made, and found the work continually held up by the old King, who gave his permission one day and withdrew it the next, she did not try to hide her irritation with these obstructions to her wishes, and the out-of-date conventions that hemmed her in.

The birth of a son in January 1859, and the fact that she nearly lost her life, greatly increased the Princess's popularity, but her complete happiness was dimmed when it was discovered that the baby had a deformed and crippled arm, and for a time she could not rid herself of the conviction that this was in some way her fault. Her letters to her mother were, however, full of delight that her first child was a boy, and full of praise for her son's strength, his liveliness and good looks. "I feel very proud of him", she said, "and very proud of being a Mama." That summer, also, the New Palace in Potsdam became her home, and from the first she loved the pleasant white house which she was allowed to furnish herself, and was able almost to imagine herself back in England, revelling in the momentary freedom from restrictions, the light rooms leading out into the park, and, above all, perhaps, the distance from Berlin.

The death of the old King in January 1861 made Frederick William Crown Prince of Prussia, but when Bismarck was recalled from the Embassy in Paris and made Minister President and Minister of Foreign Affairs, the Crown Prince realized that all hopes of influencing his father and of bringing in a more constitutional form of government were at an end. From the first Bismarck openly proclaimed that he was going to treat "Die Engländerinn" as negligible, regarding her love of talking politics, and her liberal ideas, as the foolishness of a head-strong, stupid girl, who did not know what she was talking about.

The Crown Princess had fully realized that in Bismarck she had a formidable opponent, so when Prince Albert died, in December 1861, she felt bereft of all support, unable now to turn to her father for his wise advice in her increasing difficulties, momentarily losing all her courage and self-reliance, almost as prostrate as her mother was in her grief.

In March, 1863, she was given permission to go to England, and was able to attend the marriage of her brother, the Prince of Wales, to Princess Alexandra of Denmark. She had taken her son, Prince William, with her, and her brother Leopold was instructed to look after him during the ceremony in St. George's Chapel, Windsor, a task he evidently did not find too easy, for when he was asked how "Dear little William" had behaved, he replied rather bitterly that his nephew had bitten his leg.

On their return to Germany, the Crown Prince and his wife found that the King was falling more and more under Bismarck's influence and was contemplating altering the Prussian constitution and curbing the freedom of the Press. Deeply disturbed by what he considered to be a reactionary move, the Crown Prince, in a speech he made at Danzig in June, openly declared that he was not in agreement with this policy, and as a result received a furious letter from his father, commanding him to retract what he had said, charging him with disobedience, and warning him that if he continued he would be deprived of his army command and his place on the Council.

The incident caused a tremendous stir in Germany. For a time the Crown Prince and his wife were in a precarious position, deprived of several members of their suite, cold-shouldered by their relations, abused and criticized by the general public.

Greatly distressed by the letters she received from her daughter, Queen Victoria had shown one of them to Lord John Russell. When he said that the Crown Prince had shown great courage, and that the "hope of any future good" depended on his being able to persevere in the attitude he had adopted, she was somewhat comforted, but at the same time continued to be anxious, feeling that the position of her daughter and her son-in-law might be irretrievably damaged if they continued to antagonize the King and his powerful Minister. She was therefore greatly relieved when the Crown Prince yielded to his father's wishes, withdrew his proffered resignation, and agreed to make no further statement on constitutional matters, nor to voice his own opinion in any circumstances whatsoever.

The war with Schleswig-Holstein found the Crown Princess, for the first time, at variance with her relations in England, and especially with her brother the Prince of Wales, and she complained bitterly to her mother about the pro-Danish attitude of the British Press and, "the continual muddling and interfering of England in other people's affairs". When, two years later, Bismarck declared war on Austria, and she had to see her husband leave for the Front, to fight against her brother-in-law, Prince Louis of Hesse, and her cousin the King of Hanover, she declared that she was as proud of being a Prussian as of being an Englishwoman, and rejoiced in the defeat of Austria and the German states who had sided with her.

It was while her husband was away at the Front that her younger son, Prince Sigismund, died of meningitis, after only three days' illness, and in her sorrow she forgot all political differences and became only a woman, heartbroken at the loss of a child who, she told her mother, had been more to her than any of her other children, and in whom she had thought to see a likeness to her father.

By many writers, both English and German, the Crown Princess has been accused of despising her eldest son because of his crippled arm, of showing him no tenderness or understanding, and of making no secret of her preference for her younger children, in this way alienating the affection he might have given her and arousing in him the bitterness of a thwarted, frustrated nature. It has often been said that she showed a heartless inhumanity in forcing him to learn to ride, even though he suffered agonies at first, falling off over and over again because of his lack of balance; but she knew that in his position, as heir presumptive to the throne, it was essential that he should be able to sit a horse. She had to harden her heart to his suffering, and if she was sometimes unable to control her impatience, it can scarcely be wondered at. In the letters she wrote to the Queen, the constant references she makes to Prince William, the pride with which she speaks of his good looks, his intelligence, his patience and courage, show that she was not devoid of affection for her eldest son, and that in those years before he had attained manhood this affection was returned.

The question of the Spanish Succession raised the spectre of war again in Europe, and gave Bismarck the opportunity he sought, for he had encouraged the nomination of Prince Leopold of Hohenzollern to the throne of Spain fully realizing that it would arouse violent opposition in France, and when Prince Leopold, for the second time, refused to accept the proposed honour, and the Emperor Napoleon wrote a strong letter to King William requesting that the offer should not be renewed, Bismarck cunningly twisted the words of the King's reply in such a way as to give France an adequate reason for declaring war.

[ 11 ]

As soon as her third daughter, Princess Sophie, born June 14, 1870, had been christened, and her husband had left for the Front, the Crown Princess threw herself with her usual ebullient enthusiasm into working for the wounded, eventually obtaining permission to run a small hospital of her own in Homburg. But here again, she met with nothing but opposition, and received no thanks for the work she did. Because she was directing a hospital of her own, she was accused of running down the German medical system, of calling the doctors dirty, the nurses lazy and incompetent. Because she had expressed disapproval of the bombardment of Paris, she was called pro-French. Because anti-German articles appeared in the British Press, she was suspected of being in sympathy with the general feeling in England. "In Berlin", the Crown Prince wrote in his diary in December, 1870, "the order of the day is to vilify my wife." A few months later, writing to her mother, she spoke of the cruel and unjust accusations that had been heaped upon her, and of the many tears she had shed.

After the defeat of France, and the proclamation of King William as Emperor of Germany, things for a time went more smoothly, and when the Prince of Wales visited Berlin in June, 1874, in order to attend the confirmation of Prince William, the former tension between the brother and sister was completely forgotten, and the Crown Princess wrote and told her mother how kind, amiable and considerate "Dear Bertie" had been. "Sometimes", she added, "I feel too young for a mother with a son already confirmed, and then at times so old", and she continued to describe the ceremony of Prince William's confirmation, and to say how sad she felt that in two days' time he would be leaving for school, where he would stay for three years and from there go into the Army, while his brother, Prince Henry, went into the Navy. "It is", she said, "a kind of break-up. . . . I feel giving them up like this very much."

It was while studying at the University in Bonn that Prince William frequently went to stay at Darmstadt, with his aunt,

Princess Alice. His visits were not always welcomed by the little princesses of Hesse and their brother, who found him rather a disturbing element in their peaceful family circle. Although it is not generally known, there can be little doubt that he was greatly attracted to Princess Elizabeth of Hesse, but it is not certain whether she herself refused his proposal, or whether he ever actually asked for permission to marry her, but, judging from a letter the Crown Princess wrote to her mother, some years later, in which she said that it "had not been considered advisable for him to marry a cousin", there must at some time have been a question of their engagement.

Whatever Princess Elizabeth may have thought of her cousin, to Princess Augusta Victoria of Schleswig-Holstein-Sonderburg-Augustenburg he appeared as the hero of all a young girl's dreams. Dashing, vivacious, eagle-eyed, handsome, his restless exuberance and mercurial temperament fascinated her, even though she was at times puzzled and bewildered. Perhaps he was flattered by her all too evident adoration, perhaps he found her rosy-cheeked Germanic prettiness soothing, realizing that he would always be able to dominate her; he became engaged to her when he was only twenty-one, and married her in 1881.

After the death, in 1878, of her favourite sister, Princess Alice, tragedies and sorrows darkened the life of the Crown Princess, and when her youngest surviving son, Prince Waldemar, died in 1879, there was a note of profound sadness in her letters to her mother. "I thought", she said, "that I could have been of some use to him. He is gone. I can be of but limited use to Henry, and of none at all to William." For she was already becoming estranged from him, an estrangement that increased after his marriage. This state of things was encouraged by the Prince's wife, by the old Empress Augusta, and most of all by Bismarck who, fearing his parents' influence and the ideals of a more liberal, constitutional government, did all in his power to alienate the heir presumptive, instilling into him his own principles of autocratic power and military glory, flattering him, pushing him forward on all occasions, and in so doing completely ignoring the Crown Prince's senior rank and position. It was Prince William who, in August, 1886, was invited to the meeting of the Emperor of Austria and the Emperor of Germany at Gastein. It was Prince William, again, who was sent to Russia to attend the ceremonies for the coming of age of the Tsarevitch. And, being young, inexperienced and conceited, he failed to see that he was being used as a tool against his father by people far cleverer than himself. He thought he had been singled out because of his own knowledge and intelligence. He followed Bismarck blindly in all things, joining with him against his parents in opposing the marriage of his sister, Princess Victoria, to Alexander of Battenberg.

It was an inexpressible sorrow to his mother to see him turning against her, becoming hard and abrupt in his manner, ignoring any advice she ventured to give him, contradicting her almost rudely when she expressed an opinion. She, who a few years earlier had said, in one of her letters to the Queen, that there was a bond of love and confidence between them that nothing could destroy, now wrote in a very different strain. "One must guard against the fault of being annoyed with one's children for not being what one wished and hoped, what one wants them to be," she said in one of these letters. "One must learn to abandon dreams, and to take things as they come, and characters as they are. . . . But it ends in one's feeling rather solitary." In May, 1886, describing a meeting she had had with Prince William, she said sadly, "a little civility, kindness and 'empressement' go a long way, but I never get them from him. . . . It is very painful for a soft-hearted mama to feel so plainly that her own child does not care whether he sees her or no, whether she is well or ill."

Many other women have had to learn this hard lesson, but, for the Crown Princess, the tragedy was intensified by her unpopularity in Berlin, by the blaze of limelight always focused upon her, by the joy with which her enemies gloated over her discomfiture, and also by the adoration of the common people for her daughter-in-law, in whom they saw the German ideal of a perfect wife and mother, interested solely in her husband, her children and her household.

The year 1886 brought also to the Crown Princess the beginning of her beloved husband's illness, an illness that was to end in the irretrievable loss of all that he and she had dreamed of, when they at last became rulers of Germany.

The storm of abuse let loose upon her, and the accusation that she had refused to listen to the German doctors and had called in Morel Mackenzie, are well known, and have been written about time and again. But it has now been abundantly proved that it was the German doctors and not the Crown Princess who asked for Morel Mackenzie's opinion. When, in his mistaken diagnosis, he declared that the Crown Prince was not suffering from cancer of the throat and advised against an immediate operation, it is easy to understand that in her agony of mind she was ready to believe him, and that she clung desperately to the hope that an operation would not be necessary, and that some other cure might be found. During those long torturing months with the endless journeys from place to place, to Ems, to England, to Switzerland, to Venice, to Baveano, and finally to San Remo, she tried to keep up her courage, tried to hope that a miracle might happen, and because, for her husband's sake, she hid her harrowing anxiety and fears under an assumed cheerfulness, she was called indifferent and unfeeling, and was charged with callousness. It was said she had forced the Crown Prince to take part in the Jubilee festivities in London, and she was held responsible for his increasing illness, and blamed for keeping him so long away from Germany.

On March 9, 1888, the old Emperor William, who had come to be considered almost deathless, passed away, and it now became imperative for the new Emperor and Empress to leave the peace and sunshine of San Remo, and return to Berlin. It was a summons she had prayed would not come till the spring, dreading the effect of the bitter climate of Berlin. "Six weeks more might have set Fritz up," she said in a letter to Queen Victoria, still clinging to the forlorn hope that the illness was not fatal, still unable to believe that the man she loved so wholeheartedly was doomed. But when, before leaving San Remo, the Emperor, no longer able to speak, pinned his Order of the Black Eagle on her chest, and handed Morel Mackenzie a tablet on which he had written, "I thank you for making me live long enough to reward the valiant courage of my wife," she at last broke down, flinging herself in an agony of grief into her husband's arms.

The Emperor Frederick, who might, if he had lived, have saved not only Germany but Europe from disaster, reigned for only ninety-eight days, days which passed with terrible, implacable swiftness for his wife. In April, 1888, she had the consolation of a visit from her mother; and Bismarck, who had an interview with the Queen, conceded that "Grandmama had been quite sensible", for she had eventually agreed with him that, now that Prince Alexander of Battenberg had been forced to abdicate from the throne of Bulgaria, and was merely a private person, a marriage between him and Princess Victoria of Prussia was out of the question, and managed even to convince the Empress that the idea must be abandoned.

Early in May the Emperor insisted on being present at the marriage of his second son, Prince Henry, to Princess Irene of Hesse. A week later he asked to be taken to his old home, the New Palace at Potsdam, where he died on June 15, having, in a last interview, placed his wife's hand in the hand of Bismarck, his eyes raised in a mute and desperate appeal, praying him to look after her.

Hardly had his father breathed his last, when the new Emperor had the Palace surrounded with troops, forbidding all to enter or leave without permission, clattering through the rooms in his scarlet hussar's uniform, searching for the letters and diaries which had already been sent to England, turning everything upside down in his frenzied haste, totally regardless of the majesty of death, and the agony of the woman who knelt by her husband's body.

Realizing how strained the relations were between her daughter and her grandson, Queen Victoria wrote to the latter, begging him to be patient. "Bear with poor Mama", she said, "if she is sometimes irritated and excited. She does not mean it so. Think what months of agony and suspense, watching with broken and sleepless nights, she has gone through, and don't mind it."

But the Emperor William was too taken up with the splendour of his new position, to pay any attention to his grandmother, and Bismarck soon forgot the momentary emotion he had felt when he had seen the appeal in the tortured eyes of the dying Emperor. In July, scarcely a month after his father's death, William authorized the publication by Dr. Bergman of articles giving full descriptions of the beginning of his father's illness, and the treatment prescribed by Morel Mackenzie, and in August Bismarck publicly announced that the Emperor Frederick might have been saved if the German doctors had been listened to.

It was impossible for the Empress Frederick not to know that all over Germany people were saying that she had caused the death of the man for whose sake she would gladly have sacrificed her own life. The knowledge added to her grief, but she kept a proud and dignified silence, and only her letters to her mother show the seething resentment that consumed her. "I see others taking his place, knowing that they cannot fill it. . . . We had a mission, we were faithful to what we believed and knew to be right. We loved Germany, we wished to see her strong and great, not only with the sword, but in all that was righteous in culture, in progress, in liberty. We wished to see the people happy and free, growing and developing in all

[ 17 ]

that was good." As the campaign against her increased, and she was accused not only of having caused her husband's death but of giving German military secrets to France, she told the Queen that there were things she could never forget or forgive, and she could only pray that her three eldest children would one day have their eyes opened to the truth. "As William", she said in March, 1889, "does not feel for his mother, he cannot be surprised if she, who gave him so much love and care, now can only remember with pain that he is her son." When the Queen begged her to try an attempt at reconciliation with her son, she retorted that no efforts of hers would do any good. "There is no confidence, and he does not in the least understand me . . . he does not perceive how, during the whole year, he not only cruelly neglected me, but also allowed injuries and insults to be heaped on me."

Berlin, with its noise, its bustle, its antagonism, the Court where everything was so different from what she and her husband had planned; her son, with his pretentious pomposity and bluster; her daughter-in-law with her self-satisfied complacence, had all become abhorrent to the Empress Frederick, and after the marriage of her third daughter, Princess Sophie, to the Duke of Sparta, in 1889, she bought the Villa Reiss at Cronberg, not far from Homburg. The house, which had formerly belonged to a Manchester business man, was situated on a hill in the midst of the lovely Taunus forest, but it was small and ugly, and she had it pulled down, and gave an order to the German architect, Ihne, to build a new house after her own designs, a fact which caused her many detractors to say disparagingly that the building resembled an ordinary English country house and not a German castle.

The Empress had learnt to overcome her vehement impatience and intolerance, she had acquired self-control and resignation, and although her two remaining daughters had married in 1890 and 1893, and she was now alone, she filled her life with many activities and occupations, took a keen

[ 18 ]

interest in all that was going on in the world, never allowed herself to be bored, and never gave way to self-pity or useless regrets.

During the war between Greece and Turkey she once more came into opposition with her eldest son, whose hatred of Greece and the Greek royal family did not, as she said, "improve matters". She was constantly sending for my father, or asking him to forward letters and telegrams to Queen Victoria, begging England to intervene. But, in the midst of her anxiety over her daughter and son-in-law in Athens, she was always considerate. On one occasion she kept my father for the night at Cronberg, but the telegram she sent my mother, informing her that he would not be returning, was not delivered owing to some error in the Post Office. My mother, in consequence, spent a sleepless night. The Empress was greatly distressed, and wrote apologizing for being the cause of such terrible anxiety, promising that such a thing should never occur again.

My parents were frequently invited to stay at Friedrichshof, and on their first visit, my mother, who had not then realized the personal interest the Empress took in all her household arrangements, or her unconventional informality, was very much startled when, as she was dressing for dinner, the door suddenly opened and the Empress walked in unannounced. "I have only come to see if everything is in order in your room," she said, and then, laughing at my mother's confusion, "Don't be so shy, Lady Georgina. What does it matter if you are only half-dressed?"

Several times, when we were staying at Wolfsgarten, the Empress Frederick came to spend the day on her way to visit her youngest daughter, Princess Margaret, married to Prince Frederick Charles of Hesse. She was only about fifty-six at the time, but to me she seemed a very old lady, always dressed in the deepest black, bearing a strong resemblance to Queen Victoria, her hair, which had lost its former bright colour, parted in the middle and brushed plainly back from her face. I was at the time entirely ignorant of the tragedies of her life, nor did she show any signs of the impatience and furious resentment that had so often consumed her; her face had a calm tranquillity that, had I but known it, had come to her only after years of anguish. In spite of the many tears she had shed, her eyes still retained that blue-green colour that had been so remarkable when she was a girl, and still, when she smiled, lit up her face to sudden beauty. That smile always made me forget that she was either old, or an Empress, and when it was turned on me, as it sometimes was—for she loved children and would often call me up to talk to her—I was filled with elation, and probably, I am afraid, with conceit.

One year, during the time we were in Darmstadt, we took a house at Cronberg for the summer months, and I was taken several times to tea at Friedrichshof. To me it always seemed very large and imposing, and I have only a vague recollection of the actual building, of high rooms filled with beautiful furniture and pictures, and of windows opening on to a view of pine-clad mountains. The only things I remember vividly are the wide terrace, with steps leading down to the green lawns, and the lovely rose-garden which had been laid out by the Empress. I was never shy with her, and one afternoon, walking beside her through the flowering rose-bushes, I told her how that morning I had seen a snake in the woods. "Were you frightened?" she asked, and when I told her that I had been, she said that the snakes in Cronberg were not dangerous. "You must never be frightened," she continued; "you may meet many things in life which seem terrifying and insurmountable, but if you face them with courage, you will find that somehow you are able to bear them." Her words at the moment were certainly quite above my comprehension, but they must have somehow left a deep impression on my mind, for I have never forgotten either them or the woman, whose eyes, smiling down at me, held the shadows of so many past, almost intolerable sorrows.

On September 6, 1898, the Empress wrote and told her mother that the day before, when she was out riding, her horse had reared at a steam threshing-machine, that she had been thrown off, and her riding habit catching in the pommel, she had been dragged for several yards, and her right hand trampled on. "It was a very lucky escape," she added with undaunted gallantry. "Nothing of consequence happily, and I am all right today."

The consequences were however far more serious than anyone had at first suspected, for it was only a little later that she began to suffer from agonizing pains in the back, and although these were at first attributed to lumbago, they became increasingly severe and were finally diagnosed as cancer. Aware herself that there was no hope, for by now it was too late to operate, she faced what lay before her with her usual courage, telling everybody that it was only lumbago, allowing only her closest friends to know the full extent of her malady, still keeping up many of her activities, still taking an interest in world affairs and, between her bouts of pain, showing a smiling face to all who approached her.

She outlived Queen Victoria by only a few months, and when she died on August 5, 1901, her eldest son was with her. Some say that at the end they were reconciled, others pretend that she refused to forgive him; nobody knows what his thoughts were when it was all over. Was he overcome with that agonizing remorse that comes to some of us when it is too late to retract words spoken in anger, or to explain acts of unkindness? Did he remember the days of his childhood, and the love he had for his mother? Did he unavailingly regret that he had allowed himself to be influenced by people who, to further their own ends, had blackened her character and turned him against her?

"It is nine years ago today since Fritz was taken," Queen Victoria had written in her Journal on June 15, 1897. "What a calamity it was for the whole of Europe, as well as for his own

country." To the man who stood in that silent room at Cronberg had passed the throne, and the power to carry out his
father's dreams and to save Germany from the destruction
which threatened her.

Before she died, the Empress Frederick had entrusted her
private papers and letters to Sir Frederick Ponsonby, begging
him to take them to England. "It will be my duty some day,"
she had said in 1888, "to endeavour to let the truth go down to
history, and not the lies that suit Bismarck and the Government
and all those who court its favour." Those who now read those
letters must surely agree with the words Sir Frederick Ponsonby has written at the end of the book: "Calumniated,
abandoned, distrusted, and even hated as she was by Germany
in her lifetime, and for a quarter of a century after, the time has
surely come when that country must realize that in the Empress
Frederick, they had a Sovereign lady, who, in spite of her faults,
in spite of the defects of her qualities, always devoted her
energies to secure for Germany the political and cultural leadership of Europe."

The Princess Royal and Prince Frederick William of Prussia, at the time of their marriage

The Grand Duke Ernst Ludwig of Hesse with his daughter, Princess Elizabeth

Princess Alice, Grand Duchess of Hesse

# The Grand Duke Ernst Ludwig of Hesse

WHEN Ernst Ludwig of Hesse was a small boy of three, Miss Moffat, his English nurse, watching a tree being planted in the gardens of the New Palace at Darmstadt, replied to his question as to how long it would take the tree to grow, adding inadvertently, "Anyhow I shall be dead long before it has grown." Little Prince Ernst Ludwig, looking up at her with blue eyes, suddenly darkened by fear, burst into tears; "I don't want you to die alone," he sobbed. "We must all die together."

That fear of a solitary death weighed, it seemed, on the child's mind, for, after his only brother had been killed by falling from a window, he came one day to his mother, and buried his face in her lap. Smoothing the tumbled curls from his hot forehead, she asked what was the matter. He looked up at her, his little face puckered with anxiety, "When I die," he whispered, "you must die too, and all the others. Why can't we all die together?" Then, with a wail of distress, "I don't want to die alone, like Fritty."

Sensitive, imaginative, and affectionate, it was he who fretted and pined when his parents went away, he who of all the children missed them the most. He it was who seemed always able to read his mother's thoughts without asking a question, who knew if she was unhappy or anxious, and without being told guessed, when, as was so often the case, she felt tired and ill. "I fancy," Princess Alice told Queen Victoria, "that seldom a mother and child have understood each other, and loved each other as we two do."

As quite a small baby he had been passionately fond of music, of flowers, of colours and the sound of words. He had been able to sing in tune before he had reached the age of three. Whenever his mother played the piano he would get up

B
[ 23 ]

and dance, making up the steps, and always keeping perfect time. Very early he showed signs of that artistic temperament which was so marked in his later years, and had been, maybe, inherited from his ancestress, Caroline Henriette of Zweibrucken Birkenfeld. She had married the Landgraf Louis of Hesse in 1741, and had ruled over the Principality while he was away at the wars, cultivating the society of artists, writers and musicians, Herder, Goethe and Grimm being amongst her closest friends.

Up to 1872 his childhood had been undimmed by sorrow, and he had been a happy little boy, spending the winters in the white palace at Darmstadt, and the summers at Kranichstein learning to ride the Shetland pony that had been the gift of his grandmother, Queen Victoria. Spoilt and petted by his three elder sisters, he was taken sometimes to stay at Osborne or Balmoral, or to the castle of Heiligenberg, where his great-uncle lived. He was not, perhaps, always at ease with the four Battenberg boys, being unable to join in the rough games they played with the two young Russian Grand Dukes, Serge and Paul—games which his eldest sister Victoria seemed to enjoy, but which he avoided, preferring to stay on the terrace, with his mother, and the Empress of Russia, or to wander round the gardens admiring the flowers.

The fearful shock of his younger brother's death in 1872 affected him profoundly, and nearly every night he would wake from an uneasy sleep, screaming that Fritty was falling out of the window. He was, indeed, unable to get over the loss of the little boy who had been his constant companion, or to forget the horror of the moment, when he had seen him falling to his death.

It is believed that when, in 1878, he was himself seriously ill with diphtheria, and heard that his little sister Marie had died, he was so heartbroken and distressed that Princess Alice, disregarding the warnings given her by the doctor, took him in her arms to kiss him, and comfort him, in this way catching the disease herself. Whether he ever realized that he was partly responsible for his mother's fatal illness, is not known, but it is certain that he felt her loss more acutely than did his sisters, and even many years later there was always under his gaiety and high spirits a profound melancholy which often kept him sleepless at night, and showed itself in the poems he wrote. "I have a soul that sings", runs the translation of one of these poems, "and like a bird in a cage, It voices its sorrow and grief, It twitters and laughs, It cries and laments, in unending joy, and unending pain."

After spending several years in the University at Leipzig, he passed his military examination in 1886 and joined the First Guards Regiment at Potsdam, returning to Darmstadt, however, when his father died in 1892, to take up his position as the reigning Grand Duke of Hesse. His good looks and charm had made him popular in Berlin, he was an excellent dancer, he was entertaining and amusing. "Of all the German Princes," Max Wauer says, "he was the one who gave the impression of a man of the world." The officers of his regiment missed him when he left, and in Berlin there were no doubt many aching hearts, but in Darmstadt he was welcomed with enthusiasm, and young girls on their way to school often went a long way round in order to pass by the Palace, in the hopes of catching a glimpse of the gay and good-looking Prince who was their ruler.

His three elder sisters had all married, and for the first two years after his father's death his youngest sister, Princess Alix, who had not yet attained her twentieth year, acted as hostess for him, undertaking all the duties of a reigning Grand Duchess, carrying them out with conscientious devotion, in spite of the agonizing shyness from which she suffered.

In 1892 my father had been appointed to Coburg, an assignment which did not meet with Queen Victoria's approval, as she did not consider it suitable for "Mr. Buchanan who had a young and pretty wife" to be accredited to the Court of her brother-in-law, Duke Ernst of Saxe-Coburg-Gotha, whose morals, where women were concerned, left much to be desired. Consequently, when the Chargé d'Affaires at Darmstadt died unexpectedly, she signified her wish that my father should take up the vacant post, and appointed a bachelor to Coburg.

I was about six years old at the time, and a portrait painted by a German artist, soon after we came to Darmstadt, shows me sitting in a high-backed chair, dressed in a white muslin frock with a blue sash, and, a blue ribbon tied round my straight, fair hair. A smug, sedate, and, I am afraid, rather a priggish little girl, and certainly one of my earliest recollections bears out this fact.

It was not very long after we had arrived in Darmstadt and my nurse had taken me for a walk in the Emil Garden, which adjoined the small palace belonging to Prince Joseph of Battenberg. Having wandered for some time through the grounds, we went to sit on a bench near the little artificial lake, when a very lovely lady, dressed in deep black, accompanied by another smaller lady, also in black, passed by, and stopped to smile down at me with the bluest eyes I had ever seen. "Is this the little Buchanan girl?" she asked my nurse, and I wondered why the latter blushed as she got up to reply.

"Your name is Meriel, isn't it?" the lady asked, and although she was still smiling I thought, child as I was, that her eyes were sad. "My brother and I are giving a tea-party on the terrace, would you like to come and join us?"

And, remaining stolidly seated, I looked up at her with rather reproving eyes. "My mother does not allow me to go to tea with strange people," I replied in a prim little voice.

The flush on my poor nurse's cheeks got deeper, and she pulled me quickly to my feet. "Of course you will go to tea with Her Royal Highness," she said, and added in a sibilant whisper, "You must mind your manners and curtsy. Don't you know this is Princess Alix of Hesse?"

My recollection of the actual tea-party is rather dim, and I don't think I enjoyed it very much, for when Princess Alix, telling my nurse to go back and fetch my mother, led me up to the terrace, I recall being overcome with embarrassment, because the slender young man she introduced as her brother kissed my hand with laughing gallantry. I was rather frightened, also, by his other sister, Princess Louis of Battenberg, and although I was immediately attracted to her eldest daughter, Princess Alice, I was too shy to respond to her friendly advances, and I ended by further disgracing myself by upsetting a cup of milk all over the table.

Although the Prussians were already assuming their arrogant effrontery, in those days Southern Germany still retained an atmosphere reminiscent of the fairy stories of Grimm and Hans Andersen. Old castles with turrets and battlements, rising above little clustering towns, Baroque palaces with orangeries and formal avenues of lime trees, where the inhabitants still lived surrounded by time-honoured traditions. Villages with steep red roofs, where storks built their nests, narrow cobbled streets, where chattering white geese paraded in single file, and where little girls, with stiff yellow pigtails, dropped shy curtsies to passing carriages. On Christmas Eve every mansion and every cottage had its pine tree, decorated with coloured candles. At carnival time everybody, young or old, rich or poor, went out in fancy dress, and mysterious figures in black or scarlet dominoes invaded the houses of their friends and acquaintances, or followed them in the streets, whispering embarrassing remarks in their ears. At Easter everybody gave parties where eggs, dyed all the colours of the rainbow, or made of chocolate or marzipan, were hidden in unexpected places, and became the property of anyone lucky enough to find them. And always there was the sound of music. Torchlight processions of students singing, as they marched through the town; bands playing outside a house where somebody was celebrating a birthday; bands again accompanying a party on a day's picnic, or playing in some beer-garden or open-air restaurant.

[ 27 ]

In spite of being small the Court of Darmstadt had a glamour of its own, and although some of the chamberlains, the ladies-in-waiting and attendants were old, there was a gaiety and informality about it that was unusual in some of the small German Courts of those times, many of which were bound by frigid rules of etiquette, by icy unbending conventions, and an almost inhuman precision.

The Grand Duke Ernst Ludwig was only twenty-four when his father died, and he had no use for lugubrious faces, stiff manners and hushed voices. He wanted movement, colour and gaiety all about him, his rapid speech, his quick gestures, his bright blue eyes, which could on occasions be clouded with melancholy, all expressed his mercurial temperament, and some of those around him were often perplexed by his rapid changes of mood, found his restless activity somewhat exhausting, his love of practical jokes sometimes embarrassing.

Full of enthusiasms and new ideas, he was already beginning to make many changes in Darmstadt. He had done up some of the rooms in the New Palace according to his own taste, he had laid out the gardens; he would sometimes go unexpectedly into the flower shops in the town and give them directions about rearranging their windows and their floral decorations; he was taking a keen interest in the Court Theatre, would often attend rehearsals, design the costumes and scenery himself, would help generously to produce new shows and encourage new artists. He was, Princess Marie of Roumania once said, "an inventor of amusements", and certainly he was always thinking out some novel form of entertainment, some new diversion, some different way of bringing gaiety and change into the ordinary routine of life.

The most extensive renovations he began to make were probably those at the old hunting-palace of Wolfsgarten, which lay in the midst of woods, half-way between Darmstadt and Frankfurt. He turned the moat which formerly surrounded it into a flower garden, with pergolas of rambler roses and golden pumpkins. He modernized the main building, which faced the stables at the far end of the central quadrangle, with, on either side, small, one-storied houses all built of red sandstone. The principal building, with its high, pointed roof, approached by two flights of steep stone steps, contained the reception rooms, the private apartments of the Grand Duke, and the rooms reserved for royal guests; the little houses, on either side of the courtyard with its smooth lawns, its shady trees and stone fountain, were occupied by the ladies and gentlemen in waiting and visitors, the whole comprising a hundred and eighty rooms. The name Wolfsgarten (garden of wolves) had been given to it because of the wolves which in the old days had inhabited the surrounding forests, and, with the wild boar, and deer, had provided abundant sport for the former Landgrafs of Hesse, two wolves still being kept in a cage at the edge of the woods, just outside the big wooden gates which enclosed the buildings.

Here at Wolfsgarten, the Grand Duke spent all the summer months, with guests constantly coming and going. His sister, Princess Alix, did not always appreciate these guests, her inherent shyness making it almost a torture to be forced to receive strangers. Diffident and restrained, she often appeared cold, and almost hostile in her manner; she was unable to unbend and enter into the sometimes rather boisterous games and practical jokes her brother enjoyed. Already, then, she was irresistibly drawn to mystical matters, and would often steal away to her room to read books on occultism. There was a shadow of haunting sadness in her eyes, a sadness so apparent in the picture Kaulbach painted of her that many people who saw it declared that she was fated to bring misfortune.

Yet she was so gentle, so generous, so full of sympathy in those days, and I know that my parents never forgot the kindness she showed them, when, during our first winter in Darmstadt, I nearly died from pneumonia. One day, during that long illness, I can still recall drifting out of feverish unconsciousness to find her kneeling by my bed. "Look, Lady Georgie," I heard her say, "she has come to. She has opened her eyes. I am sure she is better, she smiled at me." That is the picture of her I shall always remember, and when I think of her now, I do not see her as the bitter, hard-faced woman I was to know, many years later as Empress of Russia, but as that young golden-haired girl kneeling by my bed, in her simple black dress, her lovely eyes smiling at me with such inexpressible tenderness.

When the Grand Duke was invited by his grandmother, Queen Victoria, to Balmoral and met his cousin, Princess Victoria of Edinburgh, the Queen, who had arranged the meeting in the hopes that these two grandchildren of hers would finally become engaged, was overjoyed when the plans she had made were successful. But Princess Alix could not understand her brother's infatuation for the tall, dark young girl, with the rather sombre violet eyes; in her opinion the daughters of the Duke of Edinburgh were too sure of themselves and too forward in their manners, and she deeply resented the fact that this cousin, who was four years her junior, would in future take precedence of her in Darmstadt. It was with a heavy heart that she attended their wedding at Coburg, and when, during the ceremonies there, the young Tsarevitch of Russia again asked her to marry him, she accepted his proposal, the knowledge that she would now not have to share her home with her sister-in-law being perhaps yet another motive for her to overcome her reluctance in the change of religion.

It was a lovely spring day when, after their wedding at Coburg, which had been attended by Queen Victoria, and many other royalties, the Grand Duke and his bride made a state entry into Darmstadt. Bands were playing, church bells were ringing, the town was gaily bedecked with flags, the streets were full of happy, cheering crowds, and I was taken to see the procession from a window in a friend's house. In an open carriage, filled to overflowing with bunches of roses, or irises and lilac, the Grand Duchess, looking very slim and young, in a pale mauve dress and a flowered toque, raised her head, in answer to her husband's gesture, to smile at my parents, and I thought how lovely and romantic she was. I was indeed thrilled, by what seemed to me a traditional love story with the inevitable happy ending.

A few days later there was a gala performance of *Hansel and Gretel* at the Court Theatre, and as a very great treat I was allowed to go. By chance our box happened to adjoin one of the royal boxes, and to my intense excitement I found myself sitting next to the Tsarevitch, who had come on a short visit to Darmstadt. I was much more interested in him than in what was going on on the stage, for I had been told that he was going to marry Princess Alix, and here was yet another thrilling romance to fire my imagination—the heir to that faraway throne in Russia, and a beautiful golden-haired Princess! What fairy tale had ever been written to equal this in legendary splendour?

Slight and erect in his gold-braided hussar's jacket, decorations sparkling on his chest, the Tsarevitch turned once or twice to look at me, and every time no doubt found me staring at him with rapt attention. When the witches' kitchen blew up, with a quite unexpected noise, and I gave an involuntary exclamation, he turned again, his grave, gentle eyes alight with a smile of amused kindliness.

Later that evening, when I had been taken home to bed, my parents went on to a reception at the Palace. My father had been instructed to discuss some particular matter with the heir to the Russian throne, but when he found an opportunity to approach him, the Tsarevitch said that he had been very amused to find me sitting next to him, asked how old I was, and my name. "I am afraid," he added, "your little daughter had rather a shock when the witches' kitchen exploded. Please

B*                          [ 31 ]

tell her from me that she had all my sympathy. I was very frightened too." And with a friendly handshake he turned away, leaving my father with his message undelivered. "I could", he commented rather bitterly in a letter to Lord Sanderson at the Foreign Office, "have wished my daughter at the ends of the earth."

It was not very long before the marriage which Queen Victoria had planned for her two grandchildren began to show signs of discord. Ardent and impatient of constraint, with a temperament alternating between high spirits and a brooding melancholy, the Grand Duchess resented the many duties she was expected to carry out, and the conventions and restrictions of a small German Court. She forgot to answer letters; she postponed paying visits to boring old relations; at official receptions she often caused great offence by talking to somebody who amused her, and ignoring people whose high standing gave them importance.

Although she shared her husband's artistic tastes, and her paintings of flowers were almost professional in their perfection, she was imbued with a restless activity, and never wanted to stay doing the same thing for long at a time. Like her sister, Princess Marie of Roumania, she was a superb horsewoman and whip, and completely without fear. The Grand Duke, on the other hand, had no great love of riding or of horses generally, and would often arouse her impatient contempt because he refused to accompany her when she had some of her white horses from the Imperial stables in Vienna harnessed to her high dog-cart, sometimes in a tandem, at others in a four-in-hand, or all six together, driving them at a reckless speed along the dusty roads, trying to forget, it seemed, in the pace and the danger, her seething discontent. On other days she would ride out into the woods alone on Bogdan, the fiery black stallion which had come from the Russian steppes, returning hours later to find that an important engagement she had made—and completely forgotten—had had to be cancelled owing to her absence. When her husband reproached her, she would fly into a temper, and accuse him of being lazy because he had not gone with her.

The birth in 1895 of their daughter, Princess Elizabeth, for a time eased the situation between them. The people of Darmstadt were overjoyed, and Queen Victoria hoped that her grandchildren would now settle down, and that there would soon be other babies, especially an heir to the Grand Duchy of Hesse.

In 1896 the Grand Duke and Grand Duchess attended the coronation of the Emperor Nicholas in Mosow, going on from there to stay with Prince and Princess Yusopoff at Archangelskoi. After the fantastic splendour, the gaiety and glamour of those days, the Grand Duchess returned, more restless, more unhappy, more dissatisfied than ever. For in Russia she had met again her cousin the Grand Duke Cyril, and the fondness they had always had for each other as children had turned into something deeper. Headstrong and passionate by nature, and married to a man she had never really loved, the Grand Duchess rebelled against the ties that bound her, the restrictions that surrounded her, she refused to take the necessary precautions when she once more became pregnant, and was heartbroken when the baby, which would have been a boy, was born prematurely.

It was impossible to keep anything secret for long in a little town like Darmstadt, where everybody knew everybody else's business, almost before they knew it themselves. The strained relations between the Grand Duke and his wife soon became a subject for comment and conjecture, not only in Court and military circles, but at the afternoon gatherings, where old ladies met to drink cups of coffee, topped with whipped cream, and discussed the latest rumours in sibilant whispers. The Grand Duchess was in love with this handsome cousin of hers. Oh, a remarkably good-looking man, someone had seen his photograph and had been quite overcome. The Grand Duchess

had let that black horse of hers loose in the courtyard at Wolfsgarten, and the animal, which was really wild, had made
straight for the Grand Duke, and torn a piece out of his trousers,
whereupon, she had just laughed. One afternoon, it was said,
her husband had come into her room, whistling a tune which
was in his head, when she asked him to stop, and he had not
done so, in a fit of ungovernable rage she had thrown down a
whole tea-table laden with china. It was said that the Grand Duke
was paying visits to a certain lady in town. It was said that the
Grand Duchess had been furious because she had found him in
bed, writing poetry, on a lovely summer's day. It was said that
she had called him a coward because he had refused to go out
with her in the dog-cart, when she was driving her six white
horses.

Stories grew more colourful, more malicious, with every
repetition. Criticisms were passed from mouth to mouth of
the dances, the fancy-dress parties, the private theatricals in the
Palace, the succession of visitors at Wolfsgarten, the thoughtless gaiety of the life that was led there, the picnics, the races at
Frankfurt, the late hours that were kept, the games of cards
which were played, the ceaseless entertainments.

In time these rumours reached the ears of Queen Victoria.
Greatly disturbed, she sent for my father, asking him so many
searching questions about the relations of her grandchildren
that he became embarrassed and perplexed, and at last said
diffidently that certain things had been told him in confidence,
both by the Grand Duke and the Grand Duchess, and he was
afraid that he could not betray the trust they had put in his
discretion. The Queen, who was not accustomed to being
opposed, was silent for a minute, and my father wondered
anxiously whether he had hopelessly displeased her. At last
she gave the little shrug of the shoulders, so characteristic of her.
"I quite understand," she said gently; and then, with a sudden
mist of tears in her eyes, "I arranged that marriage. I will
never try and marry anyone again."

Certainly my father's position cannot have been an easy one, for although the Grand Duchess would sometimes laughingly call him, "My kind schoolmaster", there were other days when her quick temper would flare up, and she would tell him, in no uncertain terms, that he had no right to dictate to her, or to criticize her actions. Very often, also, I saw my mother's eyes reddened with tears on her return from the Palace, and when I asked what was the matter, she would reply a little uncertainly, "Never mind, darling. It is nothing really, but the Grand Duchess was cross with me." But when she had been cross it never lasted for long, and the next day a letter would arrive, begging my mother to go and see her again, saying that she could not get on without her, that she was the only friend she had, and the only person who understood how unhappy she was.

Several times, during the eight years we were in Darmstadt, my father's name was sent up to the Queen for promotion, and every time she refused to give her permission for him to be moved to another post. She wanted Mr. Buchanan to remain where he was, she said, because he had such a good influence on her granddaughter and had gained her confidence. She would see that his career did not suffer. She was not ungrateful, for in 1897 she sent two Jubilee Medals to my parents, enclosing a letter, saying that she hoped they would accept them, "as a mark of her gratitude for their great kindness to her grandchildren". It was, I believe, the Prince of Wales, who, in 1900, told his mother that she was prejudicing my father's advancement in the Diplomatic Service, by keeping him so long in Darmstadt, and reluctantly the Queen at last gave her consent for him to be posted as Counsellor to the Embassy in Rome, and at the last audience he had with her, at Balmoral, gave him the C.V.O.

The first time I went to Wolfsgarten was soon after our arrival at Darmstadt, when the Grand Duke gave a children's party. He had broken his collar-bone in a fall, and I had been given strict instructions by my parents to express their sympathy. The fact that I had to deliver this message weighed heavily on my mind during the train journey to Langen and the drive from the station through the woods, and when the Grand Duke received us at the head of the stone steps leading into the Palace, I was breathless and paralysed with shyness. I don't remember what I said, but the garbled version I probably gave of my parents' message evidently pleased him, or else he was touched by my crimson-cheeked embarrassment, for his face lit up in a smile, and I remember the heavy gold bracelet on his wrist flashing in the sunlight as he stooped to pat my head.

After his marriage, and the birth of Princess Elizabeth, we spent most of the summer months at Wolfsgarten, one of the little houses at the side of the Palace being placed at our disposal. I loved that little red house, whose front windows looked out into the courtyard, the back ones facing the former moat and the distant woods. The scent of roses from the pergola was always in the small, light rooms, the song of birds and the raucous voices of the two scarlet macaws, who, on fine days, were tethered to their perches in the courtyard, drifted in through the open windows. Although it was so deep in the country, there was always life and movement. Carriages driving up to the flight of steps leading to the entrance into the Palace, horses being led out from the stables, guests coming down after luncheon to sit drinking coffee under the trees. Gay, laughing groups of people collecting to go to the races at Frankfurt, or to drive out on some excursion or picnic. The Grand Duchess and her sister Princess Marie of Roumania, going out riding on their two black horses. Servants hurrying to and fro carrying trays of drink down to the tennis court, or the luggage of somebody who had just arrived.

Generally we went to have breakfast on the other side of the courtyard in one of the little houses belonging to Fräulein von Grancy, the head lady-in-waiting, who, in her grey silk dresses and lace caps, always seemed to me to have stepped straight out of the pages of *Cranford*. My father and mother always had their other meals in the Palace, whilst I spent most of my days with Princess Elizabeth, under the charge of her English nurse, Miss Wilson, a capable, fresh-faced woman in her white *piqué* dresses, possessed of endless patience and a warm, kindly heart, in spite of her occasional sharp reprimands, which were no doubt fully deserved. The mornings were always spent in the pine woods near the tennis court, where there was sand for us to build castles with, a swing, and a high wooden pole with long ropes, ending in loops, in which one could sit and whirl oneself round and round. At eleven a Court servant would come out with mugs of milk, and plates of cucumber sand-wiches, and even now I can never eat a cucumber sandwich without its flavour bringing back to me those lovely mornings, the scent of sun-warmed pine trees, the distant voices from the tennis court, and Princess Elizabeth with her bright chestnut curls digging in the sand.

In the afternoon we would always go out driving, sometimes in one of the big, open carriages, through the forests of beech and pine, out into the highways, through sleepy little villages, where children came out to curtsy, past fields of golden corn, of poppies and cornflowers, where farmers doffed their hats, and smiling women with bright-coloured handkerchiefs tied over their heads called out a greeting to their little Princess. Sometimes we would pay a visit to some old castle, where other little girls lived strange, shut-in lives, surrounded by ceremonial rules which nowadays would appear fantastic and absurd. On other days we drove out in the Russian pony-cart, shaped rather like an Irish jaunting-car, to take tea in the woods, to pick bilberries and wild strawberries, and the little yellow mushrooms that looked so poisonous and tasted so good, cooked in cream and eaten sizzling hot.

In the evening my favourite entertainment would be to sit at the window of my room, long after I was supposed to be in bed, and watch everybody going to dinner in the Palace, all dressed in their evening clothes, their smartest uniforms, their ribbons and decorations. The most striking figure was always Mr. Hugo Wemyss, for whom I had a romantic adoration, and who, when he was staying at Wolfsgarten, invariably donned his tartan kilt in the evening. When it was raining it was especially amusing to watch the procession of people emerging from the houses, for then planks of wood would be laid down across the courtyard, and stout ladies would balance themselves precariously on the narrow boards, one hand holding up a dripping umbrella, the other clutching up a long satin train and a multitude of petticoats.

Hidden in the woods there was a small pond, where on warm days people would go and bathe, in spite of the duckweed that covered it, the bulrushes all around it, and the mud into which one sank up to one's ankles. On one side there was a steep slope, and here the Grand Duke had built a water-chute. This was at once a terror and a delight to me, and it was used almost exclusively by the men, few of the women being brave enough to risk the rapid descent and the inevitable wetting from the muddy spray that drenched all the occupants of the boat when it reached the bottom of the wooden chute, and hurtled its way into the pond. One day, however, the Grand Duke and Prince Nicholas of Greece persuaded my mother and one of the ladies-in-waiting to go with them, having previously arranged to deliberately upset the boat. My mother had that day put on a new pink muslin dress, with a multitude of small frills, which I very much admired, but when she returned, after her immersion in the muddy waters of the pond, it presented a truly lamentable appearance, and shrank to such an extent that, greatly to my delight, she was forced to pass it on to me.

Sometimes even the Grand Duchess, forgetting her sombre discontent, would indulge in a sudden spurt of merriment. One day when everybody was sitting out in the courtyard after luncheon, a servant, who was handing round the coffee, looked up with a startled exclamation and hurried forward to intercept two peasant women in checked aprons and with coloured handkerchiefs tied over their heads, who were coming in through the big open gates leading into the woods. "You must not come in here. This is private property. It is strictly forbidden," I heard him say, and then, nearly dropping the tray of coffee cups, he gave a gasp of dismay as he recognized in the two women, whose entry he had tried to stop, the Grand Duchess and my mother.

Certainly for a little girl those summers were full of fascination and enchantment—listening to the echoes of Court scandal which I was not meant to hear, and so often did; watching the arrival and departure of guests; the groups sitting under the trees, or wandering in the gardens after dinner; the lovely dresses of the Grand Duchess and her sister, Princess Marie; the gleam of jewels in the moonlight, the sound of music drifting out from the windows of the Palace. So many people came to Wolfsgarten, names that now belong to a forgotten past, but in those days were well known and renowned. The Empress Frederick, the Duke and Duchess of Sparta, the Grand Duke Serge of Russia with his beautiful wife, the lovely Crown Princess of Roumania, the Emperor and Empress of Russia with their little daughter, the Grand Duchess Olga, the Crown Princess of Austria, and her sister, Princess Louise of Coburg, who, coming for a two-day visit brought with her thirty-four hats, pinning them to the muslin curtains over her windows, because there was no room for them in the cupboards. The Prince of Wales used to come to lunch after his annual visit to the Rosenhöhe, and the grave of his sister, and in September, 1897, the German Emperor and Empress, arrived with a great fanfare of clattering horses and sabres, a blaze of uniforms, and much pomp and display.

In 1897 the Grand Duke and Grand Duchess attended the Diamond Jubilee in London, The Grand Duchess had, I think, no great love for her grandmother at that time. She resented her power and her control, and the fact that, because of her age and her rigid principles, she the granddaughter had to resign herself to an irksome allegiance to her marriage vows. But to the Grand Duke the Queen was always, "My own darling Grandmama", and he gladly submitted himself to her wishes, obeyed her without question, and did everything in his power to please her.

Unfortunately, the letters the Queen wrote to my father during the years we were in Darmstadt were packed away in one of the trunks stored in the Embassy when we had to leave Russia in 1918. But in the royal archives at Windsor there is a letter my father wrote to the Queen, in July, 1900, which shows the interest she took in all that concerned her grand-children, and how much she liked to hear the minutest details concerning them. The Grand Duchess had recently had another miscarriage and my father began his letter, by informing the Queen that he was staying at Wolfsgarten, and was glad to say, "that he finds the Grand Duchess much improved in spirits since the last time he had the honour to see Her Royal Highness a week ago. Though it will be long before the Grand Duchess gets over her great sorrow, Her Royal Highness is gradually beginning to resume her daily occupations, and to take an interest in her former pursuits. Her Royal Highness proposes to spend the greater part of the summer at Wolfsgarten, and is at present taking a course of salt baths, which, it is hoped, will strengthen Her Royal Highness. The Grand Duchess told Mr. Buchanan this morning how deeply she has been touched by Your Majesty's affectionate sympathy, and said she hoped soon to write to Your Majesty herself. The Grand Duke is looking remarkably well, though he is grown somewhat thinner. His Royal Highness has lately become fond of bicycling, and the regular exercise which he thus takes seems to agree admirably with His Royal Highness. Princess Elizabeth is also very well, and is as devoted as ever to the Shetland pony which Your Majesty gave her. The pony follows Her Grand Ducal Highness about like a dog, even running up the flight of stone steps after her into her nursery."

How well I remember that pony running loose in the court-yard, Princess Elizabeth throwing her arms round his neck to kiss him, or, in her frilly white hat, being held on the saddle by her mother. She loved visiting the stables, and fondling the beautiful white Lippizaner horses from the famous stud in Vienna, their names in gold letters over their stalls—"Maestoso Africa, Maestoso Mercurio, Maestoso Theodastra." Bogdan would allow nobody but the Grand Duchess to enter his stall; he was let loose every afternoon, galloping at full speed round and round the courtyard, his long black tail streaming out behind him, with bared teeth and flaring nostrils making a dash at some Court lady or gentleman, chasing them in flurried trepidation up the steps. As soon as the Grand Duchess called him he would go gently up to her, bending his proud head to caress her hand, following her quietly back to his stable.

In the late autumn of 1900 we left for Rome, and although I did not realize it at the time, nothing I have since known has ever replaced in vivid, stirring stimulation, or unalloyed happiness, those golden summer days spent at Wolfsgarten. With the death of Queen Victoria in January 1901, the marriage between her two grandchildren which had been so near her heart, came to an end. For now that there was no longer any fear of hurting or displeasing "Grandmama Queen" the Grand Duchess decided to gain her freedom, and leaving her husband, went to live quietly in Coburg, waiting for her divorce that would at last enable her to marry the man she had loved for so many years.

The scandal attending her separation caused a great stir in the Europe of those days, where divorce was not accepted with the leniency of modern times, and she fiercely resented the opprobrium cast on her name, the stern disapproval of her uncle, King Edward VII, and the indignation of both the

Emperor of Germany and the Emperor of Russia, and more especially the latter's wife, the Empress Alexandra. For a woman with the pride and fastidiousness of the Grand Duchess, those years must have been hard to endure, and the letters she wrote to my mother were full of resentment and exasperation at the uncharitable treatment she was receiving from some of her relations. Had she not sacrificed years of her youth because of her grandmother's prejudices and had she not now the right to some happiness in life?

Yielding generously to her wishes, the Grand Duke allowed Princess Elizabeth to spend six months of the year with her mother, counting the days till she returned to him, sending her, when she was with him, every day to Fräulein Texter's school. Everyone in Darmstadt adored the little girl who was such a familiar figure in the little town, driving out with her father, or running through the streets, followed by her dog, which she insisted on taking with her to school. "Princessin Sonnen-schein", they called her, because of her bright curls, her mischievous naughtiness, and the laughter in her pansy-blue eyes. "Princess Sunshine", the name which had once been given to her aunt, the Empress of Russia, a name which seemed fated to bring tragedy and disaster to its holder.

In the autumn of 1903 the Grand Duke took his daughter with him on a visit to Russia, going first to stay with the Emperor and Empress at Belovej, one of the Imperial shooting-palaces, intending to go on from there to St. Petersburg. The four young daughters of the Empress were also at Belovej, and there were shooting-parties, excursions, picnics in the forest, games and romps through the big rooms of the Palace, laughter and merriment every evening. Then, early one misty autumn morning, Princess Elizabeth awoke with a start of agony, wide-eyed, panting for breath, burning with fever. When the Grand Duchess Victoria, summoned hastily by telegram, arrived two days later, it was only to stand beside a shadowed, silent bed, where, between masses of tawny golden chrysanthemums, her daughter lay asleep, deaf to her agony of self-reproach, beyond the call of love, or joy, or sorrow.

The terrible swiftness of her death caused many rumours to circulate at the time, and it was said—and firmly believed by many—that there had been a plot to poison the Emperor, and that the dish which had been specially prepared for him had been given by mistake to his little niece. These rumours were later denied. Princess Elizabeth, it was said, had died of an attack of meningitis. Others again declared that it was para-typhoid that had carried her away so suddenly. Whatever the cause, the world is a little poorer for not having known that elfin charm, those bright brown curls, those laughing star-like eyes.

Heart-broken, and with a sadness that defied all description, the Grand Duke returned to Darmstadt, bearing with him the little coffin of his daughter to be laid to rest on the Rosenhöhe, and the people watched the funeral of their Sunshine Princess with sorrowing hearts and tear-reddened eyes. They felt that something had gone out of their lives which could never be replaced, and passed through the quiet streets, telling each other in hushed voices that November was always a fateful month for the royal family of Hesse, a month which often brought mourning and loss, and a funeral winding its way through the town, beneath the cold, grey skies.

How slowly the time passed for the lonely, unhappy man in his empty palace, how long the days seemed, how quiet the rooms, where formerly there had been so much movement and animation. But finally his divorce was ratified, and in 1905 he married Princess Eleanore of Solms Hohensolms. She had not the romantic charm, the elegance, the artistic tastes of the Grand Duchess Victoria. The Court of Darmstadt lost some of its brilliance, there were fewer entertainments, fewer visitors came to Wolfsgarten; the old ladies trotting along the streets had no gossip from the Palace to discuss over their cups of coffee. The new Grand Duchess was popular and beloved. She kept up the hospitals and nursing-schools, the orphanages and institutions that had been begun by Princess Alice. She never forgot appointments, she never failed to answer letters, she never offended even the dullest people, by neglecting to talk to them, and she bore her husband two fine sons, Prince George Donatius, and Prince Louis of Hesse.

The Grand Duke regained some of his former vivacity and his former interests. He laid out a new rose-garden on the Rosenhöhe, be built a new mausoleum and a new gate. The artists' colony he had started earlier was flourishing, and he built new factories to encourage the making of glass and painted china. In 1911 he organized a big music festival in Darmstadt. More and more he devoted himself to the arts, more and more, as the years passed, his hatred of violence, in any form, increased.

When the First World War broke out in 1914 the fact that he was half English by birth and wholly English in sympathies caused him to be looked on with a certain suspicion, and, as two of his sisters were in Russia, and one in England, he was accused of corresponding with the enemies of Germany. On account of his principles, and his English relations, he was excused from active service at the Front, dedicating himself to the care of the wounded, visiting the hospitals, going with his wife in her ambulance train, spending money with liberal generosity.

The Revolution in Russia, the collapse of Germany, and the flight of the Emperor William, brought the world he had known falling in ruins around him. To a man of his vivid imagination, to whom cruelty and brute force were abhorrent, the fate that had overtaken his two sisters, the Empress Alexandra and the Grand Duchess Elizabeth, was a nightmare that almost robbed him of his reason. But he was not lacking in courage, and when the wave of communism sweeping over Germany reached even quiet little Darmstadt, and a deputation from the newly-formed People's Government invaded the

Palace, he met them with an intrepid, unflinching determination, refused all their demands, told them proudly that he would never abdicate, and sent them away cowed and overawed.

Retiring eventually to Wolfsgarten he lived there quietly but still retaining an almost royal state. His eldest son, George Donatius, had married the beautiful Princess Cecilia, daughter of Prince and Princess Andrew of Greece, and he and his wife and their two little sons George and Alexander, and their baby girl Joanna, shared the palace at Wolfsgarten with the Grand Duke and his wife.

It was seldom now that guests drove in through the big gates, there were no excursions to the races at Frankfurt, dance music no longer floated out into the summer night, but children's laughter still echoed in the rooms, two sturdy little boys played in the sand-pit among the pine trees, and ladies- and gentlemen-in-waiting still went across the courtyard to dine in the Palace, although they now no longer wore so many jewels and decorations, and the children playing in the pine woods no longer had those wafer-thin cucumber sandwiches which I had so much enjoyed in the past.

The years were passing, and for the grandson of Queen Victoria the shadows were falling. He who had so much loved life and movement, and animation, was forced to lie still. Devotedly the Grand Duchess nursed her husband through the long illness that attacked him when he was sixty-eight, and ended with his death in October, 1937.

A short time previously Prince Louis of Hesse, who had been working in England, had become engaged to the daughter of Sir Auckland Geddes, and the widowed Grand Duchess, anxious to be present at his wedding, left her husband's body on the Rosenhöhe to await burial and accompanied her eldest son, his wife, and their three small children in the plane which was to take them to England. Once again it was the month of November, and once again that month brought death to the royal family of Hesse, for the plane crashed in flames, and there were no survivors.

And so Prince Louis, so tragically and suddenly succeeding as Grand Duke of Hesse, travelled sadly back to Darmstadt with his young wife, and the bodies of those who had started out to be present at his wedding were buried with the body of his father on the Rosenhöhe. Once more Darmstadt saw a funeral of its royal family under the grey November skies.

"I don't want to die alone," little Prince Ernst Ludwig had said tearfully when he was a child. His wish had been fulfilled, for he was joined in the grave by his wife, his eldest son, his daughter-in-law and his three grandchildren.

# Princess Alice of Hesse

WHEN their eldest daughter, Victoria, known as the Princess Royal, married Prince Frederick William of Prussia in 1858, both Queen Victoria and her husband—more especially the latter—were for a time woefully dejected, missing, more than had at first seemed possible, Vicky's high sweet voice, her bubbling sense of humour, her unquenchable gaiety, even her occasional outbursts of wilfulness. For several months the Prince Consort remained inconsolable, but after a time the Queen was able to find comfort, and a most satisfying companionship, in her second daughter, Princess Alice, who had not yet attained her fifteenth year.

When she was only twelve months old Prince Albert had called her the "beauty of the family", but later on he sometimes referred to her as "poor, dear little Alice", finding in her none of the quickness of mind, the brilliant mental capacity, of her elder sister. As a child she had been slow in learning, had preferred to play with her brothers, had excelled them in endurance and courage, and in daring horsemanship. As the years passed, a greater gentleness and consideration for others made itself apparent, she was beginning to take an interest in music and the arts, and although she still enjoyed riding out in all weathers, she spent a great deal of her time visiting the poorer cottages at Balmoral. "She is a dear, good girl," the Queen wrote in her Journal. "I shall not let her marry, as long as I can reasonably delay doing so."

But fate decreed otherwise, for in June, 1860, when Princess Alice was barely seventeen, her great-uncle, King Leopold of the Belgians, came to stay at Windsor for the Ascot races, bringing with him Prince Louis, nephew and heir-apparent of the reigning Grand Duke of Hesse. From the first it became apparent that the tall, dark young man with the military bearing was greatly attracted to the Queen's second daughter who, although she had not Vicky's fascination and scintillating charm, was possessed of a flawless skin, had an enchanting grace of movement, soft blue eyes, and her mother's clear, melodious voice.

Five months later, managing once more to obtain leave from his regiment at Potsdam, Prince Louis of Hesse again visited Windsor, and one evening, in the Red Drawing-Room, the Queen noticed him standing by the fire, talking very earnestly to her daughter. As she passed close to them, on her way to her own room, Princess Alice coming up to her "in much agitation", told her that Prince Louis had proposed, and asked for her consent. Pressing his hand with a rather wistful smile, the Queen murmured "Certainly", said she would see him later in her room, and passed on, her heart perhaps a little heavy at the thought of so soon losing another of her daughters.

Next day the engagement was announced and was acclaimed with general satisfaction, in both England and Germany; but the months of preparation for her marriage, which should have been so full of happiness, were saddened for Princess Alice, first by the death of her grandmother, the Duchess of Kent, and then by the sudden illness of her father in December, 1861.

The Queen had not been able to believe that Prince Albert's illness could end fatally, and when, on December 14, she realized that she was a widow, she gave way to such paroxysms of grief that those around her feared that her mind would become deranged.

It was Princess Alice who persuaded her to leave Windsor for a time and go to Osborne. It was Alice who tried to uphold her, who kept petty annoyances and difficulties away from her, who dealt with all the communications from Cabinet Ministers, civic authorities and the royal household. And it was Alice who had to carry on the arrangements for her own wedding, which had been begun by her father. It was a harrowing and heartbreaking time for anyone so young and inexperienced. It changed her from a carefree girl into a grave, thoughtful woman with a wisdom and comprehension far beyond her years. It awakened in her, also, an interest in political matters which she had not known before and might not otherwise have attained.

The wedding, put off on account of the Prince Consort's death, took place at Osborne on July 1, 1862, the Queen's brother-in-law, Duke Ernst of Saxe-Coburg-Gotha, giving away the bride and only members of the family being present. The almost funereal gloom of the ceremony, the Queen's un-relieved grief, the tears shed by all her sisters, and even by some of her brothers, did not tend to make it a happy day for the bride, and she left for her new life in Germany with a heavy heart, burdened by self-reproach at leaving her mother in her lonely desolation of spirit.

By the time she reached Frankfurt, however, she had re-covered some of her youthful spirits. She and her husband were met by the widowed Grand Duke of Hesse, and his two brothers, Prince Charles and Prince Alexander, and making the acquaintance of these new relations, knowing that they were watching her critically, forced Princess Alice to put aside her own personal grief and anxiety. In Darmstadt the triumphal arches, the fluttering flags, the ringing of bells, the groups of young girls in white who threw flowers into the carriage, brought a shy flush of colour into her pale cheeks; the bright-ness of her eyes, which during the last months had been so often shadowed by tears, responded to the smiling faces all round her, to the scent of the roses heaped on her lap, and the spontaneous cordiality of her reception.

"I think you would like Alice," Prince Alexander of Hesse wrote a little later to his sister, the Empress of Russia. "She is a funny little woman, full of charm . . . very cultured, and very talented." She, on her side, found this new uncle with his ease of manner, his good looks, his wise amused eyes, very clever

[ 49 ]

and entertaining, and when she visited him and his wife, at their castle of Heiligenberg, fell in love with the house and the garden, with his daughter and his four handsome sons.

The first days at Darmstadt were entirely occupied with civic entertainments, and the receptions of the Hessian nobility, of the members of the Town Council and the English colony, of officials of all kinds. The Princess naïvely confessed to her mother that she sometimes found it very difficult to know what to say to the numerous people who were presented to her, and who "just stood there, waiting to be spoken to".

The old castle of Darmstadt, which had been built for the former Landgrafs of Hesse, had never been completed and could barely accommodate the Grand Duke, with Prince and Princess Charles and their suites. Plans were being made to build a new home for Prince Louis and his wife, but in the meantime they were given a small house, situated in the old quarter of the town among the narrow cobbled streets with their quaint revealing names—Stinkgässchen, Ochsengasse, Braune Gässchen, or Hinkelgasse. In her letters to her mother Princess Alice described her house, saying that it was sometimes very hot and airless in summer; she gave, too, minute details of how she spent her days. Getting up very early to go for long rides in the lovely woods surrounding the town, writing letters till one, going for drives in the afternoon and taking tea out of doors, sewing in the evening while her husband read aloud to her, and sometimes, when it was warm and fine, going for another drive. Prince Louis, she told the Queen, always treated her with tender consideration, and she could not describe how happy she was, and how her love for him increased with every day. There was such a feeling of security in being his wife, they lived in a world of their own which nothing could touch.

Her own happiness did not, however, cause her to forget the Queen's loss, and she was continually trying to comfort her, exhorting her to gather in a few of the bright things which remained, reminding her of the many opportunities to do good, begging for even a ray of hope that, either bodily or mentally, she felt better. "I long", she wrote on August 23, "to shelter you in my arms, to protect you from all future anxiety, to still your aching longing. My own sweet Mama, you know I would give my life for you, could I alter what you have to bear."

Realizing that his nephew's wife was feeling the cramped conditions of her small house, and the airlessness of the rooms, the Grand Duke was making arrangements to give the young couple a summer residence, choosing the ancient castle of Kranichstein, not far from the town, which had formerly been a hunting-lodge of the Landgraf of Hesse, the woods surrounding it still being reserved for the shooting of wild boar. It had not been inhabited for eighty years, but when the Grand Duke took Princess Alice to see it, she was delighted with the picturesque beauty of the building, with the lake reflecting the old grey walls, the big rooms and the surrounding woods, and looked forward eagerly to the following summer, when it would be ready for occupation.

In the autumn Princess Alice returned to England, yielding to the Queen's insistence, but aware that she was causing some dissatisfaction in leaving her new home so soon after her arrival. She was expecting the birth of her first child, and she spent the winter quietly at Windsor, while Prince Louis visited big industrial towns in England, and was also given permission to inspect some of the arsenals and military depots. In March she was able to attend the marriage of her brother, the Prince of Wales, to Princess Alexandra of Denmark, and looked very well, the Queen said, "in a violet dress, covered with her wedding veil, and a violet velvet train from the shoulders".

Her eldest daughter, Victoria, was born on April 5, and Prince Alexander of Hesse came over for the christening, making great friends with the Prince of Wales, and telling his sister, the Empress Marie, that Louis of Hesse had become quite an Englishman. "He wears", he wrote, "a Norfolk jacket, short breeches and multi-coloured garters, is very fond of sherry and horses, reads as little as possible, and never writes at all. He is the Queen's confidant, and is popular in England."

Soon after the christening Princess Alice and her husband and baby left again for Darmstadt. The Queen missed her intolerably, and felt a renewed desolation now that she was gone, and could no longer be turned to for consolation. "There is not a thing I cannot tell her," she wrote in her Journal. "She knows everything, and is the best element in a family."

Kranichstein was ready to be lived in that summer, and Princess Alice wrote happily to her mother, telling her how she had arranged the rooms, of the lovely rides in the woods, of bathing in the lake, and her hours of study and reading. She described the trip she had made to the castle of Marburg and the grave of St. Elizabeth, the Hessian saint, who was so re-nowned in Darmstadt. She spoke of the many guests she had entertained in the fine dining-room, of the visits of the Emperor of Austria, whom she found very amiable but not very talka-tive, of the King of Bavaria, of her sister Vicky, and of the Empress of Russia, who was staying with her brother, Prince Alexander, at Heiligenberg. In August, Queen Victoria, who had been visiting Coburg, came herself to Kranichstein, ac-companied by her three youngest daughters and her son, Prince Alfred. Princess Alice had to move her rooms round in order to accommodate her mother, and found room for some of the members of her suite in Darmstadt, finding it impossible to put them up herself.

The Prince of Wales was also a frequent visitor, for, after staying in Berlin and being repelled by the pompous formality of the Court and the arrogant manners of the inhabitants, he found in Darmstadt a more congenial atmosphere, and in Alice a sister whose gentle serenity was soothing after Vicky's restless energy and animation. The little town, with its white houses, its avenues of chestnut trees, its gardens which, in the spring, were full of laburnum and syringa, delighted him.

There were the surrounding woods, where one could ride for hours on sandy paths; there was the Zeppen Allée—or as it was sometimes called—the Hexen Allée, with its twisted, stunted trees; there was the shooting of wild boars at Kranichstein; there were the races at Frankfurt; there was the beautiful castle of Heiligenberg, where one was always certain to find amusing people and witty conversation.

Here in these pleasant surroundings the Prince of Wales felt he could relax and be at ease, and forget the many pinpricks that harassed him in England. The articles in the Press, which so often commented unfavourably on his movements, the Queen's severity, her criticism of his friends, her refusal to allow him to take part in matters of State, her control of his actions when he stayed with her and was not allowed to sit for more than a quarter of an hour drinking port with his friends, after the ladies had left the table, or to stay in the smoking-room after midnight.

The discord and dissension between the Prince of Wales and his mother were aggravated by the Schleswig-Holstein question which, at the end of 1863, was beginning to cast a cloud over Europe. The rival claims of the King of Denmark and Prince Frederick of Schleswig-Holstein-Sonderburg-Augustenburg, were so involved and intricate that Lord Palmerston said only three men had ever been able to understand them. "The Prince Consort, who was dead; a German professor, who had become insane; and he himself, and he had forgotten all about them." But Bismarck, who had been appointed Minister-President in 1863, had his own very decided views on the subject. He coveted the port of Kiel, he was determined to get it, and he had furthermore made up his mind that both Schleswig and Holstein were eventually to form part of the Prussian Kingdom, the Kingdom he had already envisaged in his mind as an Empire dominating the whole of Germany, not the constitutional utopia dreamed of formerly by the Prince Consort, but an invincible colossus, made of "blood and iron".

The Prince of Wales, married to the daughter of Prince Christian of Glücksburg, who had succeeded King Frederick of Denmark in 1863, was naturally enough inclined to adopt his wife's opinion that "the Duchies belong to Papa". When, in February 1864, a force composed of Prussian and Austrian battalions invaded both Schleswig and Holstein, the Prince was in favour of sending a British fleet to the Baltic. Lord Palmerston and Earl Russell were inclined to share his views. But the Queen, who had been studying some of Prince Albert's papers, had come to the conclusion that Denmark had no right to the Duchies; moreover, she was wisely determined not to allow England to take part in a quarrel that was no concern of hers. And so, in spite of the tears shed by the Princess of Wales, the Convention of Gastein was agreed to, Holstein being occupied by Austria, and Schleswig by Prussia.

In the summer of 1865 the Queen paid one of her periodical visits to Coburg and was disturbed by a message from the King of Prussia, expressing his desire to see her. The position of her daughter, the Crown Princess of Prussia, and Bismarck's treatment of her, were causing the Queen considerable anxiety, and she felt that a meeting with Vicky's father-in-law might be fraught with difficulties. So she was "much fussed" when the interview was finally arranged to take place at Darmstadt. Going to stay at Kranichstein she drove into town, was received by the Grand Duke at the old castle, and was kept waiting half an hour for the King. Warned by Bismarck not to embark on controversial subjects, the King made no mention of the speech that his son, egged on by his wife, had made at Danzig. For her part, the Queen kept silent about the letters the Crown Princess had written on the subject. "We talked of nothing but 'pluie et beau temps'," she wrote in her Journal, breathing a sigh of relief that the interview she had dreaded was safely over.

Princess Alice was able to move into the New Palace in Darmstadt in March 1866. "I can hardly fancy we are in

Princess Stephanie of Belgium and Crown Prince Rudolf of Austria

The Grand Duchess Serge
of Russia

The Grand Duchess Olga
Nicholaievna of Russia

Germany", she wrote to her mother, "the house and all its arrangements being so English." She went on to express the hope that the Queen would soon visit her again, telling her that, knowing how much she suffered from the heat, she had arranged rooms for her on the east side of the house which she thought would be always cool, even in summer.

But the joys of moving into a new house with spacious rooms, bright chintzes, and a big garden, were overshadowed by the tension of the political situation, and the threat of a war that would bring Hesse into conflict with Prussia. The Grand Duke had decided to side with Austria, should hostilities break out. Prince Louis had resigned his commission in the Prussian Guards, and as the lovely spring days passed, Princess Alice prayed desperately that her mother's letters to the King, imploring him not to yield to Bismarck's ambitions, would bear fruit. But Bismarck overrode the King. He had obtained the Emperor Napoleon's agreement to remain neutral, he had bribed Italy with the promise of Venetia, and having carefully made his plans, he declared war on Austria and on the German states who had sided with her.

In June Princess Alice had to say good-bye to her husband. She sent her two eldest daughters to England, and remained on alone in Darmstadt awaiting her confinement, her third daughter Princess Irene, being born on July 11. Meanwhile the Prussian armies, having driven the Austrians out of Holstein, invaded Hanover, sent the blind King into exile, overran Saxony, crossed the frontier into Hesse, occupied Frankfurt, and advanced on Darmstadt. "An existence of monstrous anxiety which it is impossible for those to imagine who have not lived through it," Princess Alice wrote to her mother, on July 19. She went on to describe how people were fleeing from town in every available carriage, how she had hidden many people's belongings in her house, and how anxious she was about her husband, who was with the Hessian armies threatened by the Prussian advance. Austria, defeated at the battle of

Sadowa, had been forced to make peace, and, in reply to a letter from her husband, Princess Alice begged the Grand Duke to accept the Prussian conditions and avert further bloodshed. Prince Alexander, hating with an implacable resentment Bismarck and all that he stood for, never quite forgave her. "These foreigners," he told the Empress Marie, "who want to barter the country to Prussia, and cherish the incredible illusion that the King of Prussia may prove generous to Hesse."

Peace was, however, at last agreed on. Hanover and Saxony were included in the Prussian Kingdom; Hesse lost Frankfurt and Homburg but was left free, although her revenues were crippled, and the royal family greatly impoverished. The war was over, but Queen Victoria began to wonder whether these foreign alliances that her husband had favoured were, after all, advantageous. For here was poor Alice, in reduced circumstances, having to make her children's clothes herself, with her mother sending her money to buy furniture for the dining-room. Here was Vicky replying to her appeal for leniency to be shown to the King of Hanover and the Grand Duke of Hesse, and declaring that the victors must make their own terms, even if they were hard ones, adding that those who now bemoaned their fate should have foreseen the danger they were running into. And Bertie, still proclaiming his hatred of Prussia, hardly civil to his sister when he visited Berlin to be invested with the Grand Cross of the Order of the Black Eagle. It was all very distressing, but at the same time the Queen was already contemplating the possibility of another foreign marriage for her second son, Prince Alfred, believing that his engagement with the Grand Duchess Marie of Russia might remove the strained relations left after the Crimean War. She had also allowed her third daughter, Princess Helena, to marry Prince Christian of Schleswig-Holstein, although as he now had no estates abroad, he would be able to live peacefully in England, which was, the Queen thought, very satisfactory, feeling that she really could not bear another daughter of hers going to live in a foreign country.

The many visits she had paid to the wounded in the hospitals had intensified the interests Princess Alice had always had in nursing and in medicine, an interest which her mother thought she was carrying too far, not altogether approving of the lectures she was attending which apparently concerned the functions of the human body—matters which the Queen thought rather indelicate, and best left to the medical profession. But in spite of her fragile appearance, and her generally submissive nature, Princess Alice had an unexpected streak of obstinacy in her character, and she refused to be turned from her purpose, telling her mother with gentle firmness that it was very useful to know such things, and not to be ignorant of the reasons doctors advised certain treatments. She realized that the Queen had an inherent dislike of all these matters, but, instead of being disgusted, it filled her with admiration "to see how wonderfully we are made".

Already in 1864 she had become Patroness of the Heidenreich Home for Pregnant Women, and took an active part in the organization. At the beginning of 1866 she raised funds for the care of the mentally defective. After the war between Prussia and Austria, she founded the Frauen Verein, or Ladies' Union, in order to train women of all classes to help in the hospitals, to care for the sick, and to nurse the wounded in times of war. She herself was far from strong, being a constant sufferer from rheumatism and agonizing neuralgia, but she never allowed her health to interfere with her work, and nobody ever came to her in vain for help or advice. Always she was ready to receive them with a smile, to listen to them patiently, to send them away comforted, feeling that some of their troubles and difficulties had been lifted from their shoulders.

She was, however, not universally popular. Her ideas on women's rights were considered too advanced, her friendship with Doctor David Friedrich Strauss, the famous theological writer, was severely criticized by certain sections of the public, and when he dedicated one of his books to her, the more censorious even accused her of being an atheist.

Nor did her husband's uncle, Prince Alexander of Hesse, always approve of her. He resented her having advocated conciliation with Prussia, and when she visited Berlin, soon after the war which had robbed Hesse of so many of her possessions, he was disgusted and scandalized. He criticized her inability to tolerate the company of boring people, and said that she was always dissatisfied when she returned from England, and did not attempt to hide her feeling of boredom.

It is not to be wondered at that Princess Alice, with her husband frequently called away on military or official duties, was often lonely, missing the companionship of her brothers and sisters, and the freedom of her life in England. Occasionally, in her letters to her mother, she criticized the "cold circle of Court people" who surrounded her, lamented the fact that she had no real friend to whom she could open her heart, and complained of the etiquette that circumscribed her movements, of being often alone, with nobody she could go and see because it would not be considered the proper thing for her to pay visits unannounced.

In the meantime, however, her children were providing her with a new interest. In 1868 was born her son, who was christened Ernst Ludwig, after former Landgrafs of Hesse. Three years later, another little boy was added to the family, a little boy who, although he had been given the names of Frederick William, was always called Fritty, who from the first was delicate, suffering it is believed from haemophilia, causing his mother many anxious moments, though because of that, loved more tenderly. In 1872 and 1874 she gave birth to two daughters, Alix and Marie, and her love for her children is shown in the constant references she made to them in her letters to the Queen. Ernie had such fine, big limbs, and although his nose was a little too short, such a pretty mouth and beautiful skin; he had such a wonderful ear for music, and could sing several songs without a fault, and could dance, always keeping perfect time. Victoria had such an inquiring mind, and such an aptitude for learning; she asked so many questions, and went out walking with her Papa, with her hands in her pockets, and amused him very much. Dear fat Ella had such deep blue eyes, and was so loving and funny, but not always very gentle or easy to manage. Her fourth daughter, who had been given the name of Alix, because the Germans pronounced Alice in such a dreadful way, was such a merry little person. "She is," Princess Alice told the Queen, "quite the personification of her nickname, 'Sunny'."

The outbreak of the Franco-Prussian War in 1870, meant another bitter parting from her husband, and again Princess Alice had to face a confinement alone, the telegram, announcing the birth of little Prince Frederick William, reaching Prince Louis a few days before the battle of Gravelotte. It also meant renewed dissension between Queen Victoria's children. For the Prince of Wales made no secret of being in sympathy with France, and was accused of having openly expressed the hope that Germany would be defeated. "Now perhaps Vicky will appreciate what the feelings of little Denmark must have been," he wrote and told his mother. Like most people in England the Queen at first thought that France had precipitated the conflict, foresaw an overwhelming victory for Napoleon's armies, and was acutely anxious for her two daughters in Germany, especially for Alice, who had refused her sister's invitation to go to Berlin, and insisted on remaining in Darmstadt. But when, contrary to all expectations, France fell before the overwhelming efficiency of Bismarck's armies, and the Emperor Napoleon capitulated at Sedan, the Crown Princess wrote triumphantly to her mother, boasting of the many French who had surrendered, of the blow to the immoderate frivolity of Paris, adding with a certain maliciousness, "What will Bertie and Alix say to these wonderful happenings?"

After the fall of Paris, and the proclamation of King William of Prussia as Emperor of Germany at Versailles, the Queen expressed her sorrow that nobody had shown any sympathy with Napoleon, and sent a telegram to the new Emperor of Germany, reminding him that he could now afford to be generous. Public feeling in England had become almost violently anti-German, while at the same time the rise of the Commune in Paris had a certain repercussion, speeches made in Hyde Park and Trafalgar Square even attacking the throne, and calling openly for a republic. But the serious illness of the Prince of Wales in November 1871, and the fact that he had been attacked by the same fever that had caused his father's death, silenced the voices of rebellion, and the whole country, stirred to sympathy for the Queen in her terrible anxiety, was swept by a wave of renewed affection and loyalty.

Princess Alice had spent the month of September at Balmoral where the Queen was suffering from a severe attack of gout, and was very low in spirits. On the way back to Germany, she paid a visit to Sandringham, and, allowing Prince Louis to return to Darmstadt without her, stayed on to nurse her brother. Her presence was a great comfort to the Princess of Wales, and to the Queen, who hurried down from Balmoral, and sitting behind a screen in the darkened room, listened to her son's laboured breathing, unable to do anything to help him. For a time it seemed as if all hope would have to be abandoned; then on December 14, the anniversary of Prince Albert's death, the Prince of Wales at last showed signs of recovery, and in January 1872 Princess Alice was able to return to Darmstadt, knowing that he was out of danger.

In spite of the birth of her fourth daughter in June, she found time for many new interests. She became patroness of a recently built orphan asylum. She got up bazaars and concerts, to raise funds for the Alice Hospital, which had originally been started by the British Red Cross in 1870, and at the end of the war was handed over to the Hessian authorities. During the summer she took part in the General Assembly of the Women's Diet, in order to inaugurate kindergartens on the Fröbel system, and to make provision for the better education of girls in the schools.

The year 1873 seemed to dawn with a promise of happiness, untroubled by any threat of war, with the Prince of Wales fully recovered and able to visit her again, and her children, even little Fritty, all in good health. In the spring she was able to fulfil a long-cherished wish and make a journey in Italy, returning to Darmstadt in May, to wait the arrival of her brother, Alfred, who was coming to meet the Grand Duchess Marie of Russia at Heiligenberg, their engagement having been at last agreed to by the Empress Marie.

On the morning of May 29, an unforeseen tragedy fell with terrible swiftness on the New Palace in Darmstadt, leaving Princess Alice crushed and broken, with her health seriously affected.

On that lovely spring morning Prince Louis had gone off very early to inspect one of his regiments, and the children came as usual into their mother's room while she was still in bed. The three eldest girls were already at their lessons, but Princess Alix was playing with her toys, while her two brothers, Ernie and Fritty, in exuberant spirits, chased each other round the furniture, and through the open door into the adjoining room, leaning out of the open windows to chatter to each other, to point out the flowers in the garden, the lilac then bursting into bloom, a blackbird singing on a may-tree.

Exactly how the accident happened has never been clearly ascertained. One story was that Fritty, leaning out too far to talk to his brother, overbalanced; another averred that running too fast towards the open window he was unable to stop himself; while still another rumour has it that the baby Princess Alix, joining in her brother's game, was somehow involved, either pushing Fritty in play, or failing to hold on to him. Whatever the cause, the fall onto the stone terrace below the windows proved fatal, and the little boy, who only a few moments earlier had been so full of life, never recovered consciousness.

[ 61 ]

How gravely the shock of that accident affected Princess Alice is indicated in the tone of her letters to the Queen, for, from that day onwards all she wrote bore the stamp of an almost overwhelming weariness of both body and mind, and time and again phrases occur giving proof that she no longer felt the strength to fight against her despondency and ill health. "Darling Mama, I don't think you quite know how far from well I am, and how absurdly wanting in strength." Another time: "How low and miserable I feel in these rooms, especially when I go to bed, I cannot tell you." All that had once given her joy was now a torment. The house she had loved was full of haunting memories, she could not bear to look out of her windows into the garden that had once so delighted her, she did not know how to comfort Ernie, who kept crying for his brother. Trying to accept her loss with resignation she wrote to her mother on October 7, telling her that perhaps she should be thankful that her son had ended his fight so soon. "May we all," she continued, "follow in a way as peaceful, and with so little struggle and pain, and leave an image of as much love and brightness behind." When she wrote those words, how little she foresaw the terrible fate that awaited two of her daughters, or the accusations that were to cast such a shadow over the memory of the little girl she had lovingly nicknamed "Sunny".

In 1875 there were once more persistent rumours that Germany contemplated another attack on France. "Bismarck," Queen Victoria exclaimed, "is violent, grasping, unprincipled." There were others, even in Germany, who shared this opinion, and saw the shadow of war threatening their peace and security. In July, Princess Alice and her husband visited Baden, for the coming-of-age of the Hereditary Grand Duke, and watched the big parade in which the Emperor, the Crown Prince, and his eldest son, Prince William, were taking part. "This enormous and splendid army," she wrote and told her mother, "ready at any moment, is a dangerous possession for any country." She had, she continued, spoken to the Emperor, who had appeared distressed that anyone could believe him capable of embarking on another conflict. But neither the Crown Prince, nor the Grand Duke of Baden were reassured, and both of them had said that as long as Bismarck was in power there could be no real peace, and that he might well force another war on an unwilling country.

The Queen had written to the Emperor of Russia, begging him to use his influence, and when he visited Berlin he spoke with very decisive firmness to Bismarck. Later when he came to Heiligenberg he had a long conversation with Princess Alice, begging her to reassure the Queen. "Tell Mama," he said, "how happy I am to know that it is she who desires peace. We cannot and will not quarrel with England." Maybe Queen Victoria smiled somewhat ruefully when she read those consoling words, for the Pan-Slav spirit that was sweeping across Russia, that nation's aggressive attitude towards Turkey, and the fervour with which she seemed to be taking the part of the oppressed Balkan countries, was already causing great anxiety in England.

Prince Louis succeeded as Grand Duke of Hesse in 1877, owing to the deaths of his father, Prince Charles, and of his uncle, within a few months of each other. Her new position as "Landes Mutter" (mother of the country), with all its added responsibilities, weighed heavily on Princess Alice. "Too much is demanded of one," she wrote wearily. "It is more than my strength will stand in the long run."

During the summer of 1878 she was able, however, to come once more to England where the rest and quiet of her stay at Osborne restored her strength. She returned to Darmstadt, still looking wan and pale, but imbued with a new courage, a new resignation, and full of plans for further charitable activities.

And then, on November 8, a telegram from Darmstadt was delivered at Windsor, and opening it, the Queen was overcome with dismay at the news it contained. "Victoria has diphtheria. The fever is high. I am so anxious." Four days later came yet another message, "Tonight my precious Alicky has been taken ill."

As soon as she heard what had happened the Queen sent her own Physician in Ordinary, Sir William Jenner, to Darmstadt, but after he had gone it seemed to her that the tidings of disaster came thick and fast, for on November 13 she heard that her youngest granddaughter, "dear little Marie", had contracted the disease; the next day the Grand Duke and his son were taken ill; and on November 16 she received a message telling her that Princess Marie had died.

In spite of the danger Princess Alice had insisted on nursing her husband and children herself, going from room to room, trying to comfort and soothe and bring relief. On December she was able to tell her mother that Victoria and Alicky were out of danger, and the Grand Duke and Ernie so far recovered that they were able to go out in a closed carriage. But on December 8 Sir William Jenner telegraphed to the Queen to say that her daughter had now herself been taken ill, and that, weak and worn out as she was, the position must be considered serious.

The fourteenth of December was once more the anniversary of Prince Albert's death, and the Queen, obsessed with thoughts of her husband, and memories of "that terrible day" seventeen years ago, had, when she first woke up, almost forgotten her new anxiety. All too soon, however, the remembrance returned to her, and with a heavy heart she went as usual into the Blue Room to pray. Returning after a while to her sitting-room, she found John Brown waiting for her with two telegrams, one from her son-in-law, the other from Sir William Jenner, telling her that Princess Alice, her "dear tenderhearted sweet child", had become suddenly worse at midnight, and had passed away at seven that morning. That this overwhelming blow should have fallen on this day of all days, seemed to the Queen in her sorrow, "almost incredible, and most mysterious".

The British Press was full of tributes to the Princess who had

won all hearts by her courage and devotion; in Hesse the news
that their Grand Duchess, who was only thirty-five, had died
under such tragic circumstances, was received with grief and
dismay. Her liberal ideas, what was called by some her "interference" in the welfare of the country, had been often resented,
but the real good she had done, her gentleness and charm of
manner, had overcome many prejudices. Even Prince Alexander of Hesse, who had often criticized her political activities,
was heartbroken at the thought that this "remarkable, clever
and forceful woman" should have been taken from her husband and children, leaving unfinished so many of the plans she
had begun.

Crowds of mourners came to place their offerings on her
coffin, lying in state in the chapel of the old castle, draped by
her wish in the Union Jack and covered with a violet velvet
pall. A deputation from the Court Theatre, in which she had
taken so much interest, placed on it a wreath intertwined with
pale pink ribbons. A cross of dark green foliage came from
Princess Charles of Hesse; cushions of flowers from the many
charitable organizations she had run; wreaths from the civic
authorities of all the neighbouring towns. An old peasant
woman from the Odenwald sent a tiny garland of rosemary;
two little orphan girls she had once befriended, a small, crumpled bunch of violets.

All day the slow procession passed, the busy life of the little
town was hushed beneath the grey December sky, the white
Palace she had planned so joyfully and furnished with such
loving care, was shuttered and silent.

"Sweet darling Alice," the Crown Princess of Germany
wrote to the Queen. "She was my particular sister, the nearest
in age, the only one living in the same country with me. It
often tormented me to see her so frail, so white . . . though it
only added additional charm . . . seemed to envelop her with
something sad and touching, that always drew me to her all
the more." To the Prince of Wales the death of his sister was

an irreparable loss, and those who saw him at the funeral hardly recognized in the bowed figure the jovial man whose gay, genial laughter they had known in the past. Nor, as time passed, did he forget this favourite, best-loved sister; every year, whatever he was doing, however pressed and busy, he returned to Darmstadt to visit the mausoleum on the Rosenhöhe and kneel before Boehm's effigy of Princess Alice, lying at rest with her youngest daughter in her arms.

When I was a child in Darmstadt I was once taken to the Rosenhöhe, and I can recall my feeling of awe, as I stood before that white, recumbent figure so ineffably peaceful and serene. I was taken, too, for walks in the woods at Kranichstein —walks that were always filled with a certain, rather pleasurable sense of danger, when I saw through the undergrowth low dark shapes moving ponderously about, or sometimes heard in the distance the savage grunt of a wild boar. But the old grey castle itself seemed to me like the enchanted palace of the Sleeping Beauty, its walls and battlements reflected in the waters of the lake, deserted and silent, dreaming of the days when a young bride had moved so busily through the empty rooms, when music and laughter and children's voices had resounded along the passages.

"Does no one live there now?" I asked my German governess. Sighing sadly, she replied, "No, not now. The Grand Duke had it closed many years ago. You see, she died, your English Princess who lived here once, who was so good, so much loved by all who knew her. Some people say they have heard her voice calling to her children, others pretend they have seen her face looking out of the window. But no one ever comes here now."

An empty, silent house, the echoes of a young sweet voice calling to the children who were no longer there; grey walls and battlements, yellow leaves drifting from the autumn trees. An enchanted castle, with only memories of past happiness and dead laughter to fill its deserted rooms.

# Crown Princess Stephanie of Austria

AMONG my mother's many dresses was one I had always specially coveted, a dress of pale mauve satin, so rich in texture that although she had possessed it for nearly twenty years and it had been altered several times to suit the prevailing fashions it always looked new, its shimmering lustre undimmed by time. All round the hem, and half-way up the skirt, it was embroidered with diamond wheatsheaves, which shone and sparkled with every movement, and there was diamond embroidery on the bodice, and silver lace which somehow never seemed to get tarnished.

Again and again I begged my mother to let me have that dress. Once she even allowed me to try it on and I can still vividly recall the thrill of excitement when, standing in her bedroom in St. Petersburg, I put it over my head and the gleaming folds of satin rustled round my feet. In the long looking-glass I saw myself transfigured into an entirely different person, and dreamed of sweeping into a ball-room with diamonds round my neck and in my hair. But when I turned eagerly to my mother, she shook her head. "No, I am afraid it is too old for you," she said firmly, and then, with a little smile, "I promise I will give it you, when you get married."

At that moment the promise seemed as if it might have been fulfilled, but the war and the Russian Revolution intervened, and in 1918 we had to leave St. Petersburg, and were allowed to take only three small cabin trunks with us on the long and perilous journey to England, while all our evening clothes, our Court trains, and velvet, fur-lined evening cloaks, had to be packed away and left behind.

Eight months later the Embassy was raided, by order of the Cheka. Captain Cromie, the Naval Attaché, was killed while trying to prevent the Red Guards from entering the building; the Consul and his staff were arrested and taken to prison; and the soldiers of the Revolution surged through the empty building, and broke into the ball-room where all our trunks had been stored, together with the furniture and belongings of some of the members of the British colony who had fled from the terror in Russia. An Englishwoman who remained on in St. Petersburg during the first years of the Revolution told me how she went to the Embassy and saw the orgy of destruction in the ball-room. The shattered mirrors, the tables and chairs, broken and overturned, the cupboards and trunks burst open, some of the contents still lying scattered on the floor. But everything of value had been taken away, including the mauve satin dress whose ultimate fate I have always longed to know.

That dress had once belonged to the Crown Princess Stephanie of Austria, and I remember how one day, when she was staying at Wolfsgarten, she came into our room, carrying it on her arm. "I want you to have this, Lady Georgie," she said to my mother. "It was chosen for me by Rudolf, and I wore it the last time I went to the Opera with him. I shall never be able to wear it again."

At that time I was only a very little girl, and I knew nothing about the tragedy of Mayerling, or the broken dreams of this tall, fair, young woman, who never looked really happy, in spite of her beautiful clothes and jewels. She deeply offended me when my mother first presented me to her, for, staring at me with her unsmiling, hard blue eyes, she remarked curtly that it was a great pity that my hair was so straight. "When I was your daughter's age," she added, turning to my mother, "my hair reached nearly down to my ankles, and was so curly that I could hardly get the comb through it."

Now, after all these years, I can smile at the agony of self-conscious humiliation that overwhelmed me. Knowing the story of Princess Stephanie of Belgium, married when she was barely seventeen to the Crown Prince Rudolf of Austria, I find it hard to feel anything but pity for a woman who, in spite of all her faults, was so cruelly used by fate.

"Wherever I go, I find a Coburg in the ranks of my enemies," Napoleon once exclaimed. Many years later, Bismarck was to say with a certain impatient contempt, "Coburg is the stud farm of Europe." It was undoubtedly Princess Stephanie's grandfather, Prince Leopold of Coburg, who was chiefly responsible for raising the family of a small German principality to such pre-eminence in Europe. One of the most outstandingly handsome men of his time, he had himself married Princess Charlotte, daughter of George IV of England; after her premature death in childbirth, and his subsequent election to the throne of Belgium, he had chosen as his second wife Princess Louise Marie of Orleans. It was he who had planned the marriages of his sister Victoria, widowed Princess of Leiningen, to the Duke of Kent, and of their daughter Queen Victoria, to his nephew Prince Albert of Coburg. In 1835 he had forced another nephew, Prince Ferdinand of Coburg Kohary, to become the husband and consort of Queen Maria da Gloria of Portugal. It was he again who arranged the marriage of his beautiful niece, Victoire, to the Duc de Nemours, and of her son with a daughter of the Emperor of Brazil.

When his eldest son, Prince Leopold, Duke of Brabant, was barely eighteen, he took him to Vienna, choosing as his bride the Arch-Duchess Marie Henriette, daughter of the Arch-Duke Joseph of Austria. "The bride looks so unhappy," the Duchess de Dino wrote to a friend. "I pity the young Duke also, as these two children are being forced into an unwilling marriage." But King Leopold had no consideration for a boy and a girl who, he thought, did not know their own minds and would soon settle down and be content, even as he had done with his second wife, forgetting apparently that he had once been in love, and had known happiness in that all too brief marriage with Princess Charlotte of England.

The animation, the gaiety and wit, that had made the Arch-Duchess Marie Henriette so popular in Vienna, were soon quenched after she had left Austria with her young husband. Four weeks after her marriage, she wrote to a friend bewailing her fate, and crying out pitifully that she could only hope that God would not allow her to live much longer. Yet, hard and bitter as she became in her misery, she never, it seems, blamed her father-in-law for having forced her into a loveless marriage, and during his last illness in 1865, she was the only member of his family King Leopold could bear to have near him, and she never left his side, remaining with him until the end.

Even before his father's death and his succession to the throne, King Leopold II had entertained soaring ambitions for the future of his country, and had dreamed of colonial expansion to rival the growing power of the British Empire. He, too, had found nothing but disappointment in his marriage, for although he had not approved of his wife's former high spirits, the bleak reserve in which she shut herself away was equally irritating, and he found her unresponsive silence intensely boring. The fact that their first child was a daughter was an added and bitter disappointment, for he wanted to found a powerful dynasty to carry on his plans for the future. When, after the birth of the longed-for heir in 1859, another daughter, Princess Stephanie, was born, he took very little pains to hide his vexation, avoiding the company of his wife, immersing himself more and more in his geographical studies, his plans for colonial development, and his frequent intimacies with other women.

The death of his only son, in 1869, was a shattering blow that nearly undermined his reason. For weeks he could hardly speak or eat, his sleepless nights haunted with self-reproach at not having insisted that his son should never be left alone or unguarded, should never have been permitted to run any risks of accident. For the little boy, playing with his toy boat, had fallen into the pond, taking a chill that resulted in pneumonia, which, in spite of all efforts to save him, ended fatally. The thought that his throne, and the wealth he was beginning to amass, would now pass to his brother, Philip, Count of Flanders, and his son, Prince Albert, was so galling and mortifying, that it compelled the King to live with his wife again. But when a third daughter was born, in 1872, he could hardly contain his furious resentment, and his rage was so violent that his horrified household had to guard his wife's door, in terror that he might do her some harm. From that day onwards he and the Queen hardly spoke to one another, meeting only at meals, when they went to church, or when some national festival or State occasion made it necessary for them to be seen together. Neither of them, it seemed, made any attempt to show their daughters any tenderness or affection.

In such circumstances it is hardly to be wondered at that both Princess Stephanie and her elder sister, Princess Louise, retained dismal memories of their childhood. Their daily life in the castle of Laeken was Spartan in its rigid severity, and their mother seemed almost vindictive in the harshness with which she brought them up. Their rooms were never heated and their windows were always kept wide open, whatever the weather. They were forced to get up at five in the summer, and at six in the winter, and make their own beds; they were not allowed to speak to one another while dressing, nor was the maid in attendance permitted to help them in any way. All the morning they did lessons in an icily cold schoolroom, they were taken for long, dreary walks in the park every afternoon, and were seldom allowed to play games like other children. Their only real pleasure was in the little gardens set aside for them, which they tended themselves.

But the worst part of the day was probably the mid-day meal which the girls shared with their parents; a meal eaten in almost unbroken silence, the King and Queen hardly addressing a word to one another, and their daughters forbidden to speak unless they were spoken to. When the meal which was so dismal, for all the superb excellence of the food, was over, the

Queen would retire to her sitting-room, while through the open door leading to the King's study, the two little girls could see their father with his big, black beard, pacing silently up and down. Having been well schooled, they knew that it was as much as their lives were worth to cross the threshold without special permission. Even when they were with their mother, unless, looking up from the papers she was reading, she asked them a sudden question, they did not dare address her, or even venture to speak to one another. They waited in silence, their longing eyes fixed on the clock, for the hour when they would be free to go to their own apartments.

When she was six years old Princess Stephanie had the welcome and exciting change of a visit to England; for King Leopold was always careful to ingratiate himself with Queen Victoria and traded on her old fondness for his father, her beloved Uncle Leopold. He was mindful, too, of her power in Europe. He wrote to her constantly, and went over to see her whenever it was possible, always taking with him a basket of flowers, or rare and beautiful orchids from the conservatories at Laeken, which had been built by King Leopold I, and were famous the world over. In 1870 he accepted her invitation to visit Windsor, taking with him his second daughter, whom the Queen had not yet seen.

Speaking of this visit many years later, Princess Stephanie said that Queen Victoria spoilt and petted her, and admired her long, golden hair, begging that it might be let loose from the hideous net that confined it. "My Aunt, Queen Victoria, always loved me," I remember Princess Stephanie once saying to my mother, when the Queen's name was mentioned, and it is possible that this little granddaughter of her Uncle Leopold had a special place in the Queen's heart, and that remembering her own not very happy childhood she felt a stirring of pity for this fair-haired child, noticing the stern discipline with which she was being brought up, and the lack of affection she received from her parents.

Five years later there was another break in the sober monotony of the days at Laeken, for Stephanie's elder sister, Louise, became engaged to Prince Philip, the eldest son of Prince August of Coburg Kohary. The preparations for the wedding, the trying on of the bride's and bridesmaids' dresses, the invitations to be sent out, created an amusing diversion from all the compulsory duties and the endless hours of study. The marriage had been arranged by the Queen of the Belgians, regardless of the fact that the bridegroom was fourteen years older than her daughter; but Princess Louise appears to have accepted the plans made for her future without reluctance, seeing in them an escape from the boredom of her life. She was, moreover, flattered by the attentions of this accomplished, good-looking man of the world, and happily unconscious of the misery and heartbreak which lay in store for her.

Though desolate at the thought of losing the companionship of her sister, Stephanie nevertheless enjoyed the excitement of the wedding, the parties and banquets; she was thrilled to be partnered at the marriage ceremony by the bridegroom's youngest brother, Prince Ferdinand of Coburg, never realizing that he escaped from her as soon as posssible, in order to explore the conservatories which, with their beautiful flowers, he found far more to his taste than the gawky little girl, with her fuzzy yellow hair.

When all the festivities were over, and life resumed its ordinary round, Stephanie missed Louise every moment of the day, finding her little sister, Clementine, still too young to be a real companion. She tried to fill the hours with study, with lessons in riding, dancing and deportment, and wondered when her turn would come to escape from Laeken.

She was sixteen, when, in the spring of 1880, the Crown Prince Rudolf of Austria arrived on a visit. Noticing her mother's veiled glances and her father's sudden joviality, she was not slow in guessing the reason of his visit. She did not know that he had brought with him his mistress, Mitzi Kasper,

whom he had left in Brussels. Nor did she realize that he had
already been to Dresden and Madrid in search of a bride,
finding the daughter of the King of Saxony stout, and with no
idea of personal cleanliness, and the Spanish princess plain,
and fatiguingly voluble. After these experiences, the fair young
girl, in spite of her rather unbecoming pale blue dress, made a
good impression on him; he thought her distinguished, sensible
and pretty, and declared that he was very happy. At the same
time, however, he wrote to his mother, who had reproached
him for his choice. It would be impossible, he told her, to find
a bride who would really satisfy her or live up to her expectations. "The little Belgian," he added, "will do as well as another.
No better, and no worse."

Stephanie's own impressions of the slight, dark young man
with the restless eyes, and quick, rather charming smile, were
not very clear or definite, for the only thing she could think of
was her brilliant future as Empress of Austria. The thought of
that future might certainly have dazzled the mind of any young
girl, with its promise of unlimited splendour and power, and
she is hardly to be blamed if she allowed herself to be carried
away by dreams of all that would one day be hers—the Habs-
burg jewels, the Hofburg in Vienna, the Redoutensaal with
its golden ceiling, its Gobelin tapestries and huge crystal
chandeliers, the Spanish Riding School, with the famous
Lippizaner stud of pure white, or coal-black, horses. The
fabulous Palace of Schönbrunn, with its one thousand and
forty-one rooms, its hundred and thirty kitchens, and beautiful botanical gardens. All these marvels, which her mother had
so often described, would soon be hers! No wonder that her
eyes were bright with excitement, or that colour glowed in her
cheeks, making Rudolf, spoilt and sophisticated as he was, see
her transformed and softened by her new-found happiness.

King Leopold was overjoyed that one of his superfluous
daughters was making such a brilliant marriage, and, although
the Queen had been slightly shocked when she heard that

Rudolf had brought Mitzi Kasper to Brussels, she was unable to resist the charm of his manners, and told herself complacently that he was probably no worse than any other young man in his position, and that he would settle down after marriage.

And so, in spite of the Empress Elizabeth's disapproval, and Queen Victoria's openly-expressed opinion that the Crown Prince of Austria was no fit husband for any young girl, the arrangements for the marriage went on. In May 1881 Stephanie and her parents travelled to Austria, going straight to Schönbrunn, where they were received by the Emperor and Empress, and other members of the Imperial family.

The magnificence of her wedding lived up to all Princess Stephanie's expectations. There was her entrance into Vienna, in a wonderful golden coach drawn by six white horses, through streets decorated with flags and flowers, and crowds who cheered themselves hoarse. There was the state banquet, the procession through the Hofburg to the Chapel of St. Augustin, the royal guests, the shifting colours of uniforms and decorations and jewels; and she herself, in her gown of silver brocade, the central figure in this fairy-tale pageant.

She did not know that the Empress Elizabeth, aloof and beautiful, had already nicknamed her a "Trampeltier" (hobble-dehoy) or that, in a letter to a friend, she had expressed her premonition of impending tragedy. "This girl," she wrote, "will bring unhappiness. She is a wooden doll, not fit to be Rudolf's wife." Nor did Stephanie know that the ultra-fastidious Viennese were already criticizing her pale eyebrows, the way her hair was done, and the stiff ugliness of her wedding dress. She did not hear one of the Arch-Dukes whisper to another guest, "She has the daintiness of a dragoon . . . her hands and arms are the colour of my great-coat lining".

When the brilliant ceremonies were over, and the newly-married couple set out to drive to the castle of Laxenberg, where they were to spend the honeymoon, disillusion fell like a blight on the bride, who only a few hours ago had been so

[ 75 ]

triumphantly sure of herself. The fairy tale had ended. The sun, which had shone fitfully throughout the morning, was now obscured by heavy clouds. Although it was May, a few scattered snowflakes fell against the windows of the carriage, an icy wind chilled her to the marrow. Sunk gloomily into his corner, Rudolf had apparently nothing to say to her, and in her youth and inexperience the bride did not know how to approach him, was afraid to be the first to speak. Her throat ached with sobs she could hardly control, her eyes smarted with tears, but Rudolf appeared not to notice her misery, and the uneasy silence remained unbroken.

When at last they arrived at Laxenberg, she found nothing to warm her frozen misery. No fires had been lit in the big, dark rooms, there were no flowers to give her a welcome, there was no bathroom, no hot water, no comfort of any kind. She was alone in a strange country, surrounded by strangers who appeared not to want her, and the rain, and half-frozen snowflakes, beating against the windows, seemed to mock at her lost illusions.

The fairy tale was over indeed, and the girl, who had so happily put on that silver wedding dress breathed a sigh of relief when the time deemed indispensable for a royal honeymoon came to an end, and she was able to accompany her husband on a State visit to Budapest. The reception she received when, in the national dress of the country, she made a short speech in Hungarian, and the cheers that acclaimed her youth and her golden hair, restored some of her self-esteem, and the bitter memories of Laxenberg were submerged in her feeling of triumphant exultation.

In Prague, where the Crown Prince was stationed with his regiment, the apartments in the old castle of Hradschin had been done up, and here Stephanie found some of the modern comforts she desired. But even these did not entirely bring her happiness. Occupied with his military duties, and snatching at every spare moment to go out shooting, Rudolf seldom found

[ 76 ]

time to be with her; yet he sternly supervised all her move-ments, would not allow her any liberty, kept a watch on the guests she received, criticized the way she did her hair, and told her cynically that the dresses she had brought from Belgium were fit for nothing but to be hung on a clothes-horse.

Nevertheless his letters to her, especially during the first years of their marriage, show a certain affection, beginning always "Dearest Angel", and signed, "Your Coco who loves you", or "Your loving Coco", inquiring tenderly after her health, urging her to take the greatest care of herself, sometimes, when he was on his way home, advising her what to order for dinner. But after the birth of a daughter, in 1883, and the Crown Prince's appointment to Vienna, where he and his wife occupied rooms in the Hofburg, the position deteriorated, and Rudolf spent as many evenings as possible away from his wife, drinking and gambling with his friends, or dining at some of the little restaurants in the Wienerwald.

Bored as he might be in his wife's company, he could no longer accuse her of dowdiness. Encouraged by her sister, Louise of Coburg, who was renowned for her good taste and her fabulous wardrobe, Stephanie was indulging in an orgy of extravagance, ordering new clothes, doing her hair in a different fashion, her jewels always carefully chosen to har-monize with the colour and style of her gown. Nor did she content herself with ordering one new hat or dress at a time, she would have several sent from different establishments, trying them all on in turn, giving away those she discarded, instead of returning them to the shop. Since she could never make up her mind till the last moment what to wear, and would often have to send for three or four different sets of jewels from the Treasury in the Hofburg, she was nearly always late for appointments. When Rudolf reminded her that punctuality was the courtesy of kings, or reproached her for her senseless wastefulness, she would burst into tears, and in her turn, accuse him of being unfaithful and inattentive, until, driven to distraction, he would fling out of the room, banging the door behind him.

Certainly no two people could have been more unsuited to one another, and when, after the birth of her daughter, Stephanie fell gravely ill and all hopes of any further children seemed to be doomed, Rudolf, who was devoted to his little daughter but bitterly disappointed at not having a son, seemed to give up even the pretence of being happy in his marriage. He was, at the same time, becoming more and more embroiled in political intrigues, was openly proclaiming his radical ideas, publishing anonymous articles in the papers, and holding secret meetings with Hungarians who were known to be in revolt against the domination of Austria.

His occasional outbursts of rage—or of wild dissipation—were without doubt the signs of an unbalanced character; but when one takes into account the upbringing he had as a child, this is hardly to be wondered at. His first tutor, chosen by the Emperor's mother, the Arch-Duchess Sophie, had been told that the Crown Prince needed to be hardened, and the delicate, sensitive little boy was forced to get up before daybreak and drill in the courtyard, even when snow was on the ground, and was shut up in the wild-game preserve at Schönbrunn, while his tutor, standing outside the gates, warned him that a wild boar was after him. Pistols were let off in his bedroom when he was asleep, traps of all kinds were laid for him, until at last the Empress, defying her mother-in-law, insisted on the tutor being dismissed. But by the time Latour was engaged it was already too late, and the terrors and hardships the little boy had suffered left him with shattered nerves, prone to unreasoning fears, and to fits of morbid melancholy that he tried to overcome and forget with wine and licentious pleasures.

He could, if he pleased, captivate all he came in contact with. Unlike his father, he was a brilliant speaker, and could always find the right word with which to sway his audience. In Berlin Bismarck had been amazed at his clear, mature judgement. The

Crown Princess wrote and told Queen Victoria that she found him delightful. Her son, Prince William, was charmed by his wit and good humour. He was entirely genuine in his wish to improve the lot of suffering humanity, he saw only too clearly the faults and misdirections in the administration of his country, and had he lived to be Emperor the history of Austria might have been a happier one.

Then he married Princess Stephanie of Belgium, who was bored by his interest in science, who could not understand his liberal ideas, who did not respond to his craving for affection, but spied on his movements, and bombarded him with re-criminations and reproaches, her mind set on her position and her brilliant future. The history of their married life does not leave her free from blame, but at the same time it is impossible not to feel sorry for her, and there must have been many moments when, knowing that her husband had no real love for her, and that the Empress openly disliked her, she was intensely lonely and unhappy. Nor did she find the Hofburg, for all the splendour of the State apartments, an ideal home, for the rooms which had been assigned to her were gloomy and dark, lighted only by oil-lamps, which smoked incessantly, pervaded always by the smell of cooking from the adjoining kitchen, and possessing no sanitation, and no hot water.

In spite of the criticisms of Austrian society her looks were improving. She had grown in height, had attained poise and dignity. She was no longer the callow, awkward girl who had been so severely censured on her wedding day. In her book, *Embassies of Other Days*, Walburga, Lady Paget, the wife of the British Ambassador in Vienna, describes in glowing terms her appearance at a Court ball. "The Crown Princess", she says, "was a revelation that evening. I knew that she was not considered pretty in Vienna; imagine then my amazement when I saw, walking behind the Empress, a lovely creature, very tall, with a slight but undulating figure, with a delicate rose tint on her lovely skin, scarlet lips, and a crown of corn-coloured hair above her brows. She was dressed in pale-blue velvet with a front of gold, on which pink and red flowers were embroidered. On her long train reposed beds of many-tinted carnations. Round her throat, and on her head, were large turquoises, set in diamonds. She looked an ideal Elsa of Brabant, and I wondered why the wedding march was not played. Her eyes, it is true, are not large, but they are pretty, blue, and well set, and there is a softness and peachiness about her skin which is bewitching."

I remember my mother also describing her, in a dress of pale pink with mauve draperies, and a crown of diamonds and amethysts on her golden hair. "She looked so young," my mother said, "with her pink and white complexion that one could hardly believe that she was a married woman, and one felt that, when she took off her dress and her wonderful jewels, one would see her in a little short frock with pigtails down her back."

And Princess Stephanie was not unaware of her good looks, and again and again in her memoirs one comes across sentences stressing the favourable impression she created. When she and the Crown Prince visited Constantinople, in 1884, she describes the first audience they had with the Sultan, and says that his eyes were continually fixed on her while he was talking to her husband, and that he left none of her wishes unfulfilled. Several times she made a note of the enthusiastic receptions she received on her various journeys through Austria and Croatia. When she launched a new battleship at Pola, she declared that the acclamations she received expressed a "sincere affection, a profound admiration".

In June, 1887, the Crown Prince was invited to the Jubilee in London, but Stephanie, knowing that Queen Victoria had disapproved of him, refused to accompany him. Contrary to all expectations, however, the Queen was particularly amiable to him. He had been very circumspect in his behaviour, he fascinated all who met him by his charm of manner, and the good reports she received of him, especially from her daughter, the Crown Princess of Germany, made the Queen feel that she had misjudged him, for she conferred on him the Order of the Garter, putting it round his neck herself, and kissing his cheek, which, he wrote and told his wife, nearly made him laugh.

The Crown Prince and his wife were not often together during the next year. For Rudolf was kept busy on manoeuvres, on visits to Berlin, and other missions assigned by his father, while Stephanie stayed for some time in Dalmatia, and in September, 1888, went on a voyage to Greece. When she returned to Vienna in the autumn, she was shocked to see the change in her husband. His pale, sunken cheeks, his feverish eyes, his threats to commit suicide, his outbursts of insensate rage, the few remarks he let slip regarding the political intrigues he was involved in, all filled her with intense anxiety. He was, she could see, drinking heavily. He told her that he was taking drugs to soothe his constant irritating cough, and to dull the pains of rheumatism, from which he suffered. But he refused to give any further explanation about his changed appearance and his evident state of nervous apprehension; it was from other sources that she heard that there had been a violent quarrel between him and his father, and that from that day his health had seemed to have deteriorated.

At last, seriously alarmed and full of misgivings, Stephanie decided to appeal to the Emperor herself. Instead of waiting to send a formal request for an interview, which she should have done, knowing the uncompromising etiquette that prevailed in the Hofburg, she went straight to her father-in-law's room, and ordered the Chamberlain to announce her.

Seated at his vast writing-table, with its red-shaded lamp, Franz Joseph looked up from the pile of papers in front of him, surprise and irritation at this abrupt interruption on his usually kindly face. Undeterred by his obvious vexation, and not waiting to be asked the reason of her visit, Stephanie burst into a torrent of words. Rudolf, she said, was desperately ill. Something must be done or he would die. He was drinking too much. He was taking drugs. He was in a state of nervous exhaustion that would surely lead to a complete breakdown, and drive him insane. He must be sent to another country. He must be got away from the women who were pursuing him, and from his friends, who were leading him into all sorts of trouble.

Thoroughly informed by the secret police of his son's love-affair with Mary Vetsera, the Emperor saw in his daughter-in-law's complaints the hysterical ravings of a jealous woman, and was not inclined to take them seriously. She was giving way to fancies, he told her, in his flat, rather tired voice. Certainly Rudolf was a little pale, he had remarked it himself several times, but he did not think there was anything seriously wrong, and he was certain that she need not be anxious about the Crown Prince's mental state. He had always been excitable, he was too active, would not forego either duty or pleasure. Stephanie should persuade him to rest, to stay at home a little more. After all, she was his wife, she ought to know how to make herself agreeable to him.

"I should have made a very good civil servant," Franz Joseph once said, with a certain wry humour, unconscious how apt his words were. He took his duties seriously, was at work every morning before the break of day, dipping his buttered roll into a steaming cup of coffee, eating his frugal mid-day meal off a tray placed at the corner of his desk, never failing to read through every paper placed before him. But at the same time he was unwilling to face unpleasant facts, was totally lacking in imagination, reluctant to give any decision that might upset the even tenor of his day. Kindhearted, pedantic, and phlegmatic, he was indeed the personification of an excellent servant of the public. Looking at that bland, complacent face, Stephanie knew that she had failed to move him. This, she thought bitterly, is the Emperor of Austria, the man who has unlimited power, the man who calls himself the father of his people, and yet has so little care for his own son that he will not lift a finger to save him. With a gesture of despair she turned away, her eyes blinded with tears, walking from the big room, with its panelled walls, its shaded lights and crimson curtains, leaving the Emperor once more immersed in his papers, her unwelcome interruption forgotten.

At the Opera a few nights later the Crown Princess saw Mary Vetsera sitting in a box opposite, saw her raise her glasses to stare at her shamelessly, taking in every detail of her dress and her jewels, making Stephanie feel acutely conscious that, having once more been late, she had failed to fasten all the buttons of her long white gloves.

Everybody in Vienna knew that this girl of Armenian extraction, with her black hair, her white skin, and dark, melting eyes, was Rudolf's latest mistress. Stephanie herself was not ignorant of the fact, for her husband had never made any secret of his many infidelities. She did not know, however, that the girl had several times been driven late at night to one of the back entrances of the Hofburg, in Rudolf's carriage. Nor did she know that, making her mother believe she had gone to bed, she had crept out of the house, flinging on her fur coat over her nightdress.

"Look well at the little Vetsera," Rudolf is reported to have once said to his wife. "She will be my death." My mother, who had known the girl well in Vienna, had been horrified and disturbed by the almost fanatical frenzy in her eyes when she spoke of Rudolf. "I will never let him go," she once exclaimed, when my mother tried to reason with her, "I will die with him, if there is no other way, but he shall not leave me."

On January 27 1889 a big ball was given at the German Embassy in honour of the young Emperor William's birthday, several members of the Imperial family being invited, as well as the Diplomatic Corps, and all Viennese society. The Crown Prince and Crown Princess were also present. During the course of the evening Stephanie, in a red velvet dress, trimmed with gold, came face to face with Mary Vetsera in the crowded room, the girl staring at her insolently, and turning away without even dropping a curtsy.

The incident had not passed unnoticed. Stephanie, seeing her husband dancing with this girl who had been so rude to her, heard the whispered comments and sat with a white set face, leaving as soon as possible. She called angrily to her footman, who was slow in bringing her white ermine cloak, and was rebuked by her husband, who would never tolerate discourtesy to servants.

Early the next morning Rudolf came to Stephanie's room, telling her that he was leaving for his shooting-box at Mayerling, but that he did not wish her to accompany him, as his only guests were to be Prince Philip of Coburg and Count Hoyos. Promising to return for a family dinner with the Emperor on the 29th, he took his leave, and watching him go, Princess Stephanie declares in her memoirs that a cold feeling of premonition swept over her, warning her that she would never see him again, and that their life together was over.

Indeed Rudolf never returned to the Hofburg. On the 29th he sent a telegram, excusing himself from attending his father's dinner, on the plea that he had a bad cold, and did not dare risk the long drive into town. On the morning of the 30th January, Stephanie, in a crimson silk dressing-gown, was having her usual singing-lesson, when a white-faced lady-in-waiting brought her the news of her husband's death, and summoned her into the presence of the Emperor and Empress.

The tragedy of Mayerling has been written about too often to need recapitulating in all its terrible details. But in spite of the years that have passed since that January night, in spite of the varying explanations that have been given the true story still remains an unfathomable secret. Did Rudolf, behind those locked doors, shoot Mary Vetsera and then himself, because there was no hope of their ever marrying? Did she, in her hysterical love for him, force him into a suicide pact? Or, in that interview with his father, did something transpire that opened his eyes to the danger he stood in, owing to his political intrigues?

It is significant, perhaps, that among the letters found on the table in Rudolf's room at Mayerling there was none for the Emperor, and although it is reported that Franz Joseph opened and read them all, it is not known whether he found the explanation of the tragedy. Bombelles, to whom it is rumoured that Rudolf told the truth, was sworn to secrecy, and died a little later without revealing his knowledge.

Frantic endeavours were made to hush the matter up. By order of the Emperor, the first report published in the Press stated that the Crown Prince had succumbed to a sudden heart-attack, but in spite of the consent for a State Funeral obtained from the Pope, rumours spread and multiplied, and the fact that Rudolf had committed suicide soon became public knowledge. As the wild fantastic stories spread from mouth to mouth, the agony of the Emperor and Empress increased, and the girl who found herself so suddenly a widow knew that in their eyes she was guilty of having caused their son's death, because she had failed to win his confidence, and had not given him the support and sympathy he needed.

The King and the Queen of the Belgians had hurried to Vienna to be near their daughter in her hour of terrible trial, but when she begged and implored to be allowed to return to Belgium with them, her father refused to take her, and the Emperor told her sternly that it was her duty to remain in the country she had adopted when she married, and to carry out Rudolf's wishes to look after their only daughter. Queen Victoria's invitation to Windsor was also courteously declined for the same reasons, and Stephanie had to resign herself to remaining in the crape-draped gloom of her apartments in the Hofburg, to the censorious criticism she read in all eyes, and the memories of Rudolf that haunted her at every step. At last, making the excuse that the climate of Vienna was seriously affecting her health, she obtained permission to go to Miramar, taking her little daughter with her. They stayed for several months in that lovely palace overlooking the Adriatic.

Stephanie was only twenty-five when Rudolf died, and as time passed the resilience of youth enabled her to take up her life again, to find pleasure once more in clothes, in dancing and riding, and driving her four-in-hand. She had improved, not only in looks, but in her manners. She no longer interrupted when people were speaking, no longer tried to monopolize the conversation, or to air her views, regardless of whom she offended. There were many men who found her tall, slender fairness attractive, who considered it an honour to be seen in her company. Staying sometimes in Vienna, sometimes at Laxenberg, which had been given her for a residence, sometimes at Miramar, paying occasional visits to other European countries, she was learning to enjoy life. She was only too ready to put the past with its harrowing memories behind her, to carry out Rudolf's injunctions to be happy in her own way.

When I saw her at Wolfsgarten she was accompanied by Count Elmer Lonyay, and I often overheard whispered remarks which, needless to say, were not meant for my ears, regarding her friendship with this tall, good-looking Hungarian nobleman, who was so constantly by her side. Although she was debarred as the widowed Crown Princess from her former position at the Viennese Court, she was still a member of the Imperial family, and the gossip that surrounded her finally became so persistent that the Emperor, persuaded by his friend Catherine Schratt, gave his consent to her marriage, conferring on Count Lonyay the title of Prince.

Unlike her unfortunate sister, Princess Stephanie never knew the crushing burden of poverty, the ceaseless anxiety over unpaid bills, the cruel persistence of creditors, that pursued Princess Louise up to her death after her divorce from Prince Philip of Coburg. Stephanie on the other hand knew happiness and peace in her second marriage, and even after 1918, when Prince

Lonyay's estates in Hungary were seized, and, like so many others, he and his wife sought refuge in Switzerland, they were still able to keep up an almost royal state, and right up to her death, at the age of eighty-one, in 1945, she never forgot that she should have been Empress of Austria.

# The Grand Duchess Elizabeth

IN November, 1864, Princess Alice of Hesse wrote to tell Queen Victoria that she and her husband had decided to call their second daughter, born on the first of the month, Elizabeth, after the Saint so beloved and venerated in Darmstadt. "I forgot," she wrote a little later, "to tell you, in answer to your letter about Ella's name, that of course she must be called Elizabeth; only 'entre nous' Ella." For the next few months her letters to her mother were full of the sweetness of the new baby, her deep-blue eyes, her bright chestnut hair, her merriness, her loving ways, her occasional naughtiness.

In August, 1865, Queen Victoria went herself to Darmstadt, partly to see the beginnings of the new Palace that was being built for Princess Alice and her husband, and partly to make the acquaintance of her new granddaughter. In no way alarmed or intimidated by the indefinable air of power and majesty that surrounded the short, stout lady, in the sombre black dress, the baby looked up at her with laughing blue eyes, and allowed her fat cheeks to be kissed, without a whimper of protest. "She is so very good, my grandmama," she said a little later, and Princess Alice no doubt breathed a sigh of relief; for her second daughter had a mind of her own, and had been decidedly rebellious when her other grandmother, Princess Charles of Hesse, had tried to caress her. "So very tiresome," Princess Alice said plaintively, bewailing the fact that a child who was otherwise so amiable, should apparently not like old ladies.

But when, in the summer of 1865, her mother took her on a visit to Heiligenberg, and her Great-Aunt Marie held her for half an hour on her lap, the little girl was delighted, throwing her fat arms round her neck, pressing her face against the haggard, feverish cheeks of the woman who was Empress of

Russia, and who found perhaps in the exuberant affection of this lovely child a momentary balm for her aching heart.

Born Princess Marie, daughter of the Grand Duke Ludwig II of Hesse-Darmstadt, the Empress had left Germany in 1841 to marry the Grand Duke Alexander, heir to his father, the Emperor Nicholas I of Russia. It had not been a marriage arranged for reasons of State, for the Grand Duke Alexander had fallen in love with Princess Marie, when he paid a duty visit to her father at the end of his tour of Europe in 1839, and, in spite of the opposition of his parents, had insisted that she was the only woman in the world for him. But from the outset the little German Princess had not been very happy in Russia. Her mother-in-law, the Empress, had been a daughter of Queen Louise of Prussia, and, in her pride of birth did not trouble to hide her dislike of her son's marriage. Her father-in-law was immensely tall, imposing and alarming, and although he could at times be genial and gay, she was never able to get over her shyness in his presence. Because of her shyness her manner was stiff, and St. Petersburg society complained that she was cold and austere, said she had no taste in dress, no conversation, no charm. The cold, damp climate of the northern capital never agreed with her, the piercing winds, the dank, humid mists rising from the swamps on which St. Petersburg was built, affected the delicate chest she had inherited from her mother, brought on a racking cough and intermittent, recurring fever.

There could be no question of her love for her tall, splendid young husband; never, for one moment, in thought, word or deed, was she unfaithful to him, and she bore him five sons and one daughter, her frequent pregnancies still further impairing her health and sapping her vitality. Her first years in Russia had, it is true, been brightened by the fact that her favourite brother, Prince Alexander of Hesse, had accompanied her, had been given a commission in the Chevaliers Gardes, and was her constant companion. She missed him intolerably, when, after his elopement with one of her ladies-in-waiting, the Emperor banished him from Russia and even her adoration for her husband failed to compensate her for the loss of Alexander's unfailing gaiety and laughter. As time passed, she began to realize that her husband was growing less ardent, and although the possibility that he was unfaithful to her filled her with apprehension, she could not entirely blame him, knowing how often he had been forced, by her ill health, to go alone to Court festivities, and aware, too, that there were many women in society only too eager to console him for her absence.

The Emperor Nicholas died in 1855. When the period of Court mourning was over the young Empress found the burden of her great position almost beyond her strength, her growing infirmity making it a martyrdom to her when she was forced to take part in some State occasion. How often, with aching limbs, and a burning fever, she had to take that part, only those who were in immediate attendance on her, and had to help her take off the heavy Court robes, the massive tiara, knew or realized. Society grumbled at her frequent absence, and complained that even when she did appear, she showed no animation. Nobody, they murmered, could doubt her piety, her devotion to her husband, to her children, and to charity; but Russia wanted more than that, what was needed was an Empress who was always accessible, always on view, always smiling, beautifully dressed, and resplendent with jewels.

Alexander never failed to treat her with tender and considerate kindness, but after 1858 she knew, with a blinding certainty, that his heart no longer belonged to her, for the rumours of his secret meetings with Princess Catherine Dolgorouky were not long in reaching her ears. The knowledge that this girl, who was young enough to be his daughter, had completely bewitched him, was an agony that consumed the Empress, though she hid it with a cold and frigid self-control.

The death of her eldest son, the Grand Duke George, in 1865, soon after his engagement to Princess Dagmar of

Denmark, extinguished her last happiness on earth. He had always been her favourite, on him she had lavished all the love she had never been able to give her other children, and his loss left her aged and broken, and without the will to fight against the disease that was slowly destroying her.

The only time she found comparative happiness and peace was when she went to stay with her brother, Prince Alexander of Hesse, and his wife, in the castle of Heiligenberg, near Darmstadt. There she could forget the burdens and responsibilities of her life in Russia, and the increasing ascendency of Catherine Dolgorouky over the Emperor. There, in the soft air and sunshine, her health improved, and she could sit on the terrace watching her two youngest sons, Serge and Paul, playing with the four tall Battenberg boys, and with the children of Princess Alice. Although she saw her nephew's wife so often, she was not however always in sympathy with her. She disagreed with her policy of conciliation with Prussia, and was very angry at her going to Berlin with her husband in 1879. "Louis and Alice," she told her brother Prince Alexander, "are, with all due respect, possessed of the devil, in their mania for inappropriate visits."

The fact that it was Princess Alice who had first suggested the idea of a marriage between the Duke of Edinburgh and the Grand Duchess Marie, was another sore point, for the Empress had from the first been opposed to the union. After the Russo-Turkish war had broken out, and she received letters from her daughter bewailing the difficulties of her position in England, she smiled a little grimly, for had she not always said that a marriage between a Romanoff and a member of the English royal family was a mistake.

The tragic death of the Grand Duchess of Hesse, after nursing her husband and children through diphtheria in 1879, however, made the Empress forget all her former antipathy to this daughter of Queen Victoria. The misery of the Grand Duke touched her heart, and she invited the motherless children as often as possible to the castle of Heiligenberg. Both Princess Victoria and Princess Elizabeth were now growing up, and the little fat Ella whom she had nursed so often, was beginning to show signs of an almost breath-taking beauty, a beauty that the Empress saw did not pass unnoticed by her son. In the past, when Ella had been a baby, Serge had often left his games with the other boys, to lead her gently by the hand, guiding her uncertain footsteps down the steep garden paths. Now she was growing up, and he was a man, a man moreover whose thoughts even his mother could not read. He had always been so different from her other sons; those tall, handsome, boisterous young men with their exuberant vitality, their sometimes lewd conversation. Spoilt by their father, adored by St. Petersburg society, they had never denied themselves anything. Thanks to their good looks and their charm, they had always been forgiven, even for the most flagrant and notorious indiscretions. But there was about Serge a cold, mystic austerity that gave one the uneasy feeling that it concealed something hidden and secret, and somehow a little frightening. It would not, his mother thought, be easy to be his wife, and what did this lovely young girl know of men, brought up as she had been in the sheltered security of a little German court, her only knowledge of the outside world occasional visits to her grandmother in England, and that sedate, homely Court which was, it seemed, perpetually in mourning.

The Empress sighed and thrust away the problem, for her head ached, and she was finding it difficult to breathe, and she had many other cares and troubles to oppress her. The growing power of nihilism in Russia was a nightmare that filled all her thoughts, and she lived in hourly terror that the attacks on the Emperor's life would in the end prove successful. When, in the winter of 1880, a bomb exploded under the dining-room in the Winter Palace, she was already so ill that, although the blast shook her apartment, she did not notice it. Nor did she know how narrowly the Emperor, his sons, and all the members of his Court, had escaped death, thanks to the fact that Prince Alexander of Hesse, who had come on a visit to St. Petersburg, had arrived late and the Emperor had delayed going into the dining-room in order to stay and talk to him in his study.

On June 3 the Empress Marie's long martyrdom came to an end, and six weeks after her death the Emperor married Catherine Dolgorouky at Tsarskoe. The precipitate hastiness of this action aroused the furious indignation of all his family, and greatly shocked Queen Victoria. Fully aware of the unpopularity of his marriage he wrote to his sister Olga, Queen of Württemberg, explaining that as he lived in daily fear of assassination he had to do his best, without delay, to safeguard the future of the woman who had given up so much for him, as well as of the three children she had borne him.

Whatever happiness he may have had was of short duration, for on March 13, 1881, the assassins, who had for so long dogged his footstsps, made their final and successful attempt on the life of the man who had given freedom to the serfs, and contemplated giving Russia a constitutional government. In spite of warnings he had insisted on attending the usual Sunday review of his Guards; on the way back a bomb was thrown at his carriage, killing two of the cossacks of his escort and wounding several others. The coachman attempted to drive on, but the Emperor ordered him to stop. On his refusal to do so, Alexander seized the reins and got out of the carriage, the second bomb exploding near him as he went to give help to the wounded. Carried back to the Winter Palace, he died a few hours later, the document which he had signed only that morning, giving a constitutional government to Russia, still lying on his writing-table. It was torn up by his son, who succeeded him as Alexander III.

The Grand Duke Serge was in Rome when his father was assassinated, and was spared the horror of seeing that broken, mutilated body carried into the Winter Palace; nor did he have to watch the agony that followed, an agony which I once heard the Dowager Empress describe as the most harrowing and ghastly memory of her life. Serge had adored his father, and there can be little doubt that this murder had a profound and fatal effect, making him savagely reactionary, filling him with hatred of the people who had so cruelly repaid their Emperor's attempts at liberation. Maybe it also intensified his love for Elizabeth of Hesse, for he was filled with foreboding that he would meet the same end as his father. Feeling that he must snatch at the happiness this girl alone could give him, he attended the marriage of her sister to Prince Louis of Battenberg in Darmstadt and asked her father for her hand in marriage.

She did not, it seems, hesitate in accepting him, for she could never forget how gentle he had been with her when she was a child. She was too young and inexperienced to sense the fevers that burned beneath his seemingly impassive manner. Moreover, she infinitely preferred him to her cousin, William of Prussia, whose tempestuous ardour she had found very disturbing when, during the years he was studying at Bonn University, he had come to stay at Darmstadt or at Kranischstein.

Knowing that her sister the Crown Princess of Prussia was finding her eldest son intractable and difficult, Princess Alice had hoped that the example of the happy home life led by her children might be a good influence upon him, but they disliked his restlessness and complained that his rapid changes of mood made him an impossible companion. At one moment he would want to go rowing, then it would be riding, or a game of tennis, always eager to show how proficient he was in spite of his crippled arm. He would rein in his horse, or throw down his racket in the middle of a game, and order them all to come and listen to him reading the Bible. Whether he was riding, playing games, or reading, he wanted his cousin Ella to be near him, always his brilliant eyes followed her movements, and when she spoke he was silent, listening to every

[94]

inflection of her voice. No engagement, however, took place, and in 1881 he married the Princess Augusta of Schleswig-Holstein-Sonderburg. It is known that for several years, even after he had succeeded his father as Emperor of Germany, and after Elizabeth of Hesse had become the Grand Duchess Serge of Russia, he refused obstinately to meet her, never going to see her if she was passing through Berlin, and deliberately keeping at a distance, if circumstances forced them to be together on some State occasion. Questioned as to this marked avoidance of his cousin, he sometimes refused to reply, or if he did, said harshly that he could never forget how much she had meant to him in the past, and how much he had loved her.

Princess Elizabeth's engagement was a short one, for Serge was impatient for the marriage to take place as soon as possible, and although the Grand Duke of Hesse did not altogether approve of this haste, he was forced to acquiesce, and in June, 1884, he arrived in St. Petersburg with Elizabeth and her two younger sisters, Irene and Alix.

Russia, with its vastness, its strange, inexplicable atmosphere, overawed the two elder Princesses who had, with the exception of their visits to England, seen so little of the world. The huge squares, the broad streets of St. Petersburg, the Neva, which was so much bigger and wider than any river in Germany or England, the golden domes and spires of the cathedrals, the baroque immensity of the Winter Palace, the all-pervading smell of sunflower-oil and leather and cigarettes, the fountains spraying scented water, the teeming rabbit-warrens of rooms and corridors on the upper floors of the palace, the inadequate sanitary arrangements—all this was so new and unexpected that they felt bewildered and confused, unable to accustom themselves to the strangeness of these unfamiliar surroundings. They were intimidated by the crowds of servants, by the numerous ladies-in-waiting who fussed around them, by the Court attendants who were always giving them different instructions, but most of all by Serge's brother, the Emperor

Alexander, with his immense height, his broad shoulders, square-cut beard, loud voice, and hands that could straighten an iron horseshoe, or roll a silver coin into a tube without any visible effort. Alicky alone, being only twelve years old at the time, seemed to have no apprehensions; she found nothing awe-inspiring in the vast halls of the Winter Palace, with their miles of shining parquet floors, but spent hours playing at hide-and-seek round the tall pillars of marble and porphyry with the eldest son of the Emperor Alexander III who, shy and diffident with strangers, found this little girl with the bright golden curls an enchanting companion with whom he always felt perfectly at ease.

The Grand Duke of Hesse had refused to allow his daughter to change her religion before marriage, so there had to be both a Lutheran and an Orthodox marriage service. When at last the long, tiring ceremonies were over, and pale and misty-eyed, Elizabeth had said good-bye to her father and her two sisters, it must have been with an aching heart and a sense of fear, almost perhaps of terror, that she faced her life in this unfamiliar country, surrounded by strange, new relations, and with a husband who was almost completely unknown.

There is nothing to show that she was unhappy; if she suffered, she did so in silence, uttering no word of complaint. But the general feeling in St. Petersburg society was one of sympathy for a lovely, innocent young girl married to a man whose coldness of manner was said to conceal a vicious depravity. Even Queen Marie of Roumania who, as a child, adored her Uncle Serge, confessed that he was always a little frightening, that his eyes were steel-grey and cold, his lips thin, his manner very often harsh.

With the white astrakhan cap on his well-shaped head, his close-cropped fair beard, his tall, slender figure in the dark-green uniform with the baggy trousers, he was imposing and wonderfully handsome; but always one had the uneasy feeling that beneath his iron self-control, there lay secret and consuming fires. He adored his wife, he worshipped her beauty, he loaded her with presents of gorgeous jewels and furs, but he would frequently rebuke her in public if she forgot an instruction or committed what he considered a breach of etiquette.

None who saw the Grand Duchess Serge in those days could ever forget her. "She was", one contemporary writer says, "the most beautiful creature of God I have ever seen." Yet although many must have fallen under the spell of that beauty, and although she was young and gay and human enough to enjoy the marvellous clothes and jewels her husband gave her, no breath of scandal ever touched her name. Queen Marie of Roumania, who visited Russia when she was a little girl, gives a vivid description of her at some of the Court ceremonies. "Aunt Ella", she says in her memoirs, "on these occasions was so fairy-like an apparition that I would like to dip my pen in colour, so as to be able to make her live again, if only for a moment, because eyes that have never beheld her will never be able to conceive what she was. With that divine smile curving her perfect lips, with a blush on her cheeks, only comparable to almond-blossoms, and an almost bashful look in her long-shaped, sky-blue eyes. . . . Her gown, heavily embroidered in silver, is a colour which is neither blue nor green, the colour of glaciers or of aquamarine; her *kakoshnik* of emeralds and diamonds is truly a halo for her angelic face, and the gorgeous jewels, covering arms and throat, have, when she wears them, the aspect of gifts, piously offered to some beloved saint."

I cannot now say definitely what year it was, but I remember being taken to see some *tableaux vivants* in the Palace at Darmstadt, and seeing the Grand Duchess Serge taking the part of her ancestress St. Elizabeth, who was a daughter of the King of Hungary, and was married to a Landgraf of Thuringia, in Hesse-Marburg. The legend of St. Elizabeth and the Roses was a familiar one in Germany, and I had seen many pictures representing the scene where the Princess, taking food and comfort to the poor in the village, was stopped and questioned by her husband. Replying that her basket held flowers, not food, she held it out for him to see, when the loaves, meat and milk it contained, were miraculously transformed into a glowing mass of roses. The tall, slender figure of the Grand Duchess Serge, dressed in a long blue velvet robe, with a silver veil covering her lovely head, a little secret smile on her lips, and her deep blue eyes full of a mystic radiance as she held out her basket full of deep-red roses, has remained in my mind like the picture of a saint in some old cathedral window. St. Elizabeth! No one present that day had any conception of what lay ahead. No one, in the invulnerable security of that late Victorian era, could foresee how closely the fate of the woman whose beauty they applauded so rapturously was to resemble that of her ancestress who, after her husband's death in the Crusades, was driven from her home, separated from her children, and, devoting her life to the care of the sick, died at the age of twenty-four, when the Emperor Frederick II, who had vainly sought her hand in marriage, laid a golden crown on her coffin.

One summer the Grand Duchess Serge and her husband stayed at Wolfsgarten, and I remember seeing her often, always dressed very simply in the daytime, when even the ugly fashions of the time—the plainly-dressed hair and leg-of-mutton sleeves—were unable to spoil the spiritual loveliness of her face. The Grand Duke Serge adored children and in spite of the almost forbidding sternness of his face I trusted him implicitly, even when one day he took me out on the water-chute the Grand Duke had built on the pond in the woods, sitting behind me and holding me tightly round the waist. "You need not be afraid, Dushinka [little darling]," he said softly. "Even if the boat upsets I can swim and we shall not drown."

The Grand Duchess Elizabeth had adopted the Orthodox religion a year or two after her marriage, much against her father's wishes; and when, after her visit to St. Petersburg, he was told that the Tsarevitch Nicholas had fallen in love with

Princess Alix, he refused point-blank to permit another daughter of his to abjure her Protestant faith. Nor did Queen Victoria approve of these changes in religion, and she did not favour the idea of her favourite grandchild becoming engaged to the Tsarevitch. She had thought him charming, simple, and unaffected when he visited Windsor, but at the same time she felt that he lacked stability and decision. The Emperor and Empress shared her apprehensions, although for a very different reason. Princess Alix had not been altogether popular when she stayed in St. Petersburg, the Emperor had thought her a typical German, and the Empress had been irritated by her stiffness; moreover she had wanted her son to marry the daughter of the Comte de Paris, and she did not think this little Princess of Hesse with the shy, almost hostile manner, would make him a good wife.

Like his grandfather, Alexander II, the Tsarevitch Nicholas was determined that his choice was the right one. "My dream is to marry Alix of Hesse," he wrote in his diary on December 21, 1889. At last, in April, 1894, the Emperor, who was already ailing, gave his permission to the engagement, and the Tsarevitch hurried to Coburg, where a big concourse of guests had assembled for the wedding of Princess Victoria Melita, daughter of the Duke of Edinburgh, to the Grand Duke Ernst Ludwig of Hesse, who had succeeded his father in 1891. But as the wife of the Tsarevitch and heir to the throne, Princess Alix knew that she would have to belong to the Orthodox Church, and at first she could not make up her mind to change her religion. "The poor thing cried a good deal," the Tsarevitch noted in his diary, describing a long interview he had with her, which lasted till midnight. On April 8, however, came the "beautiful, unforgettable day" when, hand in hand, they went into Queen Victoria's room, to tell her that they had reached an understanding. "I was quite thunderstruck", the Queen wrote in her journal, "as, although I knew that Nicky much wished it, I thought Alix was not sure of her mind."

The Grand Duchess Serge, who was among the wedding guests at Coburg, was overjoyed at her sister's engagement. From all sides congratulations poured in, and even the Queen began to think that this marriage might bring a closer understanding with Russia. But from the outset, shadows seemed to gather round the young couple whose future appeared so brilliant, and full of promise, for when the Tsarevitch returned to St. Petersburg, he found his father's health had deteriorated, and although he was able in June to spend a few unforgettably happy weeks with Alix at Windsor, he had to forego his visit to Wolfsgarten and hurry back to Russia. A few months later, the Emperor, who had been moved to the Crimea, became worse. In October the doctors gave up hope, and Princess Alix had to cut short her preparations, and hurry away from Darmstadt. She was met by her sister in Warsaw, and travelled with her to Livadia, arriving there only a few days before the Emperor's death.

After the long, slow, mournful journey to St. Petersburg, and the long-drawn-out funeral services, the wedding was hurried on. In spite of the deep mourning it took place on November 26, 1894. "Alicky looked too wonderfully lovely," the Princess of Wales telegraphed to her mother-in-law, and at Windsor Queen Victoria gave a dinner-party in honour of her granddaughter's wedding, wore again the bright cherry-coloured ribbon of St. Catherine, and stood while the Russian National Anthem was played. "How impossible it seems", she wrote in her journal, "that gentle little simple Alicky should be the great Empress of Russia."

The coronation of the young Emperor and Empress took place in May 1896 the Emperor riding into Moscow on a white horse, followed by two golden coaches bearing his mother and his wife, the Dowager Empress in gold brocade, the Empress Alexandra in silver with a long golden train, her fair head crowned with diamonds. The rose-red walls of the Kremlin re-echoed to the thunder of the bells of Ivan Veliki, and the old Uspensky Cathedral, where all the Emperors of Russia had been crowned, was filled to overflowing with members of the Imperial family, royal guests who had come to Moscow for the ceremony, foreign representatives, and all the men and women holding high office, either in the Government or at Court. The lights of thousands of candles fell on the golden painted columns, on the dim old frescoes, gleamed on the gorgeous diadems, the decorations, the brilliant colours of the priests' vestments, the blue-and-gold, high-collared robes of the choristers.

"Most glorious and impressive ceremony," Prince Arthur wrote to his mother, omitting however to tell her that at one moment during the long ceremony the Emperor, overcome by the weight of his Imperial robes, by the heat, the clouds of incense and the smell of the flickering candles, had nearly fainted, and had let the jewelled sceptre fall from his fingers. Although it was quickly recovered, and he pulled himself together, the accident gave the superstitious yet another reason for their gloomy predictions of misfortune.

Nor was this the only accident to cast a shadow over the coronation festivities, for the tragedy of the Khodinska plain, three miles from Moscow, where a huge crowd had gathered for the traditional fair, and where hundreds lost their lives, gave to all who were present the uneasy feeling of impending disaster.

"A most untoward and horrible catastrophe took place here early yesterday morning," telegraphed Sir Nicholas O'Connor, British Ambassador in St. Petersburg, to the Queen on May 31. He described how the crowd of peasants who had slept on the field all night in their anxiety to reach the place where meals were to be given them free, surged forward in the early morning, overcoming the police. For some reason a panic started; those who were in front tripped over the uneven ground, which had been cut up in trenches, and those behind, unable to stop themselves, trampled on the fallen; others, passing over wells that had been inadequately protected by thin boards which gave way under the weight, were precipitated to their deaths.

Although the Emperor was warned that an accident had taken place, and that a few people had been crushed, the whole magnitude of the disaster, in which over two thousand people were killed or injured, was not divulged, and by the time he arrived on the scene the bodies and casualties had been taken away, although some, it was said, were hidden actually under the Imperial pavilion where he was standing.

The Grand Duke Serge, who had been appointed Governor of Moscow in 1891, had at first, as Queen Victoria feared, been blamed for the tragedy, but later it was found that the Chief of Police had failed to carry out the orders he had received, and had been culpably negligent in making arrangements. The fact that the Emperor and Empress were present that night at a ball given by the French Ambassador, was also severely criticized, but the Empress, who had returned from the hospitals in floods of tears, had begged and prayed to have the ball postponed, and was told that it was not possible at the last moment, for it would not do to offend France. But she was, Sir Nicholas O'Connor noted, evidently in great distress, her eyes were reddened with tears, and the ball was altogether a dismal affair, nobody able to forget the horror of what had occurred.

Princess Catherine Radziwill, in her books an unsparing critic of the Romanoff family, declares that neither the Empress, nor her sister, the Grand Duchess Serge, ever visited the hospitals, or took any interest in the injured; but there are other witnesses besides Sir Nicholas O'Connor to prove that both they and the Dowager Empress were unremitting in their care for those who had suffered, that they visited the hospitals every day and made liberal provision for the families of those who had died. "Aunt Ella was in despair," said Queen Marie, who was present at the coronation, and although her husband was eventually exonerated from blame, the memory of that day remained to haunt her, and she was never able to rid herself of the thought that in some way he had been guilty of negligence.

The Diamond Jubilee of 1897 brought a gathering of Queen Victoria's relations once more to London. It was the last time that some of her grandchildren, and great-grandchildren, were to see the little old lady who for so many years had been the centre round which their lives revolved, whose approval they all sought and cherished, whose anger and criticism they dreaded, even if they were thousands of miles away. They all brought gifts and offerings—a diamond chain from her younger daughters, a diamond brooch from the Prince and Princess of Wales, a diamond and sapphire pendant with Slavonic characters from the Grand Duke and Grand Duchess Serge and the Grand Duke and Grand Duchess of Hesse, besides many other gifts. When she drove through the crowded, gaily decorated streets of London, on her way to St. Paul's, in a black silk dress, with panels of grey satin, and a bonnet trimmed with white flowers, her people gave her a rousing welcome, and during all the festivities that followed she was almost overcome by the love and devotion shown her. She was, however, very tired by the banquets and ceremonies, she also missed many faces amongst the group of children and grandchildren who surrounded her, and some were causing her moments of grave anxiety. Her grandson, the Emperor William of Germany, was often so difficult and troublesome, and she feared that he had been very angry when he was told that his presence was not required at the Jubilee, as no crowned heads were invited. She was worried about the marriage of the Grand Duke and Grand Duchess of Hesse, which was not turning out a success. She had been greatly shocked when her cousin, Prince Ferdinand of Bulgaria, had gone back on his solemn undertaking and had his eldest son confirmed in the Orthodox Church. When the Emperor and Empress of Russia, with their daughter, had visited her at Balmoral in 1896 she had found "Dear simple little Alicky" greatly changed. The cold formality of her manner, and the way in which she had, without question, accepted her grandmother's gesture in giving her precedence, had hurt the Queen's feelings, and she was afraid that this favourite granddaughter of hers was becoming too imperious.

On June 28, the Grand Duchess Serge and her husband said good-bye to the Queen, before leaving for Russia, and as Ella bent her head to kiss the Queen's cheek she had tears in her lovely eyes, as if in her secret heart she knew that she would never again know the peace and security of England, never again see this small, infinitely majestic figure, who, for so many years, had been not only a grandmother, but a mother and a friend.

The disastrous Russo-Japanese war of 1904 brought to the Grand Duchess Serge a task which she accomplished in a way that would have filled Queen Victoria's heart with pride, had she been alive. As wife of the Governor of Moscow the Grand Duchess was head of all the Red Cross organizations in the town. She sent out ambulance trains and camp churches, and first-aid equipment, she organized workrooms in the Kremlin Palace, and was there herself every day, supervizing and encouraging the hundreds of women of all classes who worked there, packing endless bales of bandages, first-aid dressings, socks, shirts, pyjamas, food and provisions, for the wretchedly-equipped soldiers at the Front. Dressed always simply in blue or grey, she was indefatigable in her constant attendance, she always had a smile or a word of praise for those who worked for her, she was never out of patience, even when mistakes were made, and was always ready to do the hardest work herself.

She was on her way from her private apartments to the workroom, on February 4 1905, when a sudden explosion shattered some of the windows of the Palace. She stood for a moment, a hand on her heart, knowing with a feeling of dread chilling her blood that what she had feared—and what her husband had always expected—had happened at last. How often during the last few years had he forbidden her to go driving with him? How often had he not told her that he knew he was hated, and was sure he would suffer the same fate as his father?

Without waiting to ask questions, or even to put on a cloak, she hurried down the stairs and out into the bitter cold, where, guided by a cloud of smoke and the acrid smell of gunpowder, she came to the spot where, amidst the wreckage of the carriage and the mangled bodies of the horses, she found soldiers trying to cover with their coats all that remained of her husband.

The tears were streaming down her cheeks as she knelt there on the blood-stained snow, beneath the lovely rose-red walls, with the golden domes of the cathedrals shining against the sky, in the centre of a gathering crowd, who gazed with white, horrified faces, while soldiers and policemen held the defiant figure of the assassin in their midst. Only a few hours ago, she had said good-bye to the tall erect figure in the dark-green uniform, had seen the smile in the cold grey eyes, had felt his lips touching her cheek, had heard his voice telling her not to worry. Whatever he had made her suffer, he was her husband, he was the boy who had led her so gently by the hand in the gardens of Heiligenberg. He had known the danger that threatened him, and had never shirked his responsibilities; he had been conscientious to the last degree in carrying out the minutest details of what he considered his duty as Governor of Moscow. Yet his almost fanatical austerity, his vindictive cruelty on certain occasions, had made him hated; he was a reactionary, an autocrat, almost a tyrant; but she had been married to him for just on twenty years, and perhaps she alone knew the secret of his heart.

That afternoon, in spite of her own personal grief, she visited the fatally wounded coachman in hospital. He looked up at her with tortured eyes. "How is His Imperial Highness?" he whispered. Very gently, her face calm and composed, she replied,

"It is he who has sent me to you," and stayed beside his bed until he died. She begged the Emperor to spare the life of the assassin, and when her petition was refused she went to see the man in prison, only to find him cynically obdurate and unrepentant, boasting of an action which, he said, had destroyed a man who was an enemy of the people.

From the moment she had knelt, shivering, faint, sickened and heartbroken in the snow, she never again touched meat or fish; she divided into three parts all the splendid jewels her husband had given her, giving some to the son and daughter of the Grand Duke Paul, who was Serge's favourite brother, returning some to the Crown, and selling the rest for charity, and to found the Convent of Mary and Martha, in Moscow, to be run on the lines of the Little Sisters of the Poor.

St. Petersburg society saw her no more. Only very occasionally she visited her sister in Tsarskoe Seloe, and in 1910 she herself joined the Sisterhood of Martha and Mary, giving away all her furs and clothes, her remaining bits of jewellery, retaining nothing for herself, not even her wedding-ring. "This veil," Bishop Triphonius said when she entered the convent, "will hide you from the world, and the world will be hidden from you; but it will be a witness of your good works which will shine before God and glorify the Lord."

Living in three small rooms in the convent, plainly furnished with white wicker chairs, she slept on a wooden bed without a mattress, and with only one hard pillow. Always she took upon herself the hardest tasks, tending the fifteen patients in the hospital wing with her own hands, hardly ever sleeping for more than three hours, visiting the home for consumptives which she had also founded; always there when a patient died, taking on the long night duty when it was obligatory, according to the Orthodox faith, to repeat prayers unceasingly over a dead body.

Yet she never became rigid, or stern or morose, she even retained some of the gaiety that had made her so enchanting as a young girl. Once, when her sister Princess Victoria, Marchioness of Milford Haven, was staying at the convent with her second daughter, Princess Louise, the door of their bedroom was opened early one morning, and a small cropped head looked in on them with a laughing "Hallo". Startled, Lady Milford Haven thought at first that some mischievous boy had found his way into the convent, and was invading her room, until she realized with a rueful laugh, that it was her sister, without her veil, her lovely hair cut close to her head.

In *Secrets of Dethroned Royalty* Princess Catherine Radziwill declares that the Grand Duchess Serge continued to live a life of luxury and ease at the convent, that "she wished to pose as a victim of circumstances and aspired to acquire the reputation of a saint, which she was not". I have the accounts of a friend, and also of my mother who visited the convent when we were in Moscow, to prove that this charge is false, for they both saw the stark simplicity of those plain, whitewashed rooms, the lack of any comfort, far less of luxury, in the surroundings of the woman in the plain grey nun's dress, her only ornament a wooden cross on a white ribbon round her neck.

During the years we were in Russia I saw the Grand Duchess Serge on only two occasions: once in the Kazan Cathedral in St. Petersburg, at a Te Deum held to celebrate the Romanoff Tercentenary; the second time at the outbreak of war in 1914, when, according to old tradition, the Emperor went to pray for victory in the Uspensky Cathedral in Moscow, and to lay the plan of campaign before the wonder-working Ikon of Vladimer. Amidst the brilliant uniforms of the Grand Dukes, the generals and diplomats, the bright-coloured silks and satins worn by the women, the Grand Duchess stood out like a tall white lily in a garden of exotic flowers. Her face was pale and grave, and unbelievably beautiful, framed in her soft white veil; the plain white woollen robes, she wore on especial occasions, fell in classic folds round her slender figure. The blue mist of incense, the golden ikons, the gorgeous colours of the priests' vestments, made a shimmering background to that motionless white figure, and gazing at her, across the crowded church, I recalled again that picture of her in her blue velvet dress, holding out the roses, with that mystical, secret smile in her eyes. St. Elizabeth! In her veins ran the blood of that medieval princess who had been canonized; had she not by her life of abnegation earned that title?

But on that cloudless day of August, 1914, with the square in front of the Cathedral packed with people, praying on their knees as they waited to greet their Emperor, we did not know that the sacred Ikon of Vladimir, which Dimitri Donskoi had carried on his banner when he defeated the Tartar hordes, was not this time to bring victory to the Russian armies, and that the martyrdom of the woman who had sacrificed so much was not yet ended.

And as the long years of the war went on, and defeat and frustration undermined the morale of the army, and crippled the courage of the people, the Grand Duchess wrote over and over again to her sister, letters of warning that were angrily resented by the Empress, who told her husband to pay no attention to the "Moscow Clique" and to "Ella's bigoted ideas". At last, in December, 1916, alarmed by the reports she received, and knowing that the Emperor was in Tsarskoe, the Grand Duchess determined to go there herself and try to make him see the danger threatening the throne, to beg him to dismiss the members of the Government appointed by Rasputin, and to win back the confidence of his people.

But when she arrived at the Palace at Tsarskoe it was her sister, stern and forbidding, in her violet velvet dress, who met her, telling her coldly that she could not see the Emperor as he was just leaving for Staff Headquarters, and must on no account be disturbed or worried.

The gardens outside the windows were hidden under a mantle of snow, but in the big, golden room, with its masses of photographs and ornaments, the big picture of Marie

Antoinette and her children on the wall, the pots of azaleas and lilies, it was warm and still, seemingly secure. Nothing had changed; the armed cossacks riding in an endless ring round the confines of the park; the Court servants; the chamberlains; the ladies-in-waiting in the ante-rooms; the impregnable stronghold of Imperial power! But was it so impregnable, the Grand Duchess wondered? Were the foundations not already trembling before the gathering storm, the fury of a nation who, through incompetence and the lack of munitions and supplies, had seen its soldier sons laying down their lives in a vain and useless sacrifice? With sudden tears in her eyes she pleaded once more with her sister, begging her to persuade the Emperor to go to the Duma, to make concessions, to dismiss Rasputin, whose evil influence was destroying the people's faith in the integrity of their rulers.

The Empress had been pale at first, but now an angry flush began to redden her cheeks. "Saints have been maligned before", she said curtly, sweeping away all arguments in her proud assertion that she, as the Empress of Russia, knew the hearts and minds of her people. Listening in silence, the Grand Duchess knew that her last effort had failed. She turned away and left the big golden room, little knowing that she would never see it again. Her heart was heavy, but she knew there was nothing more she could do but work and pray for this sister who had been so dear to her, whose golden curls and gaiety as a child had won for her the nickname of "Sunny", but who now, in her mistaken policy, had hardened herself against all who disagreed with her, and refused to see the evil in the man she believed to be a saint.

From her quiet white rooms in the convent the Grand Duchess watched the cataclysm of events, the tragic blunders that sealed the doom of the Russian Empire. She heard of the Emperor's abdication, of his imprisonment with his wife and children in the palace at Tsarskoe. She saw the raging crowds surge through the streets of Moscow, the red flags burgeoning like scarlet flames on all the buildings. She listened to the rattle of machine-guns, to the screaming voices, drunk with the lust for blood.

Nor was she herself left for long in peace, for one day, in March 1917, lorries full of soldiers who had deserted, workmen, and criminals who had been released from prison, drove up to the convent doors and clamoured for admittance. Sending all the nuns into the chapel, the Grand Duchess went out alone and, standing at the open door, asked what they wanted. When they shouted that they had come to arrest her because she was concealing German officers, she said that five of them could come in and search the building. Leading the way first to the chapel, she asked them to put down their rifles at the door, and dumbly, overawed by her calm dignity, they obeyed her, stood with bared heads during the short service, followed her through the rest of the building, and went out at last to their comrades, waiting in the street, to tell them that they had made a mistake; there were no arms there, no German officers, it was only a convent full of nuns.

A few months later another visitor appeared, but this time it was the Swedish Minister from St. Petersburg, bearing a message from the Emperor of Germany to the woman he had once loved, begging her to leave Russia before it was too late, promising her safe conduct and a refuge in his country. The Grand Duchess listened with a little smile on her lips, but gently refused the offer of help. She also, she said, believed terrible things were going to happen in Russia, but she was prepared to share whatever fate awaited her adopted country, and she could not leave the sisters of her community alone. She was touched that her cousin William had remembered her, she had perhaps a moment of wistful sadness, thinking of the games they had played together at Darmstadt, and how often she had been impatient with him, but nothing could alter her decision, and the Swedish Minister had to leave, his mission unfulfilled.

"We work, we pray, we hope," she wrote to a friend in April 1918, when the First Provisional Government, too weak to control the wave of anarchy they had unleashed, had fallen from power, and the new rulers of Russia were established in the Kremlin. They knew all about the work she was doing, but they were determined that no member of the Imperial family should remain alive in Russia, and made up their minds to rid themselves of her presence. Knowing how much the people loved her, they did not dare lay hands on her, nor have her executed in Moscow, but in May they sent a detachment of Red Guards to the convent, with orders that she was to join the Emperor and Empress at Ekaterinburg. She was hurried away secretly at night, accompanied only by Sister Varvara, her former maid, who had refused to be parted from her.

Had she gone to Ekaterinburg, the Grand Duchess would have shared the fate of the Emperor and Empress; but she would have been with her sister, and the end would have been quicker and more merciful. At Perm, a little desolate town on the river Kama, she was taken out of the train, and thrown into prison, in company with two of the younger sons of the Grand Duke Constantine, and of Prince Paley, the only son of the Grand Duke Paul by his second marriage.

At first the Lithuanian Guards were lenient to the prisoners, but after a few weeks they were exchanged for Russian soldiers, who, having received orders from the Kremlin, were unspeakably brutal. Then, one day in June 1918, the prisoners were led out, and forced to walk several miles through the forest, until they reached the shaft of an empty, disused mine. One by one, the young men, who were still really only boys, and had committed no crime save that of being members of the Romanoff family, the woman who had given up years of her life to work for the poor, and the girl who had refused to leave a beloved mistress, were hurled into the deep chasm of the mine, and the soldiers, having carried out their masters' wishes, returned the way they had come through the forest.

Rumours of that crime against humanity spread in Perm, and a priest who had heard of the saintliness of the woman who had been so foully done to death, made his way secretly one night through the forest, and climbed down into the mine. Here he found the bodies of the victims, and found also that some of their wounds had been roughly bandaged, a proof that none of them had died immediately. He was a man of high and exalted courage, and knew that he stood in hourly danger of death, but he carried away the bodies of the Grand Duchess and of Sister Varvara, kept them hidden for months in rough, wooden coffins, and then, by secret, devious ways, smuggled them out of Russia, over the Ural mountains, across Siberia and Manchuria and Asia, till finally he had them placed in a small chapel in Shanghai.

And so at last, after nearly three years, the whole terrible story came to light, the Marchioness of Milford Haven was told that her sister's body had been found, orders were given for the two coffins to be taken to Jerusalem, and, in April, 1921, Lady Milford Haven and her husband went to the lovely Russian church, built in memory of the Empress Marie, wife of Alexander II, on the Mount of Olives, and knelt beside those two coffins, which, after their long perilous journey, had finally come to rest.

There are probably only a few people in Moscow who remember the woman in the grey nun's dress, who was formerly such a familiar figure, going through the streets, on her way to visit the sick. The convent she founded has been disbanded, the sisters who worked with her have been imprisoned, or sent to labour camps. In the world of today who is there to care about what happened so long ago? But those who knew the Grand Duchess Elizabeth, who saw her in the magnificence of her Court robes and the splendour of her jewels, or in her plain nun's dress, can never, as Queen Marie of Roumania said, forget that she did once exist, in all her glorious, almost unearthly beauty.

# Queen Marie of Roumania

THE Foreign Relations Department of the British Red Cross was started in 1939 with a small staff, and a few desultory inquiries for people in France or Germany. But as the war continued and Hitler's armies swept across Europe, more and more people were interned or deported, and the inquiries for missing relatives grew in number. Eventually the Foreign Relations Department moved to Clarence House, where the staff of over four hundred filled every room to overflowing.

Here in the hall through which Queen Victoria had sometimes passed on her way to visit her son, sat shabbily-dressed refugees of all nationalities, waiting to make hopeless inquiries for some missing person dear to them. Little typists, with bare legs and scarves tied over their curls, clattered noisily up and down the wide staircase which so many men and women with names well known to history had formerly ascended. Women in Red Cross uniforms, with harassed faces, hurried along the passages, with sheaves of documents under their arms. A ceaseless activity, an atmosphere of stress in which there was little time to think of the past, or to picture the bygone history of this stately house, and only here and there a reminder of former days—a tall stuffed bear in front of one of the doors, a big globe of the world in one of the passages, the nursery bars across a window!

When I worked there I often thought I saw the ghosts of three little girls in holland pinafores, their hair cut in a straight fringe across their forehead, running down the passages in front of me, standing at the door of the big green-and-gold room filled with utility office furniture, typewriting desks and steel filing cabinets, or sometimes wandering into the store-room, once their mother's private chapel and now stacked with bales of linen, packets of stationery, and boxes of soap, cleaning materials, and disinfectants.

The Princesses Marie, Victoria Melita, and Alexandra! Their spirits were always there, and always it seemed to me that their big blue eyes were full of reproach, asking me what right I had to be there, in that house which had once been their home.

The marriage between her second son, Prince Alfred, Duke of Edinburgh, and the Grand Duchess Marie, daughter of the Emperor Alexander II of Russia, had at first been suggested to Queen Victoria by Princess Alice of Hesse, who had frequently seen the young Grand Duchess, when she came with her mother on her annual visits to Darmstadt. The idea was not favourably received by the Empress, however, and the Queen was so annoyed by the discouraging reply she received from Russia that she decided to give up the project, and rebuked her favourite daughter for having exposed her to such an ungracious rebuff.

It was the Grand Duchess Marie herself who finally settled the question. On her visits to the Castle of Heiligenberg near Darmstadt, she had seen photographs of the Duke of Edinburgh, belonging to Princess Alice, and came to the conclusion that the tall, handsome son of the Queen of England was more attractive than some of the German princes whose names had been mentioned as possible suitors. In the summer of 1873 a meeting was accordingly arranged at Heiligenberg, when the Grand Duchess declared herself to have fallen in love, and begged her parents to give their consent to the marriage.

The wedding took place in St. Petersburg on January 3, 1874. Crowds of notable guests attended the ceremony, which was regarded as of great political importance, for it was the first time in history that a member of the English royal family had married a Romanoff, and after the Crimean War such an alliance was doubly significant. Sitting quietly in her room at

Windsor, Queen Victoria read the marriage service, thinking of her son and his bride, and that night at dinner wore the Order of St. Catherine pinned on her dress, and drank the health of the young couple, praying softly to herself that their happiness might last longer than hers had done.

On March 7 the Duke of Edinburgh brought his wife to London, and Queen Victoria met them at the South-Western Station, dressed in her short black jacket, trimmed with miniver, and her cloak lined with ermine. Taking her son's wife into her arms she kissed her warmly on both soft flushed cheeks. "I was quite nervous and trembling," she said, although her agitation did not prevent her noticing that the young bride had a pleasant face, that she wore a pale-blue dress, and had pinned the bunch of white heather, which the Queen had sent to Antwerp, into her white tulle bonnet.

But in spite of her mother-in-law's embraces, and the warm welcome given her by the crowds who flocked the gaily-decorated streets, the young Duchess of Edinburgh was not happy in England. She thought the climate detestable, the food tasteless and badly cooked, and London drab and uninteresting after the broad streets, the golden domes and magnificent palaces of St. Petersburg. She also deeply resented the fact that she, the only daughter of the Emperor of Russia, had to give precedence, not only to the Princess of Wales, who was always charming and considerate, but also to the Queen's daughters, who were not always so agreeable, and took no pains to hide their jealousy of her superb diamonds. Those jewels, which had been given to her by her adoring father, were viewed, too, with some disfavour by the Queen, who at the first Drawing-Room the young Duchess attended compared her tiara with those of her daughters, shrugging her shoulders like a bird whose plumage has been ruffled, her mouth drawn down at the corners, in an expression which those who knew her had learned to dread.

A few months later the Emperor Alexander came to England

with his eldest son and, sitting next to the Queen at a dinner at Windsor, thanked her for being so kind to his daughter. That evening the Duchess of Edinburgh again wore her diamond and sapphire tiara outshining in its splendour even the coronet the Queen wore over her veil, but although she noted that her daughter-in-law was again wearing her "wonderful diamonds" the Queen paid no further attention, being too engrossed in her conversation with the Emperor, recalling old times, talking of his former visit and of the many people they had known, so many of whom were now dead, or much aged and altered.

It was, indeed, thirty-six years since they had met, and the Queen, glancing at the care-worn, harassed man by her side, found little to remind her of the handsome boy with whom she had danced a quadrille to Strauss's band in Buckingham Palace, and had taught her the mazurka during those enchanted evenings at Windsor. On his side, the Emperor found it difficult to imagine that the stout, middle-aged lady with the rather pendulous cheeks could indeed be that young girl whose silvery voice and grace of movement had almost made him forget the little Princess of Hesse with whom he had fallen in love.

He was however very cordial and affable, assured the Queen that he could see no reason why their two countries should not always be on the best of terms, and promised to write to her direct should there at any time be complications and difficulties. Sitting on his other side, the Duchess of Edinburgh listened with a rather sceptical smile to all these amiabilities. She was aware that her marriage was supposed to have healed the scars left by the Crimean War, but she had frequently overheard her parents allude to the Queen as a "silly old fool", and she wondered if it would ever be possible for England and Russia to forget their differences.

The outbreak of the Russo-Turkish war in 1877 proved how frail indeed was the understanding between the two countries.

The Queen's bellicose attitude, her openly-expressed desire to show Russia that England would not be browbeaten, nearly brought about a declaration of war, and when she wrote to the Emperor, warning him that she could not guarantee British neutrality if he continued his advance on Constantinople, he regarded it as tantamount to a threat of armed intervention. "Je m'en fiche," he wrote on the margin of the letter.

The Prince of Wales was almost as violently anti-Russian as his mother. Public opinion in England was expressed in the popular song, "We don't want to fight, but by Jingo if we do." It was a time the Duchess of Edinburgh never forgot; it imbued in her a hardness, alien to her hitherto sunny nature, it filled her with an implacable resentment against the Queen, and a determination that none of her daughters should ever marry a member of the English royal family.

But whatever the feelings of the Duchess of Edinburgh towards her mother-in-law, her three eldest daughters regarded the Queen with reverent adoration. "Grandmama Queen", they called her, in order to distinguish her from that other "Grandmama Empress" in Russia. Thrilled with excitement when they were taken to see her, they were nonetheless somewhat awed when actually in her presence, but delighted and proud when she praised them for being good, or stroked their hair with her soft, jewelled fingers. "My Picture Grandchild", she called Princess Marie, and the little girl, already conscious of being prettier than her sisters, boasted that she was her grandmother's favourite.

Nicknames were very prevalent in the royal family in those days, and the three little girls were known to everybody as "Missy", "Ducky" and "Sandra". Their youngest sister, Princess Beatrice, born in 1884, was called Baby B., and still relegated to the nursery, long after the other three were already in the schoolroom. Of their only brother, Prince Alfred, they saw very little, for he was sent at an early age to be educated in Germany, a settlement having been made by the

Prince Consort that if his elder brother had no children, the Duke of Edinburgh, or his heir, should succeed to the Duchy of Coburg.

Whether they were staying with the Queen at Osborne, or living at Clarence House, the three little Edinburgh Princesses led the ordinary life of children in those days. They were brought down to the drawing-room at tea-time, in velvet or white muslin dresses, their hair brushed to a shining perfection and tied with a matching ribbon, but relegated most of the day to the schoolroom in holland pinafores, having music lessons, painting lessons, trying to master the intricacies of French grammar and the involved complexity of arithmetic, spending many an evening peeping over the banisters at Clarence House to watch their parents' guests arriving for a dinner-party. All their lives they remembered the day in the winter of 1881 when they found their mother kneeling, in floods of tears, in the blue-and-gold chapel, and were hurriedly removed by a nurse in a white piqué dress. They must be very good and not make a noise, they were told, for Grandpapa Emperor was dead.

It seemed strange when they next accompanied their mother on one of her periodical visits to Russia, to find tall bearded Uncle Sasha in the place of Grandpapa Emperor. But they were too young to know what had happened, or to grieve very long for the man whose mutilated body lay at peace in the Cathedral of St. Peter and St. Paul, across the river; and there were so many kind aunts to pet them, so many tall, handsome uncles to tease them and pull their hair; Uncle Vladimir, with his loud, gruff voice, and mischievous, twinkling eyes; Uncle Serge, austere and stern, but bending from his great height to kiss them with such gentleness; Uncle Alexis, fair and boisterous, always making fun and playing practical jokes; Aunt Minnie, who was now, it seemed, Empress of Russia; beautiful Aunt Ella with her enchanting smile. There were also the tall, bearded cossacks of the Guard, who looked so fierce and terrifying with their daggers and pistols, but were always so kind to three little girls who sometimes felt rather lost and shy in the vast immensity of those Imperial palaces.

In 1886 Admiral of the Fleet the Duke of Edinburgh was given the command at Malta, and in after years Princess Marie and her sister Princess Victoria looked back on the time they spent there as the happiest in their lives, wishing, as so many of us do, that they had more keenly appreciated that happiness, and had not taken those golden, care-free days for granted. It was here that twelve-year-old Princess Marie first got to know Cousin George, the second son of the Prince of Wales, who was then serving in H.M.S. *Alexandra*. It was here that he gave her a crystal watch with the inscription "From George to Darling Missy", a watch she kept all her life, even though in later years she had so many other beautiful jewels. It was at Malta, when the three years of her father's command were over, that she said good-bye to him crying bitterly.

After leaving Malta the Duke of Edinburgh was appointed to Devonport, but, overcoming all his objections, the Duchess decided to take her daughters to Coburg. They needed, she said, more discipline and intensive instruction, she also wanted to see more of her son who was finishing his education there. The real reason was that she wanted to remove herself from the domination of her mother-in-law, to be no longer dictated to and made to play second fiddle, and in Coburg she had a position of her own, she was able to do, and dress, as she pleased, and neither Duke Ernst nor his down-trodden, meek little wife ever interfered with her.

Autocratic, domineering, with a quick wit, and a caustic tongue, I remember the Duchess at Wolfsgarten, and also, many years later, in St. Petersburg. A stout, awe-inspiring old lady who seemed to care nothing for her looks or her clothes, who was terrifyingly dictatorial, and shot questions at me in a gruff, abrupt voice, always making me feel inarticulate and self-conscious.

Now I see that she was really rather to be pitied. She had the brains, the courage, the personality of a ruler, and she had suffered acutely from her subordinate position. She was therefore determined that her daughters should not make the same mistake. When both Queen Victoria and the Duke of Edinburgh suggested a marriage between Princess Marie and the second son of the Prince of Wales, she refused to consider it and made the girl write a stiff little note to Cousin George, telling ¡him that he must not think there was anything definite in the friendship that had sprung up between them in Malta.

Princess Marie wrote that letter with a heavy heart, but she was too afraid of her domineering mother to do other than obey. She was also forced to submit when the Grand Duke George of Russia and one or two German princes who had visited Coburg were told that their proposals were not acceptable. These men, the Duchess told her daughter, might be very good-looking and seem charming and agreeable, but they were probably always kissing maids behind the parlour door. Princess Marie had been brought up in the royal tradition; she knew that Princesses could not always follow their hearts. So she bent her golden head in meek submission, said nothing of the wonderful presents that had been sent her secretly by the Grand Duke George, and tried to put the memories of Malta out of her mind.

At that moment, a young man from a distant Balkan country had been sent to Germany with a list of marriageable princesses in his pocket and orders to forget his illicit love-affair with one of his aunt's ladies-in-waiting. Meetings were arranged between him and Princess Marie, he found her by far the most lovely of all the princesses he had seen, and, swept away by her mother's whirlwind activities, by the excitement of visits to Berlin, and to the beautiful Hohenzollern castle of Sigmaringen, before she was really aware of what had happened, Princess Marie found herself engaged to Prince Ferdinand, nephew and heir to King Carol I of Roumania. She was possibly a little sorry for this dark-haired, slender young man with the shy, rather sad eyes, the protruding ears, and nervous laugh. She knew nothing of his former engagement; his proposal had been so awkward, so badly expressed, that she felt an almost maternal tenderness for him, believing that he was seriously in love with her.

Queen Victoria was very displeased that her beautiful granddaughter's future had been settled without her wishes being taken into consideration. The Duke of Edinburgh made no secret of his dislike of this engagement to a Hohenzollern Prince, heir to the throne of a country which in those days seemed very far away, and practically uncivilized. He had had very different plans for his favourite daughter. He was exceedingly angry with his bustling energetic wife for being in such a hurry, for now the poor young Duke of Clarence was dead, and if his wishes and those of his mother had been obeyed, "Missy" would one day have been Queen of England.

There were possibly many angry arguments between him and his wife. But the Duchess of Edinburgh had made up her mind, she was obstinately determined to allow no interference with the plans she had made, and on January 10, 1893, Princess Marie was married to Prince Ferdinand of Hohenzollern in the Castle of Sigmaringen, thus once more disregarding the wishes of the Queen, who had wanted her granddaughter's marriage to be celebrated in England.

Many years later, Princess Marie told my father that no words could describe her utter misery during the first years she spent in Roumania. The heavy German atmosphere of the royal palace, the dark, stiff furniture, the thick curtains, the closed windows, stifled and oppressed her. The discipline King Carol imposed on her, mortified her at every turn. She was not permitted to go out unaccompanied, nor to have friends of her own age. She was watched and spied on, and everything she said or did was reported back to the King, while her husband, with his slavish subservience, and his dread of "what Uncle might say", refused to listen to her complaints, and advised her to be circumspect.

The birth of Prince Carol, in 1894, and of her eldest daughter, Princess Elizabeth, a year later, did not at first make her any happier, for she was soon aware that it was considered her duty to bear children, and she was conscious that in the King's eyes, she herself was not important, but that her son, as heir to the throne, had always to be considered. But as time passed her natural happy nature, and buoyant vivacity, asserted themselves, she became more sure of herself, she learnt to defy King Carol and go her own way, disregarding her husband's timid admonitions and his almost pitiful appeals not to offend "the Uncle". And the King, almost in spite of himself, began to admire the courage of this golden-haired girl who was never afraid of him. He relaxed his stern control over her movements, gave her the Cotroceni Palace to live in, and when she overspent her allowance, paid her debts with a grim, little smile, and a warning to be more careful in future.

Sometimes, also, Princess Marie was able to escape from the monotony of her life in Roumania. Once or twice she took her children to Osborne, where Queen Victoria would look at her rather quizzically and say, "Well, Missy, and how are you getting on down there?" She would take her out driving, and ask her innumerable questions not always easy to answer. When her favourite sister, Princess Victoria, married the Grand Duke of Hesse in 1894, there were also many carefree weeks spent at Wolfsgarten, the old hunting-palace in the woods not far from Darmstadt. In 1895 there was the coronation of the Emperor Nicholas II at Moscow to which both Princess Marie and her sister, the Grand Duchess of Hesse, had been invited.

After the gorgeous pageantry of the ceremonies in Moscow, darkened and saddened by the disaster on the Khodinsky field, there were the days spent at Archangelskoi, the fabulous palace outside Moscow, which the young and beautiful Princess Yusopoff had inherited from her father. The Duke and

Duchess of Edinburgh, who, since the death of Duke Ernst in 1893, had become the Duke and Duchess of Coburg, were staying with the Emperor and Empress, and some of the older guests at Yilinsky, the summer estate of the Grand Duke Serge. But Princess Marie and her husband and the Grand Duke and Grand Duchess of Hesse, had been invited to Archangelskoi, and during those enchanted summer days all cares and responsibilities were put aside and forgotten in a ceaseless round of gaiety. There were picnics and excursions, there was riding every day in the forest, boating on the lake, performances given by the Italian Opera Company in the private theatre, and dancing every night to the music of a gipsy band. "I felt as if my hands were suddenly full of sunshine," Princess Marie said later.

Beautiful, unforgettable Archangelskoi! With its three vast terraces stretching down to the distant river, its gardens laid out in imitation of Versailles, its theatre and zoo, its great library of precious books, its silver room, with the furniture which had once belonged to the Duchess of Courland.

Realizing for the first time the power her beauty gave her, Princess Marie lived in a dream, disregarding her husband's warnings that King Carol would be very displeased when he heard of all this hectic gaiety, and not even distressed when her mother lectured both her and her sister for the way in which they were flirting with their cousins, the handsome sons of the Grand Duke Vladimir.

How lovely she was in her radiant happiness and enjoyment can be seen from the effect she had on a little boy of seven. In his book *Avant l'Exil* Prince Felix Yusupoff describes how he gazed at her, unable to believe that she was real, how he followed her about, silently adoring her, and how, when one day she stooped to kiss his cheek, he stubbornly refused to have his face washed for nearly a week.

When I saw her at Wolfsgarten, she had nearly the same effect on me, and, brought up as I was by a rather sentimental

German governess, I saw in her the reincarnation of a fairy-tale princess. I was too young to know about the gossip that surrounded her name, or to listen to the tattle of the censorious who frequently misconstrued her actions and criticized her lack of formality, finding her beauty a dangerous gift for a royal princess.

Sometimes I would see her going out riding with her sister, both of them dressed in white habits, with black three-cornered hats, sitting their horses with the ease and grace of accomplished riders. Another day, dressed in a blue-and-scarlet cossack uniform, and sitting astride, she would gallop recklessly round the courtyard and out through the big gates into the woods. Sometimes I would see her starting out in a carriage for the races at Frankfurt, her lovely face framed in a blue, flower-trimmed hat; or, watching from my bedroom window, I would see her walking in the courtyard after dinner, in one of those dazzling, picturesque gowns that she knew so superbly how to wear—a white dress, covered with silver sequins, with a glittering silver scarf round the shoulders; a long black gown with a golden stole, embroidered with turquoises, a pale pink and silver dress with Grecian draperies.

One day also I was allowed to go up to the big room, on the top floor of the palace, which the Grand Duchess had turned into a studio, and there I sat entranced, watching them at work painting panels of scarlet poppies, while, stacked against the walls there were pictures of tall white madonna lilies, of deep purple irises, of big wreaths of roses, or clusters of anemones. The Grand Duchess, with her dark hair, and almost violet eyes, so often looked stern and sad, but Princess Marie was always laughing, always gave one the impression of happiness —running sometimes through the courtyard like a girl, captivating the most elderly of Court gentlemen with her irresistible gaiety; teasing Prince Albert of Schleswig-Holstein because of his bald head and solemn manner; playing with little Princess Elizabeth and making her shriek with delight; sitting down beside me, to tell me of the house she had built for her-self in one of the tall pine trees at Sinaia; of the frieze of poppies she had painted round the walls, of the tiny kitchen, and the china, decorated with poppies, with which she served tea to her guests; chuckling mischievously as she described how some of those guests arrived panting and breathless, after climbing the ladder-like stairs which led to her retreat.

Several times the beautiful, unusual clothes Princess Marie wore were severely criticized, especially by her mother who declared that she and her sister had a sinful love of dress, and liked to look different from other princesses; they must remember that in their position they were the cynosure of all eyes and ought never to make themselves conspicuous. Princess Marie would listen with a little smile in her meekly lowered eyes— darling Mama, who had allowed herself to get stout and elderly before her time, who wore drab, old-fashioned clothes, and never seemed to care what she looked like. One had to pretend to be submissive, one had to promise to obey; the scoldings never went very deep, and beautiful stuffs, glowing colours, rich embroideries were too difficult to resist. She knew also that to the people of Roumania the way she dressed constituted one of her greatest charms, bringing colour and romance into their lives, surrounding her with a glamour that appealed to their primitive romantic natures.

She was learning slowly, and with increasing wonder, to love her adopted country. The nameless magic of the Balkans, that casts a spell on all who have ever been there, was begin-ning to capture her vivid imagination. On her long solitary rides she grew to know and love the many beautiful little churches, the old grey convents and monasteries hidden away in the mountains and valleys, the low white cottages, the peasants who welcomed her with garlands of marigolds. Here she felt was the heart of Roumania. Not the cosmopolitan, rather meretricious gaiety of Bucharest, the bearded statesmen in their tightly-buttoned frock-coats, the officers in their brightly-coloured uniforms, the women in their Paris dresses and hats.

It was chiefly, however, when she accompanied King Carol in his yacht down the Danube, through the desolate swamps, with the innumerable canals, the tall willow trees, the flocks of storks, and cranes, and wildfowl, that the irresistible charm of this remote corner of Europe took possession of her. At Constantza, she looked along the lovely coast of the Black Sea, and saw in the distance a little town with a miniature harbour, mosques and minarets, low-roofed houses climbing up the steep cliff behind it. When she turned with an eager question to King Carol, he replied that the name of the town was Balcic, but that it lay on the other side of the Bulgarian frontier. She had a sudden flash of insight, telling herself that one day that little town should be incorporated in the Roumanian kingdom, and that she would build herself a house there, far away from the commotion and turmoil of the modern world, a dream house, with a terrace looking over the deep blue of the sea.

At times she was happy, but life was not always easy, and she had many battles to fight, many obstacles to overcome. Too impulsive and warmhearted, too eager to give pleasure to others, unable, as she often said, to refuse or disappoint those who asked favours of her, she did not always remember that her actions were watched, she was very often indiscreet. For a time she even left Roumania, causing Queen Victoria very great uneasiness, until, being recalled by Prince Carol's serious illness, she and her husband came to an understanding, the governess, who had caused so much mischief, being dismissed.

Her position had not been made easier by the fact that Queen Elizabeth of Roumania, better known to the world as Carmen Sylva, had returned to Bucharest after an absence of several years. She swept through the rooms of the palace with her restless movements, her flowing draperies, folding Princess Marie in her warm embrace, telling her that she was a darling child, a breath of spring, but taking complete control of the children, changing the routine of their education, not allowing their mother any say in the matter, often sending her to bed in tears.

King Carol watched his nephew's wife with suspicion, was once more trying to control her movements. He did not approve of her holidays at Wolfsgarten, in England and in Russia. He was displeased when the Grand Duke and Grand Duchess of Hesse came to stay in Bucharest one winter, saying frigidly that they were too light-hearted, too intent on enjoyment. He viewed with strong disfavour the visit of the Grand Duke Boris of Russia, whose admiration of Princess Marie was all too evident, and whose exuberance he found intolerable, especially when one day, playing at being a cowboy, he lamed one of the most valuable horses in the royal stable.

The deaths of her only brother, of her beloved father, and of Queen Victoria, following closely on one another, brought to Princess Marie the first real, overwhelming sorrows of her life. With the death of the Queen, came the break-up of the marriage of her favourite sister, the glaring scandal that surrounded her divorce from the Grand Duke of Hesse, and her subsequent marriage to her cousin, the Grand Duke Cyril of Russia. There were no more visits to Osborne and Windsor, no more happy weeks spent at Wolfsgarten. The Grand Duke Cyril had been exiled from Russia and was living quietly with his wife in Coburg, and Mama, since Alfred and Papa were dead, and the Duke of Albany had succeeded, had gone to live at Tegernsee near Munich.

So many changes, so much unrest, so great a loss in the passing of Grandmama Queen, and now that her wise, restraining influence was no longer there, her grandson, the Emperor William, was threatening the peace of the world with his restless ambitions, bringing the shadows of violence and confusion closer every day.

Roumania took no part in the First Balkan War, when the

Bulgarians advanced to the outskirts of Constantinople, and the Serbs defeated the Turks at Kumonova. She was, however, demanding compensation for her neutrality, and when hostilities broke out again between the victorious allies, a Roumanian army invaded Silistria and advanced into Bulgaria.

In his speech at the Conference of Ambassadors, convened in St. Petersburg, my father stressed the fact that the frontiers between Roumania and Bulgaria had been fixed by the Congress of Berlin in 1876, and reminded the delegates that any territory which Roumania now received would be at the expense of Bulgaria, and would weaken her position in the Balkans; words which were soon repeated in Bucharest, where they were received with indignant resentment.

Early in the winter of 1914 the Crown Prince and Princess of Roumania paid an official visit to St. Petersburg, in order that their eldest son, who had accompanied them, should make the acquaintance of the Emperor's daughter, the Grand Duchess Olga. Princess Marie was still in half-mourning for her father's mother, but she attended a small, informal dance, given by one of the leaders of St. Petersburg society, and it was there that I saw her again, no longer quite the young fairy-tale princess of my childish dreams, but regal and beautiful in a black-and-silver dress, her golden hair crowned with diamonds, and her eyes still as deeply blue as ever.

Happening to be standing near my father, I witnessed their meeting, and saw how her eyes grew dark with anger as he bowed before her. "I feel inclined not to speak to you, Sir George," she said coldly, and although she gave him her hand to kiss, she withdrew it again, with a movement that was almost abrupt in its haste. "How dared you say that my country had no right to territorial compensation?"

Rather startled and taken aback, my father replied that in his speech at the Conference he had merely quoted the terms laid down by the Congress of Berlin, but that he could not help feeling that Bulgaria had been unfairly treated.

"I have no patience with England," Princess Marie exclaimed. "She has always been ridiculously sentimental about Bulgaria, and my country has never received preferential treatment. If Roumania had taken part in the First Balkan War she would no doubt have been given the Silistria Balcic Line. Is she not to receive any recompense for her neutrality?"

"I can assure Your Royal Highness that I have most carefully studied the question," my father's voice was gentle and firm. "Roumania may be justified in her demands, but I am convinced that we are incurring grave risks in throwing Bulgaria into the arms of Germany, and giving King Ferdinand a reasonable cause for resentment."

Princess Marie was on the point of replying, but at that moment Prince Carol came up and asked me to dance. She looked at me with a sudden stare of displeasure, her eyes more darkly blue than ever, the little nod with which she replied to my curtsy being cold and unsmiling. Did she, I wondered abashed, not want me to dance with her son? Or did she regard me as equally guilty with my father, in obstructing her country's claims to compensation?

I could not find the answer to these questions and Prince Carol was smiling down at me. "I am afraid," he said, "that I am a very bad dancer, as I have never troubled to have lessons. Do you mind risking it?"

I murmured weakly that it did not matter, but I did not quite know what I was in for, as he certainly had no idea of time, talked continuously, paid no attention to the music, and steered so erratically that we kept colliding with other couples. But although I was breathless, and my feet were sore from being trodden on, I could not help feeling that this tall, lanky young man had a certain charm, and his frank simplicity, his unaffected enjoyment, his buoyant good humour, were somehow so endearing that I was almost sorry when the dance was over, and a gesture from his mother recalled him to her side.

"I hope we shall meet again," he said, bruising my fingers as he shook my hand, but the next day he left Russia with his parents. In spite of a second meeting with the Grand Duchess Olga, when the Emperor and Empress with their daughters visited Constantza in June, no closer understanding was reached, and the outbreak of hostilities, two months later, put an end to all further thoughts of the projected marriage.

The first months of war must have been cruelly trying for Princess Marie. Carmen Sylva gloated over the power and might of the German armies, and both King Carol and Prince Ferdinand, unable to forget their Hohenzollern ancestry, were warmly in favour of bringing Roumania into the war on the side of Germany. A firm, unanimous vote deciding on neutrality was, however, passed at a Crown Council convened at Sinaia in August, and a few months later King Carol died, his heart, Carmen Sylva hysterically declared, having been broken by the ingratitude and treachery of his people.

He had been a just and conscientious ruler; he had been respected and admired for his absolute integrity, his honesty, and the altruism with which he had worked for his country, but, although the people mourned him sincerely, they turned with impulsive enthusiasm to the woman who was now their Queen. "Maria Regina", the cry greeted her whenever she appeared, was taken up by the crowds waiting in the streets, re-echoed all over Roumania. While her husband wrote abjectly to the Emperor William, bewailing the difficulties of his position, the Queen refused all the blandishments of Germany, told the handsome diplomats who were sent to try and win her over that she was first and foremost an English-woman and would never forget her loyalty to the country of her birth. At the same time she wrote to both King George and the Emperor of Russia, promising them her country's active support provided that certain territorial claims were conceded.

Unfortunately, when Roumania entered the war in the summer of 1916, believing that help would be given her by the powers of the Entente and assured that the Russians were advancing in the Carpathians, England and France, sorely pressed on the Western Front, were unable to send the promised munitions. The Russians were once more driven back, enemy planes raided Bucharest, and the German and Austrian armies, overcoming the gallant but feeble resistance put up against them, swept victoriously across Transylvania, while at the same time the Bulgarians occupied the Dobroudja.

Not only had Queen Marie now to face the cruel knowledge that she was responsible for leading her country into war, not only was she forced to leave Bucharest and join her husband and the Government in their flight to Jassy, the old Roumanian capital in Bukhovina, but, before leaving she had the sorrow of losing the youngest of her children, little Prince Mircea. He was born in 1913, contracted the typhoid that was raging in Bucharest, and died on October 20, 1916, having to be hurriedly buried in the courtyard of the Cotroceni Palace, while German planes swept overhead and German guns bombarded the capital.

But in Jassy there was work to be done, and her own personal grief had to be put aside in the desperate need of the wounded, the sick, the homeless and hungry, who filled the little town to overflowing, crowding it to such a degree that there was hardly ever enough food to go round, and three or four wounded men had sometimes to share the same bed. Every day the Queen worked in the hospitals, she visited camps and first-aid stations near the Front; she led out bands of men to sweep the mountainous snow from the roads; she drove out into the country to obtain food and supplies from the neighbouring farms; and, whilst all around gave way to despair, her courage and fortitude remained unbroken. "She was," an Englishman in one of the Allied Missions declared, "a flame of resistance that no storm could put out."

From all sides troubles, hardships and sorrows pressed upon her. Her mother wrote her a letter of cruel reproach for having drawn Roumania into the war on the wrong side, and for thus being responsible for Prince Mircea's death. Prince Carol eloped with Zizi Lambrino, and married her secretly in Odessa. Her second son, Prince Nicholas, fell dangerously ill. In Russia the Revolution had broken out and she could obtain no news of her relations. The divisions the Emperor had promised her arrived only in February 1917, and, already imbued with the spirit of revolt, proved themselves no help, but rather a dangerous liability, disobeying their officers, refusing to fight or to conform to discipline.

When in January, 1918, the newly-established Bolshevik Government declared war on Roumania, her cup of bitterness was full, for King Ferdinand, overcome by the hopelessness of the situation, accepted the German ultimatum. "I am going out to meet a fate almost too dark to be conceived," she wrote to King George, who had sent her a telegram telling her that she and her children would be welcome in England, an invitation she refused, saying that she could not leave her country in its hour of sorrow and defeat.

Apart from the critical dangers of her own position, she was also desperately unhappy and anxious about her sister, the Grand Duchess Cyril, who, in the autumn of 1917, had escaped from St. Petersburg to Finland, and was living almost in penury, her letters bewailing the fate which had overtaken her, complaining bitterly that all her friends had forsaken her, mentioning particularly my father and mother.

"Ducky," Queen Marie once said, "was the most unforgiving of us all. She gave no second chance." But she herself, with her warm, generous humanity, was always ready to understand and forgive, and had she known the incredible difficulties that beset my father after the abdication of the Emperor, she would not, I think, have accused him, as she does in her memoirs, of deserting her sister.

The collapse of Germany, and the Armistice of 1918, saw the Queen back in Bucharest, welcomed with rapturous enthusiasm, with the ringing of bells, the cheering of crowds, the flutter of flags hung from every balcony and window.

Justified now in the eyes of her people, she became a member of the Government, often overruling King Ferdinand's hesitations with her firm judgement, her quick decisions. It was she who, in spite of her husband's opposition, went unannounced to the Paris Peace Conference, telling the startled delegates that she had come to give "Roumania a face in Europe". It was she who, by her persistence, obtained the whole of Transylvania, the Dobroudja, and the Bukhovina, as far as the Dniester; who brought in the Agrarian Law, and made many a profitable trade deal, so that Roumania attained a prominence never known before.

And now, also, she was able to realize that early dream, when as a young bride she had first visited Constantza, for owing to her efforts the little town of Balcic, which had so captured her imagination, was incorporated in the Roumanian kingdom, and that fleeting thought of a dream-house overlooking the sea became a reality.

"I am," she once said, "instinctively a builder." The undoubted talent she possessed for converting and constructing, was shown in the idyllic beauty of her house at Balcic, in the golden splendour of her Palace of Cotroceni, in her rooms at Sinaia, and in her old castle of Bran, in the Carpathians. Wherever she was, she always surrounded herself with beauty, with rare and precious books, with the deep glowing colours of curtains and hangings, Byzantine jewellery, and flowers massed in big bronze or pottery vases, on all the tables, on the floor, wherever there was room for them. And always, whether at Sinaia, at Bran, or at Balcic, she laid out orchards and gardens which in their beauty filled all who saw them with amazement, wondering at the exquisite grouping of the flowers that always seemed to grow for her in such profusion, and always, by some almost mystical foresight, seemed to be in the right surroundings.

But now, when so many of her dreams had come true, it seemed as if the Fates, deciding that too much had been given her, determined to frustrate her, and spoil her happiness. She had succeeded in having Prince Carol's marriage to Zizi Lambrino dissolved by the Roumanian Supreme Court, and when he went on a tour of Europe and, meeting Princess Helen of Greece, fell in love and married her in April 1921, the Queen thought that this wayward difficult son of hers would at last settle down and be content. For a time he seemed happy and occupied, learning to fly, inaugurating the First Roumanian Air Corps, taking a keen interest in education and in the Boy Scout Movement, which he had founded in 1913. But, after the birth of his son, his old restlessness returned. He became nervous and moody, bored with his wife's preference for a quiet family life, seeking the company of his former rather unsatisfactory friends, and, to the consternation of his family, renewing his friendship with the beautiful, red-haired Madame Helen Tampeano, who had recently divorced her husband and had once more adopted her maiden name of Lupescu. More and more she gained an ascendancy over him, and when he was forced by his mother to attend the funeral of Queen Alexandra in London, he made arrangements for her to follow him secretly, met her on his way back from England, and disobeying his father's order to return to Roumania without her, renounced all rights to the throne, and cut himself off completely from his family.

Three years after King Ferdinand's death, however, Prince Carol arrived unannounced in Roumania, and, ignoring the fact that his son had been proclaimed King under a regency, took over control of the country. His wife, refusing his tentative offer of reconciliation, had left Roumania, and when a few months later Helen Lupescu arrived in Bucharest, Queen Marie knew that she had lost her son, that in his eyes she belonged to a generation that was obsolete and out of date, that once more the ruthless self-complacency of youth had triumphed over age and experience, and that henceforward she herself counted for nothing in the government of the country.

To the Roumanian people the Queen had always stood as the symbol of a wife and a mother. By the side of her husband, with her children round her, she had reigned supreme, and although her impulsive, warmhearted generosity had sometimes led her to indiscretions, no one could criticize her devotion to duty. She had stood by her people during the war, she had worked for them untiringly, and suffered with them in their hour of disaster. She had never spared herself, nor had she ever failed the crowds who had waited in the streets to see her pass. Tired, and sick at heart, as she often was, she always had a smile for them, always dressed with care so that they should see her at her best and keep a memory of beauty and untroubled happiness.

But now Roumania had a King who was separated from his wife, a young man who had inherited some of the ideals of his grandfather, Prince Albert, who ruled his country with well-regulated discipline and military precision, who encouraged physical culture, inaugurated modern schools and modern education, gave them an up-to-date army and air force. But there was no assurance of stability, no example of a happy, united family life, no golden-haired Queen to warm their hearts with her spontaneous smile.

Anxious about the growing unrest in the country, the revolts and conspiracies, and the threat of civil war, but knowing that her advice would be disregarded, Queen Marie withdrew from her son's Court, living quietly at Cotroceni, at Bran or at Balcic, paying occasional visits to England, to her daughter the Queen of Yugoslavia, or her other daughter Princess Ileana in Austria, occupying her time by writing her memoirs. She was very often unhappy, very often lonely. The death in 1936 of her sister, the Grand Duchess Cyril, was a grief that undermined her resistance, and when, a year later, her own splendid health broke down, she seemed to have no strength left to fight against illness.

The patience with which she endured her sufferings, the long months when she was completely bedridden, were a marvel to those who had known her boundless energy and activity in the past. The journalists who visited her, either in her golden bedroom at Cotroceni, or in her gardens at Bran, were amazed at her unquenchable gaiety, her interest in world affairs; they could not believe that the shadow of death was so near.

Once more, in the spring of 1938, before leaving for a cure at Dresden, she journeyed to Balcic, lay for a few days on the lovely terrace overlooking the sea; had herself carried up the path, between the rows of tall white lilies, to the wooden chapel, and the garden filled with mauve and purple flowers, which she had laid out in memory of her sister. Then she said good-bye to this dream-house of her youth, knowing perhaps in her heart that she would never see it again.

For a time it seemed as if the cure at Dresden might prove successful. She became stronger, was able to move about, even talked gaily of taking up work again on the fourth volume of her memoirs. But in July her illness took a fatal turn, she asked to be taken back to Roumania, and died the day after her arrival at Sinaia.

"One feels," a friend of mine said sadly when she heard the news, "that a light has gone out of the world." But now, looking back, I think all those who knew Queen Marie, are glad that she did not live to see the Second World War, and the aftermath it brought to the country she loved. She, who had always hated and feared Soviet Russia, how could she have borne to see Roumania invaded by the Red Armies, the peasants who had gone to meet them, as friends and allies, shot down, the women raped, the houses burnt, the convents and monasteries plundered?

She had left orders that when she died her heart was to be

removed from her body, placed in a jewelled casket, and taken to the wooden chapel she had built in her garden at Balcic. Here for two years it lay in peace, near the house she had loved, above the garden where the flowers she had planted were fading for want of care. But when, in 1940, Bulgaria claimed the whole of the Dobrudja, the Queen's former aide-de-camp made a hurried journey to Balcic, and removing the jewelled casket from its place in the chapel, took it to Bran, where Princess Ileana built another chapel for it, carved out of the rock of one of the hills. When Princess Ileana herself was forced to leave Roumania, she found that the marble sarcophagus was so firmly cemented into the rock that it could not be moved, and so she had to go into exile, and leave her mother's heart behind in the country she had come to as a young, unhappy bride, and had grown to love with such selfless devotion.

Queen Marie is almost forgotten, or if she is remembered, is all too often criticized. I have heard people condemn her for the glaring publicity of her visit to America in 1927. I have heard many accuse her of being too theatrical, and surrounding herself with an exaggerated pageantry. But to me she will always remain a memory of enchantment, a fairy-tale princess walking in her lovely gowns under the trees at Wolfsgarten, a regal, golden-haired woman, crowned with diamonds, whose beauty I worshipped, even though her deep-blue eyes looked at me with such unexplained hostility.

Whatever mistakes she may have made she was never petty or trivial or ungenerous. If she brought sorrow to some, she brought joy to thousands of others by her gaiety and magnetic personality. When she came into a room she seemed to bring light and animation with her, stimulating by her appearance even the most elderly and weary statesmen and Court attendants, making them forget their aching feet and straighten their tired backs in a sudden alacrity.

At Wolfsgarten the Grand Duke and Grand Duchess were fond of organizing games in the evening, where the guests were given slips of paper with questions to which they had to give written replies. Sometimes my mother brought back a few of those slips of paper and let me see them, and there was one amongst them which I never forgot. Somebody had asked what would be a suitable epitaph for the guests who were present that evening, and a young Russian Grand Duke had written: "For Princess Marie of Roumania I would say 'A star danced when she was born!'"

# King Ferdinand of Bulgaria

O N February 4 1815, Augusta, the widowed Duchess of
Saxe-Coburg-Saalfeld, noted in her diary that her second
son, Prince Ferdinand, who had been fighting against Napoleon
and was attending the Congress at Vienna, had given her the
news of his brilliant matrimonial prospects. "He has lost his
heart", the Duchess wrote, "to the charming daughter of
Count Kohary, and his affection is returned. He is fortunate to
have captivated such an heiress. . . . God seems always to have
watched specially over dear Ferdinand."

In marrying the daughter of the Chancellor of Hungary,
Prince Ferdinand of Coburg had indeed done well for himself,
for besides being an heiress, his bride, with her golden hair, and
big dark eyes, was so lovely, that, when he first saw her,
Golowkin exclaimed, "On est tenté de chercher les ailes en la
regardant." She was, moreover, devoted to her tall, good-
looking husband. Settling on their vast estates in Hungary,
and in the Coburg Palace built for them in Vienna, they
founded the Roman Catholic line of the Coburg-Kohary
family, their eldest son becoming King of Portugal through
his marriage to Queen Maria del Gloria, their lovely daughter
Victoire marrying the Duc de Nemours, their second son
Auguste, taking as his bride Princess Clementine of Orleans,
daughter of Louis Philippe, King of France.

On his father's death Prince Auguste inherited the estates in
Austria and Hungary, and when he died, in 1881, his widow
continued to live in the Coburg Palace in Vienna, and at the
castle of Ebenthal, all her love and pride centred on Prince
Ferdinand, the youngest of her three sons and two daughters,
in whom she saw the brilliance of her French ancestors, as well
as the intellectual gifts of the Coburgs. Viennese society, on the

other hand, regarded him as a slightly absurd young man, who wore too many bracelets and rings, was interested in butterflies and flowers, and had exchanged from the hussars to a foot regiment because he was such a deplorable horseman. "Der Prinz mit der langen Nase" (the Prince with the long nose) they called him, mocking that protuberant feature, which he himself nicknamed, "The sufferer", stroking it sometimes with a wry, humorous expression, as if he had a certain solicitude for its size. At one moment he had even thought of having an operation performed, to alter the shape of a feature which he felt was making him ridiculous, but, when he asked the advice of Princess Pauline Metternich, her bright eyes mocked him maliciously, while she told him with her inimitable laugh that it would be a thousand pities to alter the shape of a nose, "which should be a permanency, like a cathedral".

But in spite of all adverse criticism and ridicule Princess Clementine continued to worship her youngest son, and her belief in his great future seemed to be justified when, in 1886, he was offered the throne of the autonomous Principality of Bulgaria, which, after the abdication of Alexander of Battenberg, had been refused by several other minor royalties, all of whom were afraid of encroaching on Russia's interests.

"He is totally unfit, delicate and effeminate," Queen Victoria said, when she received a letter from Princess Clementine, telling her the news; and she shook her head gravely over the "absurd pretentions of this foolish young cousin of mine". In St. Petersburg the Emperor Alexander III struck his great fist on the table; "La candidature est aussi ridicule que le personnage," he exclaimed furiously. In Berlin Bismarck shrugged his massive shoulders: "The Prince and Bulgaria," he growled, "are of no consequence to us. Russia on the other hand is important." In Vienna society exclaimed incredulously, "What, another Coburg on a throne!" Count Kalnocky told the British Ambassador, "He has too much the air of a *vieille cocotte* to be any good as a successor to Alexander of Battenberg."

But the most severe and sarcastic criticism came from Walburga, Lady Paget, who, in her book, *The Linings of Life*, stressed the fact that Prince Ferdinand wore too many bracelets and had innumerable affectations, asserting that he powdered his face and had so delicate a constitution that he could only consult lady doctors. "He sleeps in pink sura nightgowns, trimmed with valencienne lace," she added maliciously, and, probably, quite untruthfully.

But although all Europe laughed at this tall, young man with the fair wavy hair, and although the Emperor Alexander sneered at this "ridiculous individual", furious because a little Balkan country which his father had liberated from the Turks had passed into the hands of a Coburg, Prince Ferdinand was to astonish many people by his firmness, his resolution and courage.

He had left Vienna with no one but his friend the Crown Prince Rudolf to wish him luck and God-speed. The great powers refused to recognize him, their representatives in Sofia had been given orders to treat him merely as an Austrian officer, who was there for personal reasons. He was Prince of Bulgaria, but it was a purely anomalous position, not acknowledged by the sovereigns of Europe, who still regarded him as a junior member of the House of Coburg.

Nor can the first sight of the country he had chosen to adopt have created a very favourable impression. There was no railway to Sofia in those days, and the roads over which he had driven had been execrable, the food he had been forced to eat had been extremely unpalatable. Sofia itself was nothing but a small Turkish town, with low-built houses, narrow, winding, badly-paved streets, and quaint little shops. Although many of the inhabitants had received excellent educations in either Vienna or Budapest, they were still, in Prince Ferdinand's eyes, uncultured and middle-class. He regarded the royal palace as hardly habitable, for it had formerly been an old 'konak' or residence of the Turkish ruler of Bulgaria, and was lacking in any of the amenities and comforts he deemed necessary.

But Prince Ferdinand was rich, he was artistic, he was magnificent in his ideas of luxurious living. He had brought with him a suite consisting of the Comtes de Grenaud, de Bourboulon, de Foras, and Monsieur Dimitri Stancioff, a brilliant young Bulgarian diplomat who had been studying in Vienna, and within a short time he had created a Court which, Princess Pauline Metternich said later, was the most refined and exquisitely kept in Europe.

Count Kalnocky continued to express his supercilious contempt for "this feeble and astonishing gentleman" who, he said, only contrived to keep his position owing to his money and his vanity. In Russia, Monsieur de Giers said coldly that he would never recognize Ferdinand of Coburg. "We shall," he added, "maintain a passive attitude until he comes to the end of his tether." Lord Hardinge of Penshurst, however, who at that time was a young secretary representing Great Britain in Bulgaria, declared that, although it had been stated in certain quarters that Prince Ferdinand would not retain his throne for more than six months, few people "knew or understood his tenacity of purpose". The German consul was of the same opinion and expressed his astonishment that a young man, who had been so ambiguous and irrational, should show so much determination and firmness, should apply himself at once to studying the language of the country, and show more unflinching courage than Prince Alexander. It was true that he was a bad horseman, but notwithstanding this, he had been able to win over some of the more powerful of the army officers.

It was, however, largely owing to his mother that Prince Ferdinand was able to maintain himself so successfully, for, in spite of the difficulties of the journey, she had followed him to Sofia, had supervised the extensive alterations in the Palace, had taken upon herself the administration of the hospitals and charitable institutions in Bulgaria. With her knowledge of diplomacy, her wise, unerring judgement, her brilliant flair for finding solutions to seemingly unsolvable problems, she upheld her son against the formidable opposition of the great powers, and in the many obstructions and difficulties which beset him. "I always noticed," Lord Hardinge commented, "that political affairs went well during her presence."

The greatest thorn in Prince Ferdinand's side was probably the Prime Minister Stambuloff, who had acted as Regent after the abdication of Alexander of Battenberg and continued to rule the country with tryannical severity, tolerating no interference in carrying out measures he considered necessary, however severe and stringent they might be.

It can hardly be wondered at that Prince Ferdinand found antagonistic and repugnant this powerful leader, the son of an innkeeper, with his rough, uncouth manners, his lack of refinement, his shrewd brain, for there can have been hardly any subject on which they were in sympathy. Stambuloff distrusted the young man who had been elected ruler of his country, and made no secret of his hostility. He disliked the new atmosphere in the Palace, the French noblemen with their courteous, suave manners, the pictures of beautiful women, by Winterhalter and Angeli, on the walls; the gold and silver plate; the Aubusson carpets; the rich, gilded furniture; the priceless china. All these, he felt, were alien to the Balkans, just as Prince Ferdinand, with his royal bearing, his culture, his elegance, his love of birds and flowers, was totally unsuitable as a ruler of Bulgaria. Yet he had to acknowledge that the money this young man was spending with such generous liberality was doing a great deal for the country. The stone buildings that were replacing the humble cottages, the parks and gardens that were being laid out, the bridge across the river, the broad, paved streets, all these were transforming Sofia into a small, modern capital, with an atmosphere all its own. At the same time the forests which the Turks had destroyed so wantonly were being replanted; a new harbour, docks and wharfs were being constructed at Varna; factories were being built in different parts of the country; railway communication was being increased, and a new era of prosperity seemed to be dawning.

Notwithstanding all this, the unrest in the army continued, and the constant conspiracies to recall Alexander of Battenberg warned Prince Ferdinand that, if he wished to retain his position, he must found a dynasty, however unpalatable he found the idea of a marriage for reasons of State.

Accordingly, in June 1892, he went to England, and, leaving his mother in London, went up to Balmoral to stay with Queen Victoria. She had not seen him for five years, and she found him greatly improved, far more dignified and less affected. The morning after his arrival, he joined her where she sat on the terrace, surrounded by the usual pile of dispatch-boxes, sheltered under a green-lined parasol.

He talked to her for some time about all his difficulties and trials, told her that he was hardly ever able to go out without an escort, especially since the murders of one of the members of his Cabinet, and of his Minister in Constantinople, both of which he said had been instigated by Russia—a fact that shocked the Queen greatly, especially when she heard that the murderers were still at large. He was, he said with a heavy sigh, a sovereign and yet still unrecognized as such by the great powers. Then, perhaps watching her intently to see the effect of his words, he told her that it was of paramount importance that he should marry and found a dynasty. "He is", Queen Victoria wrote in her Journal, "devoted to his country, for whose good he only wishes to work."

Though she received him so graciously, and expressed her sympathy with his difficulties, the Queen made it quite clear that she would not countenance his marrying a British princess. Rather dejectedly he returned to London, was received by Lord Salisbury, attended a banquet at the Mansion House, and then went on to Berlin. There he was met by a sharp rebuff, for the Emperor William refused to receive him, and on his arrival in Munich he was told with uncompromising firmness that he would not be permitted to approach a Bavarian princess. By this time he was exasperated, and full of resentment, but finally in Vienna the Emperor Franz Joseph took pity on him, granted him an audience, and, seeming to forget his old antipathy, started negotiations for the hand of Princess Marie Louise of Bourbon-Parma.

Before giving his consent to his daughter becoming engaged to the Prince of Bulgaria, the Duke of Parma made it a condition that any children born as the result of the marriage should be brought up as Roman Catholics. Prince Ferdinand gave a solemn promise to carry out this obligation, while at the same time Stambuloff revoked Article 32 of the Bulgarian Constitution, according to which it was obligatory for the heir to the throne to belong to the Orthodox Church.

Princess Clementine was delighted that her son's future seemed at last to be assured, and wrote to tell Queen Victoria that her future daughter-in-law, although she was not pretty, was very intelligent, had a great deal of charm, and had, she was sure, a very unselfish and amiable disposition. Princess Marie Louise also wrote to the Queen, expressing the hope that "her most Gracious Majesty and Dear Aunt" would extend to her some of the affection and kindness she had always shown to Prince Ferdinand. Touched by this letter, written "in such beautiful English", the Queen replied, hoping that her future niece would visit her in Florence after her wedding, and adding that she much looked forward to meeting her.

The marriage was solemnized at the Duke of Parma's house in Pianore in April, 1893, and after meeting Queen Victoria in Florence, and spending a few weeks in Vienna and in the castle of Ebenthal, Princess Marie Louise, dressed in Bulgarian national costume, made her State entry into Sofia.

She had already begun to study the language, and almost a once she flung herself enthusiastically into the interests of her adopted country, visiting all the hospitals, founding new orphanages in different parts of the country, learning to sing the old folk-songs, making expeditions to monasteries, convents, and villages in outlying districts, talking to the peasants, and trying to find out their wants and their grievances. But, notwithstanding all her efforts, and her untiring work, she could not replace Princess Clementine, she was not able to give her husband the support, the companionship, the guidance in affairs of State, that he had always received from his mother, and missed more and more every day. Surrounded by intrigues and antagonism, resentful because the great powers still refused to recognize him, he was frequently in a bad humour, and knowing only too well that his wife was afraid of him, he took a malicious delight in seeing her quail.

The birth of Prince Boris, the resignation of Stambuloff, and the deaths of the Emperor Alexander III and of Alexander of Battenberg, strengthened Prince Ferdinand's position, and in 1894, free from the dictatorship of his Prime Minister, he was able at last to make advances to Russia. He sent a delegation to St. Petersburg to attend the funeral of Alexander III, who had always been his bitterest enemy. "Ferdinand", the Empress Frederick wrote to Queen Victoria, "seems bent on coquetting with Russia, in the hopes of being recognized, which he never will be."

The fact that Stambuloff, after his resignation, was not given police protection, or allowed a visa to go to Karlsbad for a cure, has often been cited as implicating Prince Ferdinand in the brutal murder of the former Prime Minister in 1895, and although no conclusive proof of his complicity has ever been given and he was actually away from Sofia at the time, the stigma on his name remained. "The late Lord Salisbury," he once told my father, "has always treated me as Stambuloff's assassin."

Only a year later he was again to incur the scandalized censure of Europe, for, after the birth of his second son, Prince Cyril, he yielded to the persuasion of his ministers, broke the solemn promise he had made to the Duke of Parma, and had his eldest son confirmed in the Orthodox faith. It was an action that greatly pleased the Bulgarian people, but for a time it completely estranged him from his wife, called down on his head the Pope's excommunication, shocked Queen Victoria, and aroused furious indignation in Austria. "A man who is capable of such infamy," Francis Joseph exclaimed, "is capable of betraying everyone, and of selling his best friend."

In France, however, he received a certain amount of sympathy, and an article in the *Revue des Deux Mondes* declared that he had given his son entirely to the country of his adoption, adding that when one accepted the government of a nation one was forced to accept obligations that took no account of private feelings or affections, At the same time he at last received the recognition of Russia, for the Emperor Nicholas consented to be godfather to Prince Boris, and appointed Monsieur Tcharikoff as Minister in Sofia, with orders to treat the Prince as a reigning sovereign. Slowly, and with some reluctance, the other powers followed suit, and finally, after Prince Ferdinand had paid a State visit to Constantinople, and had been received with royal honours in St. Petersburg, Austria was forced to recognize him as undisputed Prince of Bulgaria.

"Foxy Ferdinand", the world began to call him, not only because his pointed, red-gold beard, and his long nose, gave him a curious resemblance to a fox, but because certain statesmen accused him of resorting to underhand methods, and declared that he was deceitful and cunning, a craven and a coward. It cannot be denied that he was mendacious at times, that he had an exaggerated fear of infection, or that he took an almost sadistic pleasure in making people feel ill at ease, chuckling wickedly when he saw them getting flustered and agitated. Sharp-witted, and a brilliant linguist, he himself could, with consummate ease, keep two conversations going at the same time, never losing the thread, and bewildering those to whom he was speaking by his rapid transition from one language to another. He was well informed on all subjects, he was never at a loss, he could be supremely entertaining, but he could also be maliciously cruel, and when his mother's French lady-in-waiting became engaged to one of his Bulgarian secretaries, he sent her, as his only wedding present, an ebony box of chocolates, done up in black paper and black ribbon, with a black-edged card inscribed with the cryptic message: "Toutes mes condoléances. Ferdinand."

Yet his generosity knew no limits, and very few who were in real trouble ever appealed to him in vain. He would personally receive all those who came with tales of hardship, would give away rouleaux of gold from his private income, or would send them to the appropriate municipal authority with orders that help should be given immediately. His love for animals was also genuine and sincere, he never grudged the time or the labour of personally caring for the birds in his aviary, and I shall never forget the look of real distress in his eyes when, one particularly icy winter, he told me that some of his South American finches had frost-bitten feet.

He was tireless and liberal in his efforts to make Bulgaria more civilized, to beautify in every way possible the country by whom he had been adopted. It was entirely due to his personal initiative that the Orient Express, connecting Paris with Constantinople, ran through Sofia, thus bringing, as he said in his speech at the opening ceremony, "a new existence, contact with Europe, and the breath of new ideas, wafted towards Bulgaria from abroad". He turned an old, half-ruined monastery at Euxinograd, near Varna, into a magnificent estate, with a park full of rare and precious shrubs and trees. His little summer palace at Vrania, near Sofia, was set in an exquisite garden, which he himself had planned and laid out. His private zoo was the most perfect of its kind, and a model of perfection.

The love of birds and flowers and nature did not, however,

dim Prince Ferdinand's interest in politics, and the attainment of a Byzantine Empire, which in those days haunted many sovereigns in Europe, was to him more than just a fantasy— it was a very real and glowing dream, that became almost an obsession. In his private study was a picture of the Bosphorus, with a figure of himself on horseback, approaching the golden walls of Constantinople; and after the Declaration of Bulgarian Independence he had a portrait painted of himself in old Byzantine costume, crowned with a jewelled diadem, and holding a sceptre and an orb in either hand.

In 1899 Princess Marie Louise died, having given premature birth to a second daughter, and when my father was appointed to Sofia four years later, Princess Clementine was again by her son's side, supervising the care of his four motherless children, and still helping him with her wise advice in the administration of his country. Though she was well over eighty, her eyes still retained the fire and sparkle of her youth, and her radiant smile, her sense of humour, her vivid interest in everything, made her a personality one was not likely to forget. A little old lady, sitting in a high-backed chair, and yet, in spite of her age, her helplessness, her total deafness, filling one with a sense of reverence, because one felt that here was a great personality, a woman who would have commanded one's respect and admiration even if her ancestors had not been Kings of France.

My father had been acquainted with Prince Ferdinand when he was a young secretary, attached to the Embassy in Vienna, and he knew that he was always prone to take offence and imagine an insult where none had been intended, and the new task was not rendered easier by the lack of sympathy existing between King Edward VII and his cousin the Prince of Bulgaria. Before leaving England my father had had an audience with King Edward, and had begged him to give a friendly message, to pass on to Prince Ferdinand; but all the King would say was, "You may tell the Prince that I have not forgotten the fact that he is my cousin, but that, as long as he continues his present, double-faced policy, he cannot count on my support." This was a message my father could not deliver word for word; he had to gloss it over, and embroider it to the best of his ability.

When King Edward and Prince Ferdinand met at Marienbad in 1904, the King was greatly entertained by his cousin's witty conversation, but at the same time irritated by what he considered the unnecessary air of royal dignity assumed by the Bulgarian ruler. Prince Ferdinand, on his side, never quite forgave the King for helping himself so liberally to a dish of creamed mushrooms that hardly any were left for himself, and, as creamed mushrooms were one of his favourite delicacies, he considered this an outrageous injustice.

Later that year my father persuaded King Edward to invite his cousin to visit England, and somewhat reluctantly the King agreed, adding, however, "Tell him not to bring too many people, as I know only too well that the smaller the Prince, the larger the suite." Nor did my father receive any reward for his efforts on this occasion, for King Edward only gave the Bulgarians who were in attendance the K.V.O. and, regarding this as an indignity, Prince Ferdinand retorted by giving my father the Bulgarian Order, Second Class. When King Edward reminded him that this was not feasible, as all other foreign representatives in Sofia had the Grand Cross, he was forced to rectify his error, but he showed his displeasure by cutting my father dead, and refusing to speak to him for six months.

Shortly after our arrival in Sofia there was an incident that showed how unpredictable Prince Ferdinand was, how unaccountable his moods could be, and how easily he could impute an adverse meaning to an ordinary, harmless action, and could, out of sheer perversity, choose to see disrespect or mockery in an entirely inoffensive gesture.

At that moment Great Britain had broken off diplomatic relations with Serbia, owing to the recent, brutal murder of

Queen Marie of Roumania

King Ferdinand of Bulgaria

King Alexander and Queen Draga. When King Peter, who was suspected of having been involved in the conspiracy, paid a State visit to Sofia, we were not able to attend any of the dinners and ceremonies given in his honour. We did, however, watch the King's arrival from a window, and, happening to look up, Prince Ferdinand, sitting by the King's side in the open carriage, saw my father, and raised his hand in greeting. Somewhat taken aback at having been recognized, my father bowed and smiled, but thought no more of the incident until a few days later when M. Dobbrovitch, head of the Palace Secretariat, arrived at the Legation. He was a black-bearded, benign little man with glasses which, when he was nervous or agitated, were continually getting misted over, so that he was always having to take them off to wipe them. On this occasion he was most obviously ill at ease, and his glasses were more often off than on, for he had come, he said unhappily, on a very disagreeable mission. Prince Ferdinand had seen my father laughing at him when he was driving with the King of Serbia, and he demanded an explanation of this unwarranted discourtesy.

In reply to this unexpected bombshell my father wrote a conciliatory letter, protesting that nothing had been further from his thoughts than to dare to laugh at Prince Ferdinand, for whom he had the very greatest respect and admiration. It was, he added—rather unfairly, I thought—entirely due to his daughter's insistence that he had gone to see the arrival of the King of Serbia, and he had been very much struck with the perfection of the arrangements, and the smartness of the military escort. He trusted His Royal Highness would accept his word, and would keep the promise he had so kindly given to dine at the Legation on King Edward's birthday.

For a day or two we lived in an atmosphere of suspense, wondering whether we would have to leave Sofia, and then M. Dobbrovitch appeared again, smiling and urbane, assuring my father, his eyes twinkling behind clear, unmisted glasses,

F

[ 151 ]

that the Prince considered the whole matter closed, that he even acknowledged that he might have been mistaken, and was looking forward to dining at the Legation.

As I was not yet grown up I was not permitted to be present at the dinner, but knowing the Prince's fondness for birds, my mother allowed me to come in afterwards, chiefly to show off her parrot, which would allow me to do anything with it. Prince Ferdinand was in one of his most affable moods that evening, and few people could be as witty or as charming as he could be when he chose. At dinner he had apparently kept the whole table entertained, he had drunk the health of King Edward without a single tart or ironical remark, and had expressed himself delighted with the food and wine that had been served. In the drawing-room after dinner, when I took the parrot out of his cage and allowed it to sit on my shoulder, and gently bite my cheek and pull my hair, his shrewd, brilliant eyes smiled at me almost benignly, and he plied me with questions, sometimes in English, sometimes in French and sometimes in German, so that I got a little breathless trying to answer in the correct language. "Votre fille est exquise," he whispered to my mother, and smiled at me again, when he saw me blush, knowing very well that I had overheard his remark.

When Bulgaria declared her independence in 1908 there was another rather similar incident, but this time I was the culprit, and it was against me that the Prince's anger was directed.

Indignant at the *coup d'état* that had been sprung on them without warning, the great powers refused to recognize the new Kingdom of Bulgaria, and for a time none of the foreign representatives in Sofia were permitted any intercourse with the Palace. But when Prince Ferdinand, after the ceremonies attending his proclamation as King in the ancient capital of Tirnovo, made his solemn entrance into Sofia, I obtained my father's rather reluctant consent to go with some Bulgarian friends to the Officers' Club to view the procession.

Carefully obeying instructions I kept myself well in the

background, and was certain that the newly-proclaimed King, riding rather morosely at the head of his troops, had not seen me. Few things, however, escaped those sharp, penetrating eyes, and about a week later, M. Dobbrovitch came to the Legation in a pitiful state of nervousness, his hands trembling as he repeatedly took off his glasses. One of the English papers, he faltered, had published a scurrilous article describing the royal entry into Sofia, making fun of the whole ceremony, and adding that the procession had been an hour late "because King Ferdinand had been pleased to part company with his horse". His Majesty was very angry indeed. Having seen me on the balcony of the Officers' Club he presumed that I was the author of this article, and he regarded this as an act of insulting disrespect, particularly as he had always been exceedingly kind to me.

Horrified, my poor father protested that he could give his word of honour that I had never written any description whatever of the procession. Even if I had done so, he added, I would most certainly not have written anything derogatory to King Ferdinand. Raising his hands in a gesture of despair, and muttering that the King would expect a more satisfactory explanation, M. Dobbrovitch took his leave, his shoulders bowed under the weight of his troubles. I was certainly not popular with my family for the next few days, but luckily the inquiries made by my father were successful in discovering the author of the offending article, and when this information was sent to the Palace, M. Dobbrovitch brought an apology from the King. I also had a very lovely brooch, sent as a peace-offering.

The fact that King Ferdinand always wore rings and bracelets has often been quoted spitefully, by contemporary writers, but it was not really for personal adornment that he had such a liking for jewellery, it was rather a very real and almost passionate love for precious stones, more especially emeralds, sapphires, rubies and topazes. He nearly always carried a few of these loose in his pocket, taking them out occasionally to let them slip through his fingers, finding, it seemed, a vivid pleasure in their glowing colours, or perhaps, a palliative for the nervous irritation caused by the many difficulties that beset him.

He was magnificently generous in his gifts. My mother had lovely hands, a beauty he especially admired in a woman, so he gave her several rings and bracelets. For me he always chose a brooch or a pendant set with aquamarines, which he no doubt considered suitable for a young girl.

On one occasion, when we were leaving Sofia on a short holiday, he sent his A.D.C. to the station to see us off, with orders to delay the departure of the Orient Express. I remember how puzzled we were because the train did not start and General Markoff's nervousness, as he kept on telling me how delighted the King had been with my portrayal of "Lady Hamilton at the Spinning Wheel" at some *tableaux vivants* at the Austrian Legation the night before. At last a Court servant dashed on to the platform with a little parcel, and with a sigh of relief General Markoff handed it to me. "This is from the King," he said. "I left His Majesty trying to make up his mind what to give you. It is for you, Miss Merveille." This was a name everybody in Sofia used, but it was Prince Ferdinand who had originally invented it, finding it perhaps easier to say than Meriel.

There is a magic about the Balkan countries, that is hard to define or put into words. Distant from the feverish struggle, the noise and commotion of modern Europe, the world seems younger there, the air purer, life less hurried, and free of the race against time, the struggle for money and power, which make modern existence a vortex of unending conflict and strain. The wide mountain plateau upon which Sofia was built, the distant Balkan mountains that someone once described as a garland of violets, the strange glamour of the East, which was always present in the hot sunshine, the brilliance of the stars, the music of a shepherd's flute, the beat of a gipsy drum from a distant village.

In spite of the many improvements, the new buildings, the modern shops, the brightly lit streets, there were still many things to remind one that it was not really quite Europe. The minarets of a mosque rising above the bazaar in the old quarter of the town; small, whitewashed cottages with wooden verandas, alongside high new houses; carts, drawn by cream-coloured, long-horned bullocks, or black buffaloes with china-blue eyes, jostling the smart carriages of some foreign minister; women in black and gold, or butcher-blue tunics, their heads covered with long white veils, or crowned with flowers; men in white sheepskin coats, mingling with officers in blue and silver uniforms; and now and then a troop of nomad gipsies with scarlet and orange shawls, passing through the town on their rough-haired ponies laden with all their meagre household possessions.

But when one went to dine at the Palace, it was in a totally different world. On the wide staircase with its dark, crimson carpet were pots of flowering shrubs, azaleas or hydrangeas, and, on each step a soldier in a scarlet-and-silver uniform, his grey fur cap surmounted with a tall eagle's feather. In the big gold-and-white reception rooms, were crystal chandeliers, massed flowers, rich brocade curtains, portraits of Maria Theresa of Austria, of the Empress Catherine of Russia, of some of the beautiful women of the Second Empire. When the guests had all assembled, the King would come in, his broad chest covered with decorations, his eyeglass dangling on a wide black ribbon, his shrewd eyes taking in every detail of the women's dresses, quick to note if a minister or a secretary had omitted to wear the proper decoration. In an instant he spotted if anyone was ill at ease regarding something done, or left undone, which might incur the royal displeasure. In the dining-room there would be a long table laden with flowers, with golden plate and priceless glass; a band playing softly in the distance; food perfectly served, and perfectly cooked, for King Ferdinand was a connoisseur in gastronomy, and was instantly aware of even the slightest error in the preparation of one of his favourite dishes, a salmi, a ragout or a Boeuf Stroganoff.

The death of Princess Clementine in 1907 was a cruel blow to her son, for she had been the only woman he had ever really loved. In her death he lost not only a mother, but a companion and a friend whose wise advice and help were always at his disposal. Now he was once more alone, and when, later that year, the Grand Duchess Vladimir of Russia came with her husband to unveil a statue of Alexander II in Sofia, he appealed to her, saying that he would have to marry again, that he wanted a woman who would look after his four children, and take an interest in the national charities; but he did not want a wife who would expect affection, or even great attention.

The Princess Eleanor of Reuss-Kösstritz seemed to the Grand Duchess to be the woman most suited for this position. She was no longer young, she had served as a nurse in the Russo-Japanese war, she was unselfish, generous and kind-hearted, a woman of high courage and incorruptible integrity. Negotiations were accordingly begun, and, believing that she had been given an opportunity to do good, that she could devote herself to the improvement of hospitals in Bulgaria, Princess Eleanor agreed to the proposed marriage, which took place in the early spring of 1908.

There may have been many moments when she regretted her decision, for her husband certainly showed her no tenderness, and very little consideration, treating her always with a cold indifference that sometimes bordered on intolerance. But she accepted it all with resignation, showing a serenely smiling face to the world, always ready to do all she could to help those who were ill, in trouble or distress. She may have had her reward for during the Balkan Wars her knowledge of nursing enabled her to give invaluable assistance to the wounded, and her untiring work during those days is still remembered by all who knew her.

We left Sofia in the spring of 1909, and the last picture of King Ferdinand I have in my mind is of his taking the salute at an evening service of the Guard Regiments, camped out on the plains. The long lines of soldiers in their white summer uniforms, the last rim of the sun sinking behind the distant mountains, a bugle ringing out sweet and clear in the silence, and then the soldiers' voices singing an old traditional evening hymn, while the standard-bearers dipped their tattered flags, and here and there a horse stirred restlessly—the King, standing with bowed, uncovered head, beside him little Prince Boris, pale and wistful, now and then casting a nervous glance at his father, an aide-de-camp looking rather flushed, as if he had been reprimanded for some omission of duty, an old general, who had fought at the battle of Shipka, the tears running down his cheeks as he listened to the last note of the hymn.

This was our last day in Sofia, and the tears were not far from my own eyes. I tried to swallow the lump in my throat when, as the service ended, the King turned to say good-bye to my father and mother, telling them how much he regretted their departure. I knew that my refusal to marry one of his secretaries had seriously displeased him, and his eyes were cold and steely as I curtsied before him. Then the shadow of a smile touched his lips, "Good-bye, Miss Merveille," he said softly, and turned away with a sharp reprimand to Prince Boris who had failed to make room for him.

My father was Ambassador in St. Petersburg when the First Balkan War broke out in 1912. The Bulgarian armies, fighting magnificently, won the battles of Kirklisse and Lalle Burgas, advancing to the lines of Tchadalja. In those early days King Ferdinand must have seen the coveted crown of Byzantium almost within his grasp, but an outbreak of typhus and cholera brought on by the breakdown in supplies, insanitary conditions, and increasingly bad weather, decimated his armies, while at the same time Great Britain, France and Russia threatened to send an international fleet to the Dardanelles.

Cheated of his greatest triumph, the capture of Constantinople, he returned to Sofia in an execrable humour. He was, therefore, only too ready to pick a quarrel with his former allies; so when Serbia, disregarding the historical and ethnographical facts on which the Treaty of London had been based, claimed that Bulgaria had been awarded territories to which she had no right, he retorted that he was being robbed of the fruits of his victories, and recalled his Minister from Belgrade. The frontier incident that followed led to an almost simultaneous declaration of war, in June, 1913. King Ferdinand was blamed for having provoked renewed hostilities, so that when Roumania demanded Silistria, and Turkey, seizing the opportunity, re-occupied Adrianople, he found England, France and Russia ranged against him, and refusing to support him in his hour of defeat.

My father had pleaded the cause of Bulgaria at the Conference of Ambassadors convened at St. Petersburg, thereby losing the friendship of Marie of Roumania. He had vainly sought to make M. Sazonoff, the Russian Foreign Minister, more lenient in his attitude; he had protested against the intervention of Roumania and the harsh terms meted out to Bulgaria at the Treaty of Bucharest, fearing the result of alienating King Ferdinand, and knowing that Germany would not fail to take advantage of the new position in the Balkans.

The First World War gave King Ferdinand the opportunity he had been waiting for. "Ma vengeance sera terrible", he had growled when the Treaty of Bucharest was signed, robbing him of Silistria, Macedonia, and part of the Dobroudja. Now his moment of vengeance seemed to have come, for the attitude Bulgaria was likely to adopt in the conflict was of paramount importance, and the statesmen who had jeered at the "Old Fox of the Balkans" and had made fun of his big nose, of his fear of infection and his dream of being Emperor of Byzantium, were sending their emissaries to curry favour with him, were angling for his support, tempting him with the offers of land, of favours and honours.

The offers made by Germany were the most acceptable. The co-operation of Bulgaria with the Allies, which would have meant a successful outcome to the Dardanelles campaign was not forthcoming. There can be no doubt that Ferdinand would have preferred to have remained neutral, and it is known now that it was only with great reluctance that he was forced to take an active part, both under the pressure of Germany, and by reason of the ultimatum sent him by the powers of the Entente. It is also unjust to accuse him of accepting German bribes of indemnity for material loss, for it has been proved beyond doubt that those offers were made only after Bulgaria had entered the war. But the fact remains that he betrayed his French ancestry, and had his mother still been alive she would never have permitted him to deny his allegiance to the country of her birth, and, with her wise far-seeing judgement would have opposed his making an alliance with Germany.

The full consequence of his deplorable misjudgment was brought home to him in 1918, and with revolt spreading in the army, and the country seething with unrest, he was forced to acknowledge that there was only one way open, if he wanted to save the throne for his son. What that decision cost him no one can tell, but, once made, he did not hesitate or bemoan his fate, but, sending for the Prime Minister, M. Malinoff, handed over his abdication with a quiet, controlled dignity. A moment later, when Prince Boris, who was then barely seventeen, came into the room, the King showed a sudden grandeur that amazed the Prime Minister. "Let us," he said genially, "be the first to take the Oath of Allegiance to the new Tsar." Embracing the tall young man, whose dark eyes were full of tears, he added gently, "I am your subject, but I am also your father."

That afternoon he drove for the last time along the road he had taken nearly every day, across the bridge he had built, past the Boris Gardens and the Tennis Club he had planned and laid out, and on across the plain to the little Palace of Vrania, and the beautiful park and gardens that had been his pride and joy. Slowly, for the last time, he walked through the big, light rooms, out down the shady avenues, visiting the different greenhouses, with the rare orchids and plants, the cages and aviaries with the birds and animals he had bred and cared for. One wonders what his thoughts were, during those final hours. Did he recall his moments of triumph and success in the face of desperate difficulties? The dream of the golden city of Constantinople? And the picture he had had painted of himself in the robes of a Byzantine Emperor? Or did he think with bitterness of his mistakes? Dreams and regrets alike in vain. This was the end of the road. He was now only one of the many deposed monarchs in that year of 1918, when thrones were falling all over Europe. A man without standing, without power or importance.

That evening he left Sofia, a company of his personal guards accompanying him as far as the frontier, where they took leave, their voices broken with emotion, and tears running down their cheeks, for, although he had been difficult to please, and hard to serve, he had nevertheless won their respect, and even their affection. In Budapest he was received by the city commandant with royal honours. But ignominy and shame awaited him, for Count Berchtold, the Foreign Minister, boarded the train as it approached Vienna, and informed him arrogantly that he would not be given leave to enter the capital, or stay in Austria, as the Central Powers regarded him as a traitor. Ferdinand was forced, therefore, to give up his wish to live in his castle of Ebenthal, and had to continue his journey to Coburg, where, refusing the offer of the old castle of Ehrenberg, he settled down in a small house where he had stayed from time to time before the war.

Here, during the ensuing years, he lived in almost complete retirement. His second wife, Queen Eleanor, had died during the war, his children were still living in Bulgaria, and, although they visited him occasionally, and begged him to go to Sofia, he steadily refused all invitations, adhering to his resolve never to mix again in political matters or to intrude, either with advice or criticism, on King Boris. "My shadow," he said, "must not fall on Bulgaria. My son's work must not be disturbed."

But his life was by no means idle. He built aviaries in his gardens at Coburg, and personally tended the many birds he collected there. Sometimes he went to the Musical Festivals at Bayreuth. In 1927 he visited South America, in order to collect more data about rare birds and flowers. A few years later he made a lengthy expedition to the Sudan and East Africa. In 1930 he attended the wedding of King Boris and Princess Giovanna of Italy, but again he refused his son's invitation to visit him and his wife in Bulgaria.

Ferdinand's hair and beard were by now snow-white. He suffered more frequently from gout; but his figure was as tall and imposing as ever, the regal dignity of his manner had not deserted him. The affectations, the intolerance, the captious irritability of his youth were things of the past. He had become a benign, stately, elderly gentleman, who attended conferences of ornithology and botany all over the world, never asking for deferential treatment from his fellow scientists, but receiving it nevertheless, not so much because of his royal birth, but because of the respect in which he was held for his superlative knowledge, and for his unfailing courtesy and amiability.

The growing unrest in Europe, the murderous attempts made on King Boris, the bomb thrown by communists during an official ceremony in the Cathedral in Sofia, when a hundred and fifty people were killed, caused him acute distress and anxiety, but he kept his apprehensions to himself, and refused to make any comment, adhering with iron determination to his principle never to discuss political matters, or to give any opinion on the domestic problems of Bulgaria.

In 1936 the daughter of M. Dimitri Stancioff, who had accompanied the young Prince Ferdinand when he left Vienna for Sofia, and whose mother was a daughter of the

Comte de Grenaud, the first Grand Marshal of the Bulgarian Court, was travelling with her husband, Sir Alexander K. Muir, in Kenya. One day during their tour, the guide they had engaged to accompany them, pointed out a distant mountain, and told them that it was called Donya Sabouk. Lady Muir exclaimed that that was a Turkish name. When the guide asked her how she knew that, and she told him that she was a Bulgarian by birth, he shook her warmly by the hand. The previous year, he told her, he had accompanied the ex-King of Bulgaria on a long trip through the Sudan, Uganda and Kenya, and he could not sufficiently express his admiration and affection for the old gentleman in the linen dust-coat and casquette, whose knowledge of birds, butterflies and plants had been a revelation. He had been, the guide continued, a delightful companion during that long and sometimes tiring journey, never complaining of the heat and the dust, or the occasional discomforts, unfailingly entertaining, grateful for anything that was done for him, and wonderfully liberal in his payments. He had asked to be taken to Lake Victoria, and when they arrived there he had got out of the car, gone to the edge of the water and, taking out of his pocket a magnificent diamond Order, had pinned it reverently on his coat. "This Order," he told the guide, "was given me by my cousin Queen Victoria. She was a woman for whom I had the most unbounded respect and admiration, and here, on the shores of the lake that bears her name, I wear this Order in memory of her greatness."

When she returned to England, Lady Muir wrote to King Ferdinand, telling him of her meeting with the guide Gethin, of the mountain with the Turkish name that had aroused her curiosity, of Gethin's respectful and affectionate admiration, and the pleasant memories he had of the journey he had made with the King. In reply she received a telegram thanking her for her letter, and signed "Donya Sabouk".

The last years of King Ferdinand's life were darkened by the

Second World War, by the death of King Boris under circumstances which have never been fully explained, and by the fact that Bulgaria was once more forced to throw in her lot with Germany, until in 1944 she belatedly declared war against Hitler, and was subsequently occupied by Russian armies.

King Boris had been loved in Bulgaria, although he never quite attained the position his father had enjoyed. The frequent communist attacks upon him, his quiet courage, his sudden unexplained death, however, had a tremendous effect in the country. Crowds flocked to his funeral, and a friend who was in Bulgaria at the time told me that it was impossible to describe the grief of the people, or the feeling of impending doom that seemed to possess them. "There is no hope for us without Boris. Now that our King is gone, we are lost." Those words were on all lips, rich and poor alike.

After the death of King Boris, a Council of Regents, headed by Prince Cyril, was appointed for the baby King Simeon. But after 1944, and the gradually increasing influence of Russia, the government and administration of the country passed into the hands of the extreme communists, acting under the instructions of Moscow. Some of the Kremlin's cleverest men were sent to Bulgaria; propaganda organized with a supreme, diabolical cleverness swept over the country, cinemas were built in every village showing films glorifying Russia and the Russian way of life, whilst unknown to the audience in every cinema a machine-gun was hidden, in case the peasants should rise in revolt against the new Agrarian Law.

In January, 1945, Prince Cyril was accused, in a mock trial, of having helped Germany, by keeping Bulgaria in the war, and on February 1st he and thirty members of his Court were driven out, having first had all their clothes removed, to the cemetery, where they were forced to dig their own graves before being shot and thrown into them, regardless of whether they were still alive.

The position of the widowed Queen Giovanna, her son, and

[ 163 ]

Cyril's unmarried sister, Princess Eudoxia, had now become critical and very uncertain, but owing to the representations made by England and America they were finally permitted to leave Bulgaria in 1946. Princess Eudoxia joined her married sister the Duchess of Württemberg, and was frequently shown great kindness by Queen Mary.

"Tout s'écroule autour de moi," King Ferdinand exclaimed, when he was told of the murder of his second son. Old and ill, too feeble to travel, unable to care for the birds he loved, there was not much left for him in life. His two sons were dead. His little grandson was living in Egypt with his mother. The country he had spent the greater part of his fortune on lay cut off from the rest of Europe behind the Iron Curtain. Even Coburg, where he lived, was in the Russian Zone of Germany.

Old age always has its nostalgic memories, its sorrows and regrets. But for a man who had once been a King, looking back on the ruin of everything he had built up, those memories held a special poignant sadness. During sleepless nights, and the tedious hours of lonely, inactive days, watching the clock tick away the empty minutes, he waited only for death, passing away in September, 1948, quietly and peacefully, retaining consciousness until the end, comforted by the presence of his two daughters, Princess Eudoxia, and the Duchess Nadejda of Württemberg.

# Princess Alice of Greece

IT was the spring of 1839. Queen Victoria was not yet twenty years old, and, although the affair of Lady Flora Hastings had aroused a storm of hostile, and in some cases virulent, criticism, she was still in the eyes of many people that "Little Love of a Queen", young enough to enjoy the many entertainments of her Court, to revel in her new-found liberty, and the release from her mother's domination.

Prince Albert of Coburg was only a memory of a charming and delightful cousin, with whom she had enjoyed looking at drawings, and playing the piano, and for whom she had shed many tears when he left to return to Germany. It was also a memory that returned to her occasionally with a certain uneasiness, for she was fully aware that he had long ago been chosen as her future husband by her Uncle Leopold, King of the Belgians, and for the moment she did not want to think of marriage.

In the spring of 1839 all thoughts of her handsome cousin were driven out of her mind, for the Grand Duke Alexander, eldest son of the Emperor Nicholas I of Russia, arrived on a visit. This tall young man wore his glittering uniforms with such an air of ease, had such gentle, soft, blue eyes, and such perfect manners, that he completely captivated her. He had been her partner at a ball at Buckingham Palace, he had sat in her box at the theatre, and a few days later he came to stay with her at Windsor, and taught her to dance the mazurka. The Queen's cheeks were flushed and her blue eyes shining as she followed her partner to the exciting rhythm of the music, his strong arm whirling her round in a way she found very pleasant. "I am really", she wrote in her Journal, "quite in love with the Grand Duke."

[ 165 ]

But in spite of all the brilliant entertainments given in his honour, the balls at Buckingham Palace, the Banquet at the Mansion House, his inauguration of the Cesarevitch Stakes, one of England's greatest races, and the fairy-like grace of the little Queen, her silvery voice and the shy adoration in her rather protruding blue eyes, the heir to the Russian throne remained faithful to his intention of marrying the daughter of the Grand Duke of Hesse, whom he had met, when he visited Darmstadt during his tour of Europe. "She is the woman of my dreams," he told a member of his suite the first evening he met her, sending a message the next morning to his father, begging permission to ask her hand in marriage.

So, when Lord Palmerston took him to the Queen's room to say good-bye, and, standing on tiptoe, she kissed his cheek, he certainly returned her embrace very warmly, whispered that words could not express his feelings, and turned away without saying any of the things she had perhaps hoped to hear. Looking after him, the Queen was compelled to put her handkerchief to her mouth to hide the trembling of her lips. Everything suddenly became very dull and monotonous, now that all the excitement of the Grand Duke's visit was over, and she complained rather fretfully to Lord Melbourne that she did not have enough young people round her.

Maybe the Grand Duke also regretted those carefree days at Windsor, for on his return to Russia he found that neither his father nor his mother approved of his choice of a wife, and it was long before he could overcome their opposition to his marriage. Princess Marie of Hesse, they insisted, was known to be delicate, her mother had died of consumption, and it was possible that she might have inherited the disease. Besides, she was, after all, the daughter of a minor German prince, and not good enough for the future Emperor of Russia. There were rumours, too, that all had not been well between her father and mother. The busybodies so prevalent in the small German courts of those days never tired of repeating stories of the

Grand Duchess's flirtations, and some of them even laid stress on the fact that there had been a lapse of over fourteen years between the births of the two elder sons, Louis and Charles, and of Princess Marie and her brother Prince Alexander. Nevertheless, worn down by their son's insistence, the Emperor and Empress finally gave in, and, in June 1841, Princess Marie of Hesse was married in St. Petersburg, with all the splendour and ceremonial of old traditions.

Queen Victoria noted the date of the wedding, and her thoughts may have gone back to the tall young man with whom she had danced so often, who had taught her the wild, intoxicating steps of the mazurka. It was a pity Albert did not really approve of dancing! But the transient moment of rebellion vanished in a surge of tenderness as she glanced across the room to where he sat reading, with the light of a shaded lamp falling on his fine forehead, and grave, intent face—Darling Albert! Beloved husband! How inexpressibly lucky she was to be married to a man so noble, so upright, so good in every way. Baby Princess Victoria was asleep in her cradle upstairs. She could only hope that the little German Princess would find the same peace and happiness in her marriage.

Princess Marie's favourite brother, Prince Alexander of Hesse, had accompanied her to Russia, and was given a commission in the Chevaliers Gardes. Tall, fair, and good-looking, the white uniform with the silver breastplate suited him to perfection, and his charm of manner, and inexhaustible gaiety, soon made him universally popular in society. But, although so many feminine hearts beat a little faster when he entered a room, his numerous flirtations, and more especially his attempt to make love to the Grand Duchess Olga, provoked the anger of the Emperor who had other plans for his beautiful daughter, and considered this handsome German Prince an insufferable puppy.

Whatever the feelings of the Grand Duchess Olga may have been, she finally became engaged to the heir to the throne of

Württemberg, and, in 1851, the scandal caused by Prince Alexander's elopement with Countess Julia von Hauke, one of his sister's ladies-in-waiting, resulted in his being deprived of his commission, and banished from the Russian Court.

For the next few years Alexander and his wife led a nomad life, while he served with the Austrian army; but after the death of Nicholas I in 1855, and the accession of Alexander II, who had always had a warm affection for his wife's good-looking brother, he was restored to favour in St. Petersburg. When his brother Louis, who had now succeeded as Grand Duke of Hesse, conferred the title of Princess of Battenberg on Countess von Hauke, they finally settled down at Heiligen-berg, a beautiful estate at Jugenheim not far from Darmstadt, which had been bought for him by his sister the Empress Marie.

There may have been moments when, after the brilliance of St. Petersburg, he and his wife found life in this quiet corner of Germany rather dull and monotonous, but Prince Alexander started a collection of coins, spent many days hunting deer in the forests, and found a growing interest in the education of his beautiful daughter and his four tall sons. Compared with other small courts, Darmstadt was the centre where many royal visitors came, bringing a movement and gaiety to the quiet little town, and the Castle of Heiligenberg was frequently the scene of meetings between the crowned heads of Europe. The Emperor and Empress of Russia, with their two younger sons and their daughter, came nearly every summer for a long visit.

In July 1862 Prince Louis of Hesse married Queen Victoria's second daughter, Princess Alice. Prince Alexander went to Frankfurt to meet his nephew and his bride, finding her better-looking than he had expected, very cultured and talented, but a little too intense and prone to philosophical discussions.

A year later he went to Windsor to represent his brother the Grand Duke, at the christening of Prince and Princess Louis's daughter, Victoria. It was not the first time he had been to England but it was the first time he had met the Queen, who had become an almost legendary figure in Europe. He thought that the rumours that her mind had been deranged in her grief over her husband's death were completely untrue, but he deplored the heavy widow's weeds she always wore, was bored by the austere melancholy atmosphere at Windsor, and was irritated because smoking was strictly forbidden.

The outbreak of the Schleswig-Holstein war, and the conflict between Prussia and the Southern States of Germany, intensified Prince Alexander's hatred and distrust of Bismarck's policy. He found himself increasingly at variance with Princess Alice, who, he said, cherished the incredible illusion that a King of Prussia might prove generous to Hesse. But in spite of these differences of opinion, Princess Alice and her children continued to be frequent visitors to Heiligenberg, the interest she had always taken in the four Battenberg boys inducing her to help the eldest brother, Prince Louis, to the attainment of his long-cherished dream of joining the British Navy. In 1868 he took the Oath of Allegiance at Gosport, his first posting as naval cadet being on board H.M.S. *Ariadne*, in which the Prince and Princess of Wales were making a cruise in the Near East.

Writing to the Queen a few years later, Princess Alice told her that Louis of Battenberg had passed a first-rate examination, the glowing reports he had received making his parents very happy, especially as his younger brothers were inspired by his good conduct, and were hoping to be able to please their parents in the same way. Certainly, when he came home on leave in 1873, looking incredibly handsome in his naval uniform, he became almost a hero to his younger brothers. When his parents exclaimed at the way he had grown, his dark eyes lit up with a smile. "*I* thought you had all become a lot smaller," he said, putting his arm round his mother's waist, and kissing her flushed cheek.

[ 169 ]

Prince Alexander was shocked and distressed by the death of Princess Alice and her youngest daughter in 1878, and the tragedy that had so suddenly undermined the happy family life in the New Palace in Darmstadt, made old quarrels and differences seem petty and puerile. "In spite of her faults," he said, writing to his sister the Empress Marie, "Alice was a remarkable, clever and forceful woman," and he lamented the fact that so many of the things she had begun and planned would never be carried out, and that her husband and children would now be left like "rudderless ships".

Realizing that he had sometimes been unduly harsh in his judgement of their mother, he now did all he could for the four little Princesses of Hesse, inviting them to Heiligenberg as often as possible, and helping Princess Victoria in the many new duties that had fallen so suddenly on her young shoulders. In the past it had always been she who "romped with the boys", but those games were now things of the past. When Prince Louis came home on leave again, he found the little tomboy he had left grown into a young girl with a grave mature dignity, and as the years passed, a new enchantment replacing the old, thoughtless, childish companionship.

The death of his sister, the Empress Marie, and the assassination of Alexander II, in 1881, severed the links that Prince Alexander of Hesse had for so many years had in Russia, and although he attended the coronation of Alexander III, in 1883, he was received coldly. He found the new Emperor hostile and unfriendly, and the fact that the election of his second son, Alexander, as Prince of Bulgaria, was resented by Russia, determined him to keep away in future from the country where he had formerly enjoyed so much popularity. He was, he said rather wistfully, becoming old and useless, good for nothing but shooting deer, and collecting coins. His daughter had married, his sons were growing up, their good looks and charm regarded with growing suspicion by Bismarck, but winning the admiration of the Emperor of Germany, who exclaimed that he had never seen a handsomer family than "those Battenbergs".

Carrying out the wishes of his wife, who had always said that she would never allow any of her daughters to be forced into loveless marriages for reasons of State, the Grand Duke of Hesse gave his consent to the engagement of his eldest daughter, Victoria, to Prince Louis of Battenberg, and the marriage was arranged to take place in April 1884.

Queen Victoria had promised to be present, and both the castle of Heiligenberg and the New Palace in Darmstadt were filled to overflowing with royal guests. But beneath the bustle of preparations, the dinners and receptions, the unpacking of presents, the trying-on of bridesmaids' dresses, there was an atmosphere of strain and uneasiness. The bride's eyes were often filled with tears, the bridegroom was preoccupied, the Grand Duke of Hesse was pale and distracted and carefully avoided being alone with his mother-in-law, Queen Victoria, who arrived a few days before the wedding accompanied by her youngest daughter Princess Beatrice.

Queen Victoria was in deeper mourning than ever for her son, the Duke of Albany, who had died two months earlier. She was immersed in her grief, and although she noted, with an ominous tightening of the lips, the marked attention the bridegroom's handsome brother was paying Princess Beatrice, she failed to observe the grave faces and the nervous manner of some of the older guests. She was the Queen of England and they were all afraid of her, not only because of her unrivalled position and her power in Europe, but because that small, insignificant figure in the everlasting black dresses inspired an incomprehensible awe in all who came in contact with her. And so, uneasy and apprehensive, they condoled with her, talked of the situation in Khartoum, of the unrest in Bulgaria, and Russia's aggressive attitude, and none of them dared mention the subject predominant in their minds, or warn her that the Grand Duke of Hesse, who had, as she believed, remained faithful to the memory of his wife, had contracted a secret marriage with another woman who had already been divorced.

It was the Prince of Wales who finally had to undertake the task of telling her the truth. He had also to interview Frau Kolenin, and try to persuade her to sign a document annulling the secret marriage, an interview that must have been extremely painful, and resulted in her having hysterics and threatening to kill herself.

Finally, however, the marriage was dissolved by the Courts, and although the Queen found it hard to forgive her son-in-law, whose action, she told Prince Alexander, was "simply beyond expression", she nevertheless came to Darmstadt again a year later, to be present at the christening of Prince and Princess Louis's eldest daughter, Princess Alice. It was also to give her formal consent to the engagement of Princess Beatrice to Prince Henry of Battenberg, stipulating, however, that he must relinquish his commission in the German army, and take up his residence in England, because she could not bear to be parted from her youngest daughter, who had been her inseparable companion for so many years.

After the death of Prince Alexander of Hesse, in 1887, Prince Louis inherited the estate of Heiligenberg. When my father was appointed to Darmstadt, in 1902, I remember going to play with Princess Alice and her younger sister, Princess Louise. Many things in those far-away days have now become hazy and indistinct in my mind, but I have a very clear recollection of that lovely white castle, of the terraced gardens with their steep, winding paths, and of the little wooden cottage where Princess Alice and I played at being housewives, sweeping the floor with miniature brooms and, under the guidance of a nurse, trying to make cakes and scones for tea.

Prince Louis of Battenberg was often away at sea, but on his occasional visits his grave dark eyes always smiled at me, and sometimes to my supreme joy he would gently stroke my hair.

Princess Louis was in mourning for her father, the Grand Duke of Hesse, who had died in 1901, and I remember her as always dressed in black, her dark gold hair brushed plainly back from her forehead. "I should have been the man of the family," I once overheard her say to my mother, and it is true that her lack of personal vanity, her firm handshake, her direct, sometimes rather abrupt, manner, gave an almost masculine impression. She was, however, a woman whose absolute integrity seemed to shine out of her bright blue eyes, whose clear, reasoning brain was remarkable, whose honesty and singleness of purpose made one feel that one could never tell her a lie or indulge in subterfuge or evasion, a woman who had faced the many sorrows life brought her with unflinching courage, for whom it was possible to feel nothing but respect and admiration.

I was too young to realize all this at the time, and, in spite of her unfailing kindness I stood rather in awe of her. It was her eldest daughter, Princess Alice, who was my ideal, a paragon of perfection, whose golden hair and big, dark-brown eyes filled me with admiration and envy. I wanted to copy her in all things, to wear a comb or a slide instead of a ribbon round my hair, to be as tall and slender as she was, to hold myself with that grace and dignity, that seemed to come to her so naturally. Even her slight deafness, which gave her sometimes a rather faraway look, as if she was living in a world of her own, was an added attraction in my eyes, and in my zeal to try and copy her I would often pretend not to hear what people were saying, receiving a sound scolding in consequence, and being told sternly not to be rude and inattentive.

When we stayed at Wolfsgarten during the summer months, Princess Louis was often there with her two daughters, and her little son Prince George, and here I was more than ever envious of Princess Alice, who, being a year older and a member of the family, was allowed many privileges denied me. She knew or was related to so many of the royal guests who came to stay at the old red hunting-palace in the woods, and whether it was the Empress Frederick, the Prince of Wales, the Emperor and Empress of Russia, or the Crown Princess of Roumania, she was always at her ease, and never tongue-tied, self-conscious and awkward, as I so often was.

I envied her, moreover, because when she and her sister, Princess Louise, were in Darmstadt, they went for daily lessons to the finishing-school for English girls run by a Fräulein Texter. I longed to go there too instead of having to do lessons at home, with the prim daughter of a German pastor who was my daily governess. Fräulein Texter was distantly related to Goethe, and, after the death of the Grand Duchess of Hesse had been called in to educate her youngest daughter, Princess Alix. I have only a very vague picture of her in my mind, a stout, redoubtable old lady, with a loud voice and a beaming smile; but I remember being taken to private theatricals given by the girls in the school, and having tea at a long table laden with simnel cakes, gingerbread, cream buns, pots of honey and cherry jam, and cups of chocolate covered with whipped cream. I wishing more than ever that my mother would allow me to go and have lessons there, if it meant having things like that every day.

In June, 1900, Princess Alice's younger brother, Prince Louis, was born, but in the autumn of that year my father was appointed Counsellor to Rome, and with the death of Queen Victoria, in January 1901, and the subsequent divorce of the Grand Duke and Grand Duchess of Hesse, our links with Darmstadt were broken. I never saw Princess Alice again, although, when two years later I heard of her engagement I wrote her a letter which I am afraid never reached her. She had met Prince Andrew, the third, and best-looking, of all King George of Greece's tall, handsome sons, when he was doing his military service in Germany. She met him again when she went to stay with Queen Alexandra in London, and Prince Andrew, no doubt aware that she was on a visit to his aunt, arrived unexpectedly and lost little time in approaching Prince Louis to ask for his daughter's hand in marriage.

Those who saw Princess Alice when she returned to Darmstadt, could have little doubt of her radiant happiness. She was barely seventeen, and she was still pursuing her studies with Fräulein Texter. A friend of mine, who was there at the time, told me how one day in the early spring of 1902 she went into a room to find Princess Alice crying bitterly, her pink muslin dress crumpled, her fair hair falling in disorder round her shoulders. She had not, she explained through heart-rending sobs, had a letter from Andrew for over a week, in spite of the fact that she had written to him every day. He must be ill, he might have had a serious accident, or perhaps he had changed his mind. Even when she was told that it was probably only due to some delay in the post, she refused to be comforted, but the next morning she arrived at the school with her face transfigured, all tears forgotten, for the mail had brought five letters which had been held up in the post from Greece.

Her wedding has been described to me by several who were present, as one of the loveliest as well as one of the gayest they remembered. Seldom had the little town of Darmstadt been so full, seen so many royal guests at once, known so many entertainments. It seemed as if just for those few days, all who were there threw away the cares of State, all political difficulties, all personal problems, as if, knowing that time was drawing short, they wanted to capture and enjoy those hours to the full, indulging in youthful amusements, in practical jokes, in gales of laughter.

The night before the wedding there was a gala performance at the theatre, and Queen Alexandra, in a dress embroidered with mauve sequins, and wearing a tiara of diamonds and amethysts, looked lovelier than ever; but Lord Gosford, who was in attendance on her, stood entranced, gazing up at the box where the Empress of Russia, in delphinium-blue chiffon,

[ 175 ]

sat beside her sister the Grand Duchess Serge. "I am looking at the two most beautiful beings in the world," he said in a hushed tone, when somebody asked him what he was staring at. "I did not know such beauty could exist."

Owing to the difference of religion, there were two marriage ceremonies. The Emperor of Russia had brought his own choir from St. Petersburg, to sing at the Orthodox marriage service. The various, complicated rites of the ceremony had been carefully explained to the bride by Prince Nicholas and Prince Christopher of Greece, and she had been warned that the priest would ask her two questions, the first being whether she consented of her own free will to become the wife of Prince Andrew, the second whether she had at any time promised her hand elsewhere. Bewildered by the long, unfamiliar ritual, and unable to hear what the priest was saying, she gave the wrong answers, quickly correcting herself when Prince Christopher, who was holding the wedding crown over her head, gave her a sharp nudge with his elbow.

When the marriage ceremonies were over, there was a banquet in the old castle, and, sending away all the servants, the Grand Duke of Hesse acted as butler, assisted by Prince Nicholas, Prince Christopher of Greece, and the bride's two young brothers. The meal was very hilarious and merry, even the Empress of Russia laughing like a girl, when Prince George of Greece snatched the tiara of his aunt, the Duchess of Württemberg, and put it on his own head. A big crowd had gathered on the square in front of the old castle, to see the bridal pair drive away in their open carriage, pelted with rice and confetti by the guests, the Emperor of Russia forcing his way through the throngs of people, to run after the carriage, and empty yet another bag full of rice over Princess Alice. Leaning out, she gave him a sharp tap on the head with one of her shoes, leaving him standing, roaring with laughter, in the middle of the cheering crowd.

The first years in Greece must have been happy and carefree,

for the country had recovered from the defeat and humiliations of the 1897 war with Turkey, and peace seemed assured.
The frequent political upheavals, and the growing strength of
the Military League, formed in 1909, should, it is true, have
been a warning of things to come, but Princess Alice was too
young to see the danger, and was perhaps only secretly glad that
the decree prohibiting princes of the royal blood from holding
responsible positions, forced her husband to resign his commission, and kept him at home.

Almost as soon as she arrived in Athens, she began to learn
Greek, taking lessons with Princess Nicholas of Greece, who
was a daughter of the Grand Duke Vladimir, and had been
married to Prince Andrew's brother for about a year. Thrown
together as these two were by fate and circumstance, sharing
the same tragic destiny, the same difficulties and hardships, it is
difficult to visualize, in those first years, two women so entirely
different in tastes, character and upbringing. Princess Alice
with her fair hair, her soft brown eyes, her simplicity and quiet
composure; the Grand Duchess Helen, brought up at the brilliant Court of St. Petersburg, her lovely, curling mouth seeming to be made for laughter, her dark eyes scintillating with
gaiety and humour.

I saw Princess Nicholas several times when she came to stay
with her mother in St. Petersburg, before the First World
War, but one unforgettable picture of her has remained in my
mind. On New Year's Day 1914, I happened to be passing the
door of the Vladimir Palace, when her carriage drove up,
having just brought her back from a ceremony in the Winter
Palace. "Come in and see my dress," she called out. I followed
her into the hall, and when the servants had closed the heavy
glass doors she slipped off her long sable cloak, to show me the
old traditional Russian Court robes, opening over a white
satin petticoat, richly embroidered with gold. Her dress itself
was of pale blue brocade, shot with gold, and she wore a
necklace of diamonds and turquoises, the diamond *kakoshnik*

that crowned her dark, curling hair, glittering with iridescent fire as she moved. She was an entrancing figure, smiling at me mischievously as she revealed the real reason of her calling me in, when she asked me to tell my father that she wished a certain officer in the Gardes à Cheval to sit next to her at the dinner we were giving that night. "I am afraid he will not be very pleased," she said as she gave me her hand to kiss. My father's dismay, when I gave him her message, bore out her words, for it meant changing all the places at table, and up-setting the careful arrangements of precedence.

Happy as she was during those first years in Greece, Princess Alice had to adapt herself to many new conditions and to a certain amount of discomfort; for the Royal Palace in Athens was far from an ideal residence, especially during the winter months, when the vast halls and corridors were icily cold, and even her private apartments inadequately heated by china stoves, and lit by oil-lamps. The only bathroom had taps which seldom worked, or, if they did, never produced a drop of hot water. Often when the weather was bad King George would play battledore and shuttlecock with his sons in one of the ball-rooms, or, followed by all his children and grand-children, would lead a race on bicycles through the State halls and passages, in an attempt to keep warm. Even in those early days Princess Alice took a keen interest in all the charitable organizations of the country, and especially in the School of Greek Embroidery that had been started by Lady Egerton, wife of the British Minister in Athens. She would spend hours there every day, learning the intricate stitches, and the mingling of beautiful colours, in order to be able to pass the art on to others.

The summer months were generally spent at Tatoi, in the middle of the pine forests north-west of Athens, where King George and Queen Olga had built several small houses near their Summer Palace, to accommodate all the members of the family. Here the three little daughters of Princess Alice would spend many happy days in the adjoining farm, watching the cows being milked, cream and butter being made in the dairy, and the chickens, turkeys and peacocks fed. Most afternoons they went for long picnics in the woods, with the three daughters of Prince and Princess Nicholas, who were their inseparable companions. Their favourite was the youngest, Princess Marina, who, even as a baby, showed a personality, a gay, enchanting sense of fun, which put her far above her sisters. There were also visits to Prince Andrew's villa at Corfu or to England, where the little girls played together on some seaside beach, unnoticed, and unrecognized, by the holiday crowds surrounding them.

Days of tranquil happiness, with no word to warn them that the world they knew, seemingly so permanent and secure, was on the point of disintegration, that new forces were stirring beneath the surface, breaking the bonds which had for so long held them enthralled, sweeping away the guilty and the innocent, the evil and the good, in their triumphant onslaught on the strongholds of Europe, destroying the old autocracies, the old tyrannies, only to replace them by a despotism far more relentless, ruthless and inexorable.

The outbreak of the Balkan War, in October 1912, which at first united Greece, Serbia, Bulgaria and Montenegro against Turkey, and then set them snarling at each others' throats, cast the first shadow on the even, peaceful existence of the Greek royal family. Prince Nicholas and Prince Andrew immediately rejoined their regiments, under the command of their eldest brother, the Duke of Sparta. On March 13, 1913, as King George was peacefully walking in the streets of Salonika, he was struck down by an assassin. The centre and nucleus of the united circle was irretrievably destroyed, and although the Duke of Sparta, who succeeded his father as King Constantine I, was adored by the country and acclaimed as the victor of Salonika, the wisdom and gentle humanity of King George, his unpretentious far-seeing judgement, were lost to Greece at a moment when they were most needed.

A tall, handsome, powerfully-built man, I had seen King Constantine at Wolfsgarten, where he and his wife were frequent visitors when on their way to visit Queen Sophie's mother, the Empress Frederick, at Cronberg. I remember, too, one afternoon in the gardens, hearing him say to my father, half jokingly, "You know there is an old legend that if one day a King Constantine and a Queen Sophie ascend the throne of Greece the great Empire of Byzantium will be restored, and Constantinople will once more become the capital of Greece. If that prophecy is fulfilled, Mr. Buchanan, I will ask for you to be Ambassador." I can still see the smile on my father's face as he replied, "I shall be greatly honoured, Sir." They were words spoken in jest, but underneath lay the thought that was always present in the minds of those who knew and loved Greece, the memory of the heritage they had lost but still dreamt of reclaiming.

After the Treaty of Bucharest had been signed, on August 10 1913, peace seemed to be once more assured, but the day after the birth of Princess Alice's fourth daughter, June 27 1914, the first shot was fired in the war that was to change the face of Europe, when Arch-Duke Franz Ferdinand and his wife were murdered in Serajevo.

Those weeks of tension, when peace hung in the balance, must have been very hard for Princess Alice, and for her sister-in-law, Queen Sophie, whose brother, the Emperor William, was being duped and hoodwinked by the military party in Germany. She had adored him as a child, but there had been many moments when she had been at variance with him. During her father's fatal illness, when he had treated her mother so cruelly she and her two younger sisters had stood out against him. When, after her marriage, she had adopted the Orthodox religion, he had refused to see her, or permit her to come to Germany, a verdict she had found hard to forgive. On August 2 1914, he sent his threatening, almost blackmailing, telegram to King Constantine, informing him that he was concluding a treaty with Turkey and Bulgaria, and that in the event of war he would regard Greece as an enemy nation if she did not side with Germany.

Owing to her deafness, Princess Alice cannot always have followed the heated discussions that took place at the weekly dinners in the Royal Palace at Athens during those months. King Constantine argued that his only course was to remain neutral, as the country would be reduced to cinders by the fleets of Great Britain and France, if she threw in her lot with Germany. On the other hand, if she joined the Entente she would be unable to withstand the onslaught of the German, Austrian and Bulgarian armies who would immediately invade her. Prince George, married to Princess Marie Bonaparte, and Prince Nicholas, whose wife was a Russian Grand Duchess, were eager to side with the Entente. Queen Sophie said little but her eyes were shadowed with memories of her childhood. What must Princess Alice herself have thought? With her mother, who, in spite of her German father, had always been so intensely English, with two brothers serving in the British Navy, and her father, who had resigned from his post as First Sea Lord, because of the cruel and unjust attacks made against him by certain sections of the Press and the public? "These divisions in the royal family are quite unbearable," Queen Victoria had written to her daughter in 1877, little foreseeing the conflicting loyalties, the tragic dissensions, that were to divide so many of her grandchildren, and great-grandchildren, in the future.

When Turkey entered the war, Sir Edward Grey asked Greece for assistance. King Constantine was ready to give it, but unhappily at this point Russia intervened, and by refusing to allow the King of Greece to take part in the campaign in Asia Minor, for fear that he might lay claim to Constantinople, altered the course of the war. When it became known that Constantinople had been promised to Russia, King Constantine, bitterly resenting the fact that his co-operation in the

Dardanelles had been rejected, finally decided to remain neutral. In view of the many mistakes that had been made, he was convinced that the Entente would not send him troops in sufficient number and that Greece would be annihilated by Germany. He might, he wrote to the Princess of Saxe-Weimar, in that case be called a hero, but he preferred to try and save his country from the horrors of war.

In 1915 Salonika was occupied by a force of British and French troops, and the next year Prince Nicholas was sent on a mission to Russia. At the same time his brother, Prince Andrew, went to Paris and London. Both were charged with messages assuring the Governments of the Entente that King Constantine had never had any secret understanding with Germany or Bulgaria, that he had no intention of attacking the forces of the Entente in Salonika, and that any attacks being made were the work of guerilla bands, acting on their own initiative.

It was while they were both away that summer that the terrible fire at Tatoi broke out. It raged for forty-eight hours, costing the lives of eighteen people, and destroying miles of beautiful forest. It is known now that a strange car with four men had been observed touring the forest on July 7, and a few hours later the fire started in several places at once. This left little doubt that it was a calculated act of incendiarism, carried into execution because of the rumours that a secret wireless set had been installed in the Summer Palace, and was being used for communicating with Berlin.

The King and Queen were living at Tatoi at the time, and went out to investigate, as soon as the news of the outbreak was brought to them. Caught in the raging inferno, and finding the road blocked by a wall of fire, they had to abandon their car, Queen Sophie running for a mile and a half with her youngest child, Princess Catherine, in her arms, while the King, accompanied by his son Prince Paul, his aide-de-camp, and several soldiers, continued on their way to try and find the cause of the outbreak, The King, who knew every path in

Princess Alice of Greece

The Grand Duchess Cyril of Russia

the forest, finally reached safety with his son, but his aide-de-
camp, and five soldiers who had gone by another path, lost
their lives, and neither the chauffeur nor the car were ever seen
again.

In Russia, meanwhile, Prince Nicholas had found the Emperor sympathetic, asserting his entire confidence in King
Constantine's integrity, but Prince Andrew had been received
with hostile suspicion in Paris and in London, and had been
horrified by the daily placards in the streets, proclaiming in
flaming letters: "Tino's new treachery", or "Allied plans betrayed to Germany by Tino". Disheartened by the failure of his
mission, he returned home only to find the situation rendered
still more critical by an arbitrary note from the Entente demanding the unconditional surrender of all Greek arms, a
demand which placed King Constantine in an impossible
position, knowing as he did that if he agreed, his people
would brand him as a traitor, whilst if he refused the British
and French would use force.

Nor was he long left in doubt, for on November 30 an
international force was landed at Piraeus, and when shots were
fired at them by a few thoughtless hotheads, a skirmish ensued,
in which several French and British sailors were killed. In
retaliation, Allied warships bombarded Athens for two hours,
most of the shells falling near the Royal Palace.

Princess Alice, working as usual at the School for Greek
Embroidery, had heard the reports that the Palace was in
danger, and had seen the wounded brought in from the streets.
She drove home through a rain of bullets, to find that one of the
nursery windows had been broken by a shell. She hurriedly
removed her frightened, crying children to the cellars, where
Queen Sophie had already sought shelter.

It was soon after this that the Queen wrote to the Kaiser
appealing for assistance. She had not forgotten the horror of
the fire at Tatoi nor the bombardment of Athens; the blockade
which brought such misery and starvation to the people broke

her resistance, and in her desperation she turned as a last resource to her brother. Her letters are still quoted as evidence of her treachery, and at the time they certainly strengthened the rumours that the royal family was in touch with Berlin.

Owing to these rumours, and the continual attacks on the British and French forces in Macedonia made by Greek bands the Government of M. Venizelos was recognized, in the spring of 1917, and early in June, M. Jonnard, who had been appointed High Commissioner in Athens, demanded the instant abdication of the King. He promised that his second son, Prince Alexander, should succeed to the throne, that the blockade would be immediately lifted, and that there would be no reprisals on those who had resisted the landing at Piraeus.

There was no possible alternative for King Constantine. He had been sincere in his desire to save his country from the horrors of war, his conscience, he declared firmly, was clear of any act of treachery, but public opinion was against him. In England and France he was regarded as a man who had conspired with Germany, who had been irresolute and unstable, had not kept faith. No consideration was given to the many conflicting difficulties that had beset him, nor was any word in his defence allowed to find its way into the Press. To his own people he was still, however, a beloved King, and for days a weeping crowd surrounded the Palace in Athens, seeking to prevent his departure. But he and his family embarked on the steamer *Sphacteria* from a village on the Gulf of Euboea, Prince Nicholas and Prince Andrew following them into their exile in Switzerland a few weeks later.

Only those who have been uprooted from their homes, who have had to leave everything they loved, can know what exile means, but the royal family of Greece had to face not only the heartbreak of banishment from their country, and the new and unfamiliar shortage of money, but also the suspicion and distrust with which they were surrounded. The English nurse who had looked after the children of Prince and Princess

Nicholas for many years, was informed by the British consul in Lausanne that if she did not give in her notice she would be deprived of her passport. Queen Sophie was not permitted to have any intercourse with her son King Alexander, and even when he was in Paris for a few days, and she tried to telephone, she was told sharply that she could not speak to him. Princess Alice was treated more leniently, and in September 1917, was permitted to visit her father and mother, spending a few happy weeks with them and her sister Princess Louise, able to see her two brothers, and some of her many friends in England.

In 1918 she and her sister-in-law were in mourning for many of their relations whose fate in the Russian Revolution was now being gradually made known to the world. After incredible hardships the Grand Duchess Vladimir, mother of Princess Nicholas, had succeeded in escaping to Switzerland, but, worn out by all she had undergone died soon after her arrival. There was no hope for those who had not been able to get away. How often, as the months passed, and she heard the news of the murder of the Emperor and Empress, of the Grand Duchess Serge, must Princess Alice's thoughts have gone back to her gay and radiant wedding-day, when the future had seemed so bright and full of promise; how often must she have recalled the picture of the Emperor of Russia, laughing like a schoolboy as he ran after her carriage to pelt her with rice, of beautiful Aunt Ella, of the Empress Alexandra, in her dress of delphinium-blue chiffon.

King Alexander of Greece died from blood-poisoning, after having been bitten by a monkey, in October 1920. His grandmother Queen Olga was appointed Regent until a further decision had been reached, and when, a little later, a plebiscite voted almost unanimously for the recall of King Constantine to the throne, he and all the members of his family received a rapturous welcome on their return to Athens.

But the joy of returning home amid that enthusiastic welcome was soon overshadowed. King Constantine was once more forced to make a decision between peace and war. He had from the first been bitterly opposed to the campaign in Asia Minor, conceived by Venizelos, and rapturously sponsored by Lloyd George. He felt that the Greek army was not sufficiently well equipped, but he was afraid he would again be accused of pusillanimity and treachery; so, unwillingly, with a heart full of foreboding, he took up his Headquarters at Smyrna.

In the summer of 1921 Prince and Princess Andrew had gone to live in their villa at Corfu, and there on June 10, Prince Philip was born, but when her husband had to take up the command of the Fifth Army Corps, stationed at Janina, Princess Alice was left alone with her children.

At first it seemed as if King Constantine had been wrong in his foreboding of failure, for in the spring of 1922, the Greek armies swept forward victoriously, and almost reached Ankara. But the brilliant leadership of Mustapha Kemal, and the superior forces he commanded, arrested the advance, and drove the Greeks back in confusion. The Turkish soldiers took terrible revenge for the alleged cruelty of their enemies. Sedition and revolutionary disorders broke out, the terrible fire at Smyrna added to the irretrievable disaster, and in September, 1922, King Constantine was forced once more to abdicate. He died at Palermo in January 1923.

Recalled from Asia Minor and deprived of his command, Prince Andrew joined his wife and children in Corfu, but he had been there only a month when he received a message from the new Government of Greece, demanding his presence at the trial of the six ex-ministers who had been arrested, on the pretext of being responsible for the defeat in Asia Minor. It was impossible to refuse although the message was couched in peremptory terms that made Prince Andrew apprehensive and uneasy. He set out for Athens, only to find that his anxiety had been well founded, for he was arrested as soon as he landed, and placed in solitary confinement, charged with desertion from his post and culpable negligence.

King George, who had succeeded to the throne, was living at Tatoi, himself practically a prisoner. He was powerless to help his brother, who was not allowed to write or receive letters, or even to call in a dentist when he was in agony from a broken tooth. Prince Christopher contrived once only to smuggle in a message concealed in a packet of cigarettes. Replying to this, Prince Andrew said that he had given up all hope, and described a visit he had had from the Minister of War. The latter had asked how many children he had, and when he replied that he had four daughters and a son, had shrugged his shoulders and remarked laconically, "What a pity. The poor little things will soon be orphans."

Careless of the very real danger to herself, Princess Alice had come to Athens where she was permitted to see her husband daily. But in spite of a strongly-worded protest from the British Government, the six ex-ministers were executed, and Prince Andrew was condemned to death. Captain Gerald Talbot, sent out from England in response to Queen Olga's appeal for help, arrived too late to save the six ministers, but by his resolution and courage he succeeded in having the sentence, passed on Prince Andrew, commuted to one of banishment, and, despite the threats of the extremists, smuggled both Princess Alice and her husband on board a British warship, which took them to England, stopping at Corfu on the way to pick up the children.

That visit to her widowed mother must have been heartbreaking for Princess Alice. Her father, Prince Louis, whom she had adored, died in September 1921, only a few weeks after he had been appointed Admiral on the Retired List, an honour that Lord Lee of Fareham said "righted a great wrong, but came seven years too late". It was, perhaps, because England held too many memories for her that she and her husband finally left for Paris, where they were joined by Prince and Princess Nicholas with their three daughters, now also once more in exile, for the Greek Government had deposed the dynasty, and issued an edict forbidding any member of the royal family to remain in the country.

Taking a small house at St. Cloud, near Paris, Prince and Princess Andrew settled down with their children, and lived a quiet but happy family life for seven years, Prince Philip attending an American kindergarten, where he reached the third grade. The Prince and Princess had started a shop for Greek embroidery, hoping to raise funds for the many Greek exiles in Paris, but it failed to make money. They were determined that their son should have a chance of making a career, and when he was nine years old, and his sisters all married, he was sent to England to live with his grandmother, Lady Milford Haven, and share the education of his cousin David.

The little fair-haired boy was too young to remember the gardens and the sunshine of Corfu, or his flight in a British warship, but although at St. Cloud he had sometimes seen his mother crying, and had wondered perhaps why his father looked so grave and careworn, he was homesick at first in England, and missed the gay companionship of his sisters and his untrammelled freedom of movement. For in Kensington Palace there were many rules and restrictions, and when somebody gave him a toy trumpet and he was not allowed to blow it, because the noise might disturb his great-aunt Beatrice, whose rooms were near his nursery, it was very hard to understand.

When he was thirteen there was another change in his life and he was sent to Professor Kurt Hahn's school in Germany, which was run on progressive lines and aimed at developing personality and leadership. But Professor Hahn was forced to leave Germany by the Nazi régime because of his Jewish descent, and coming over to Britain founded a new school at Gordonstoun in Scotland. Here Prince Philip shared everything on an equal basis with his schoolfellows, learnt to sail his own boat, and gained experience in seamanship. From here he joined the British Navy, won the King's Dirk as the best cadet in 1939, and when Greece entered the war was posted to H.M.S. *Valiant*, took part in the battle of Matapan, and the bombardment of Bardia, was mentioned in dispatches and was awarded the Greek War Cross. In 1942 he was promoted first lieutenant, and was drafted to H.M.S. *Wallace*, for the invasion of Sicily. Two years later he became first lieutenant on H.M.S. *Whelp* and sailed with the Pacific Fleet for the Far East under the command of Admiral Fraser, being among the first to enter Japanese waters after the bombardment of Hiroshima.

For his mother those years of separation were filled with sadness. The many trials and sorrows of her life had undermined her health, had broken her resistance and her courage. When her four daughters married, while they were still in their teens, and Prince Andrew sold the house at St. Cloud and moved to the South of France, Princess Alice was undergoing cures in different sanatoriums, trying to regain her strength. The terrible air accident, in 1937, when the most beautiful of her daughters, Princess Cecilia, was killed, together with her husband, the young Grand Duke of Hesse, her mother-in-law, and her two little sons, was yet another almost overwhelming blow to her resistance; but some inner spiritual force seemed to give her back her strength, enabling her to rise above the many tragedies that had beset her, restored her serenity, her composure and resignation.

King George of Greece had been recalled to the throne in 1935; and a few years later Princess Alice returned to Athens, taking up once more her many charitable works, trying to forget her own heartache in unceasing work for others even more unfortunate than herself. She was in Athens when war broke out in 1939. Her husband, Prince Andrew, who had remained in the South of France, died of a sudden heart-attack in 1944. During the German occupation, she and her sister-in-law, Princess Nicholas, now also a widow, remained on in Athens, working every day in the crowded hospitals under the aegis of the Red Cross, respected and unmolested by the Germans but refusing to accept any favours from them.

To both of them, brought together once more by fate, those years of the war were fraught with intolerable sadness, separated as they were from all their relations, living under enemy occupation, witnessing the sufferings and hardships of their people, while King George and the other members of the family lived in exile in Egypt. Beyond all else they had the unceasing, heartbreaking anxiety about their children, divided in their different loyalties, in danger on opposing fronts. Princess Alice had her brother and her son fighting in the British Navy, while her three daughters were living in Germany, married to German Princes. Princess Nicholas had one daughter the wife of Prince Paul of Yugoslavia, another the wife of Count Toerring in Bavaria, and her third, Princess Marina, married to the Duke of Kent.

All the time there was unrest and sporadic fighting between the divergent elements in Greece. The E.L.A.S., or People's Liberation Army, had been supplied by England with arms in order that they should continue to resist the German invaders, and Mr. Churchill was one of the few people to foresee the menace of these guerilla bands under their communist leaders. He knew that they were making use of the arms they had been given, and were taking advantage of the general state of chaos in the country to seize power and set up a totalitarian state.

Because he continued to support the Government of King George of Greece established in Cairo, Mr. Churchill was accused by certain factions in England of "sentimental fondness for kings and princelings". Even after his personal visit to Athens, and his report on the situation, the Labour Party continued to oppose the sending of British troops to Greece, declaring that England stood in danger of losing the friendship of the Greek people. "There is not the slightest proof that E.L.A.S. are attempting a dictatorship," Mr. Bevan asserted, and workers on the Clyde came out on strike because they had been told that British soldiers were fighting communists.

It seemed impossible to convince people of the true situation. The stories of thousands of Greek children torn away from their parents and deported into Soviet-controlled countries were discounted and regarded as fantastically exaggerated. Even the fact that British soldiers who had been taken prisoner by E.L.A.S., had been starved and beaten, and some of them shot down in cold blood, aroused only a momentary indignation, in the minds of those who refused to acknowledge the growing menace of Communism. "Merely the breaking of eggs for the omelette of the new world order", Mr. Laski observed blandly, when, having accompanied Sir Walter Citrine to Greece, he was shown categorical proof of the cruelties perpetrated by E.L.A.S., and the massacre of innocent civilians.

During the dark winter of 1944 Athens was the centre of bitter fighting. The inhabitants lived for weeks without water, light or fuel, while the spies of E.L.A.S. tapped the telephones, stole what little food there was, disguised themselves as patients in the hospitals and from the roofs of buildings fired on passers-by in the streets. At last, aided by England and America, and upheld by their own invincible courage, the people of Greece threw off the menace of terror. The guerilla bands were gradually driven back into the hills, order was restored, and the plebiscite of 1946 recalled King George to the throne. On his death a year later, worn out by all he had undergone, he was succeeded by his younger brother, Prince Paul, who, with Queen Frederica, now rules over a people proud of the fact that they belong to the only country in Eastern Europe where the liberty of the subject is still respected.

When her son married in 1947, Princess Alice was among the wedding guests in Buckingham Palace, and a year later she founded the Nursing Sisterhood, which now occupies all her time. She had at first planned to establish it on the lovely island of Tinos, but, finding that there was not enough money, for so extensive an undertaking, took up work in Athens, devoting her whole life to the care and training of the Nursing Sisters under her charge, following in the footsteps of her aunt the Grand Duchess Elizabeth of Russia, living simply and austerely, tall and slender in her grey nun's dresses.

"I am afraid we should hardly recognize each other now, if we were to meet," she wrote recently, and certainly the fair-haired girl I knew so long ago, and the happy, laughing bride of that brilliant wedding-day, belong to the past; but the woman who has taken their place, with the drawn features framed by white veils, has a beauty of her own, and her dark-brown eyes retain the spiritual, dreaming serenity, which I admired and loved when I was a child.

# The Grand Duchess Cyril of Russia

"DUCKY," Queen Victoria said in 1889, after paying a visit to the Duke of Edinburgh at Clarence House, "is nearly as tall as her mother and such a handsome girl."

Princess Victoria Melita of Edinburgh was only about thirteen at the time, but already she showed signs of the good looks, the tall, perfectly developed figure, the deep-set, almost violet, blue eyes, the imperious carriage of the head that distinguished her in later life. Dark, and with a rather sallow complexion, she lacked the brilliant colouring, the radiant animation of her sister, Marie of Roumania, but she had a certain regal magnificence that made her outshine every other woman in the room; strangers immediately asked who she was.

She had been very unhappy in her first marriage to the Grand Duke Ernst Ludwig of Hesse. He had fallen in love with her, and he was handsome, intelligent and artistic, but her heart had always really belonged to her other cousin, the eldest son of the Grand Duke Vladimir of Russia. From the outset she had found exasperating Ernst Ludwig's exuberance, his restless activity, his occasional fits of melancholy, or lethargic indolence, while his aversion to any form of violent exercise, and his almost timid apprehension of horses, filled her with contempt. Moreover she fretted at the restrictions of the Darmstadt Court; her inherent intelligence and capabilities needed wider surroundings, a greater scope, more colourful variety.

During the years we were in Darmstadt it was chiefly to my parents that she turned for sympathy in her troubles, her discontent and dejection. My father, who often rebuked her headstrong wilfulness, was, she said, her "kind schoolmaster", while my mother was her "old gamp" to whom she turned for consolation, certain of a sympathetic hearing and wise advice.

[ 193 ]

Many things had to be packed away when we left Russia in 1918, many others have been mislaid, or maybe thrown away by mistake, in incessant moves and upheavals, but, looking through some old papers the other day, I came unexpectedly across a letter the Grand Duchess wrote to my mother from Wolfsgarten, in May 1899, shortly before she had her last miscarriage. It is a letter typical of many she wrote, which unfortunately are no longer in my possession.

Dearest Lady Georgie, [it runs] To me it seems ages since we met and chatted. I need badly a talk with "my old gamp". You must come here soon again. But just these next few days are full of people coming, and we could not be to ourselves. But as soon as we are free, may I let you know, and then you will come, won't you? I want to pour lots of woes and complaints into your long-suffering ears. I feel an aged old cripple, and am in consequence very miserable. I doubt that I ever will be well again, and I really do take care now. I scarcely move a step, and lie on my sofa all day, even for meals, during which I have endless conversations with old Ploetzer. Otherwise life is joyless. Today we have the Grand Duchess Anastasia, the Grand Duke Michael and the Apollos to play tennis. Miserably I sit and look on, and am a dumb nonentity. Something must be done, I cannot go on like this. I want lots of advice from you. A kiss to you in waiting. Victoria Melita.

It was without doubt only Queen Victoria's age and her supremacy in Europe that forced the Grand Duchess to bear the irksome bondage of her marriage for so many years, but how often she railed against her grandmother's rigid principles, her unalterable horror of divorce, and her frequent stern admonitions, only my father and mother knew. Hardly was the Queen dead, when she left her husband and sued for divorce, marrying the Grand Duke Cyril in 1905.

In those days divorce was still rigorously disapproved of,

and for a princess of royal blood to leave her husband, and marry another man, was an almost unheard-of scandal. The Empress Alexandra of Russia, who as Princess Alix of Hesse, had opposed her brother's marriage, and had never liked her sister-in-law, on her occasional visits to Darmstadt, not troubling to conceal her dislike—was now full of flaming resentment. Her brother, she said, had been treated abominably, it was preposterous that his former wife should marry a member of the Romanoff family; she would not tolerate her in St. Petersburg, she refused to receive a woman who had behaved so disgracefully, she never wanted to see her again. A marriage between first cousins was not approved of by the Orthodox Church; the Emperor, who had been displeased at the publicity surrounding the divorce of the Grand Duke and Grand Duchess of Hesse, yielded to his wife's insistence and banished the Grand Duke Cyril from Russia, depriving him of his rank, his honours, and his income from the Crown.

The affair caused a tremendous sensation in St. Petersburg society. The Grand Duke Vladimir, who had always been known for his fiery temper, stormed into the Emperor's room, towering in his great height over his nephew's slender figure. No member of the Imperial family had ever been so grossly ill-treated, he roared in that stentorian voice of his. What had his son done to deserve to be expelled from Russia? He had married a woman he had loved for many years. Surely he had the right to some happiness in life? Give him a lecture, maybe, but why heap disgrace on him in this way? It was preposterous, unfair, disgraceful. Finally, it is believed, he tore the decorations from his chest, flung them clattering down on the table in front of the Emperor, and marched out of the room, shutting the great gold-studded door behind him with a resounding bang.

Notwithstanding his uncle's fury the Emperor remained adamant in his decision, and it was not till 1909, after the death of the Grand Duke Vladimir, that his son was reinstated and recalled to Russia. When we went to St. Petersburg in the late autumn of 1910, the Grand Duke and Grand Duchess Cyril were installed in their small brown palace with their two little girls.

The Grand Duchess had kept up her correspondence with my mother, and when we had our first audience with her she was full of unfeigned delight at the incredible luck of my father being appointed Ambassador to St. Petersburg. She apologized laughingly for her bad behaviour in the past, kissed my mother warmly on both cheeks, talked of old days and old memories, and of her radiant happiness in her second marriage. Turning to me, she kissed me also, "and so this is Meriel, grown up," she said, adding with a sigh, "It makes me feel very old."

From time immemorial it had been the custom for the Tsars of Russia to attend the ceremony of the Blessing of the Waters of the Neva at Epiphany, but a few years previously, one of the guns firing the salute from the fortress facing the Winter Palace across the river, had been loaded with shrapnel, which struck the pavilion where the Emperor was standing, tore one of the flags to ribbons, and broke a window in the Palace. Nobody had been severely injured, and the Emperor had not moved or turned his head, but, in the fear of a similar incident occurring, he had been advised not to attend the ceremony again. During the ensuing summers, however, cholera had raged in St. Petersburg, and the Russian people—superstition always mingling with their religion—had declared that this scourge had come upon them because the "Little Father" had not in person blessed the waters of the Neva. Shortly after our arrival, in January, 1911, the Emperor announced his intention of once more attending the Epiphany ceremony. Coincidence or not, it is a fact that the following summer there was no recurrence of cholera in the city.

The day was one of brilliant sunshine and icy wind. The yellow Imperial standard, flying over the fortress, blew taut against a sky of clearest blue, golden domes and spires glowed with almost unbearable brilliance above the snow. On the white frozen surface of the Neva a small wooden pavilion had been built, covered with crimson velvet hangings, and, close to it, a round hole had been cut in the ice down to the sullen, black waters of the river. Inside the Winter Palace the warm, hushed stillness was full of a subdued murmur of voices, a rustle of silken skirts, soft footsteps and the jingling of spurs. Court servants in gorgeous liveries, wearing queer round hats, covered with ostrich feathers, lined the staircase. A mass of coloured uniforms thronged the vast rooms through which we passed. St. George's Hall with its high marble pillars, the Armorial Salon, the Throne Room, with its red velvet hangings, in every one of them there were Cossacks in vivid crimson, in white, brown or blue, hussars with scarlet, fur-trimmed dolmans slung over their shoulder, tirailleurs, in dark green; there were officers of the Gardes à Cheval, and the Chevaliers Gardes, looking like figures out of *Lohengrin*, in white, with gold or silver breastplates and helmets, and mingling among them were older Court ladies, in their traditional dress of olive-green velvet, and young Demoiselles d'Honneur in deep ruby velvet, their fresh faces framed by velvet *kakoshniks*, and soft white veils.

Sunshine flooded through the long glass windows facing the quay of the room where all the diplomatic body had assembled. At a given signal everyone pressed forward to stand near the open gallery which ran the whole length of the big room, and a sudden hush stilled the chattering voices as the procession of Grand Duchesses, led by the Dowager Empress, passed on their way from the private chapel, where they had attended divine service, to one of the inner rooms of the Palace. In the sudden hush the only sound was the murmur of the long trains of many-coloured velvet or brocade, the rustle of gorgeous robes opening over the embroidered underskirts of stiff white satin. The blaze of jewels that covered their *kakoshniks*, the long white veils, seemed to set them in a world apart, made all our dresses look somehow insignificant, our hats either absurd or dowdy.

In that procession, following the white-velvet, sable-trimmed train of the Dowager Empress, the Grand Duchess Cyril looked magnificent, her train of cornflower-blue velvet lined with silver, a tiara of sapphires and diamonds blazing on her head, her blue eyes alight with happiness. Now, I felt, she had come into her own; these were the surroundings she needed, this was the setting that suited her. Here she belonged! Slowly, with the rustle of her heavy train, with the fire of her jewels, she passed; slowly the heavy doors closed behind her and behind the others who had walked in that long procession; and the world suddenly became commonplace and ordinary again with a buzz of voices, with little giggles, with here and there perhaps a sigh of envy, with self-conscious gestures, as hats were adjusted and hair patted into shape.

Outside on the quay the ceremony of the Blessing of the Water was taking place. Watching from the windows, we saw the Emperor cross the road to the pavilion, followed by the Grand Dukes, tall and splendid in their brilliant uniforms, the Cossacks of the Imperial Guard, old generals, and gentlemen of the Court, all standing bare-headed in the icy wind. In their brightly coloured vestments the priests began the service, the sound of their voices coming to us dimly through the closed windows. Then, following the Emperor, they stepped down onto the ice, the silver cross was dipped three times in the water, the flags were sprinkled, the guns thundered a salute, the bells of all the churches rang out across the snow.

One might, I thought, have been looking at an illuminated page of history, when the Tsar descended from the Kremlin, accompanied by the Strelitsi in their many-coloured kaftans, by the Court magnates and Boyars in their robes of velvet, to be received by the Patriarch on the ice of the river Moskwa. They were then rowed three times across the open space of water, that had to be stirred all the time to prevent it from freezing. Ritual and pageantries of long ago, handed down through the centuries! My eyes still dazzled by the procession of Grand Duchesses, I watched the dramatic ceremony on the ice, with the fortress frowning on the opposite shore, and the spire of the Cathedral of St. Peter and St. Paul rising like a golden flame into the sky. In my ignorance, I thought that the Russian Empire was enduring, impregnable and secure.

The Grand Duchess Cyril had become the leader of the so-called Smart Set in St. Petersburg. No party was considered complete without her, the lovely—and very often unusual—clothes she wore, were examined minutely, and sometimes copied, the colour and decorations of her rooms were discussed, admired, and envied, invitations to any entertainments she gave were angled for assiduously by everybody in society. She was always kind to me, very often insisting on my taking part in the dances and parties of the young married women, to which girls were not generally invited. I thoroughly appreciated this, finding the "Bals Roses" as they were called, infinitely more amusing than the "Bals Blancs", which were given exclusively for débutantes.

But on one occasion her kindness caused me a great deal of unhappiness. "It would be so wonderful if Meriel could marry Sandro, it would be such fun to have her with us," she told my mother; but it all came to nothing. I shall never forget the day she sent for my mother and me to tell us that her attempt to arrange things had failed. Seeing my stricken face, she told me to go into the next room to talk to her two little daughters, while she explained what had happened. I was feeling coldly sick and miserable, and was finding it hard to control my tears as I sat on the floor, watching Princess Kyra, fair and rather solemn, and dark chubby little Princess Marie building a castle of bricks. "Sister," Princess Kyra admonished, "you must not put the bricks there. The tower will fall down." When it collapsed, with a rattle of bricks, which in my ears sounded the death-knell to all my dreams, she shook her head gravely, "I told you so, sister," she said, "you will never be able to build a castle unless you are more prudent."

Probably it was all for the best, but at the moment I imagined myself broken-hearted, and when Sandro told me later that if only the Grand Duchess had let well alone things might have been very different, I was inclined to blame her for an interference that was actuated by the kindness of her heart and her desire to help.

In spite of all her social engagements and her official duties she continued with her painting, and in the summer of 1913, when we took a small house at Tsarskoe, where she was staying with her mother-in-law, the Grand Duchess Vladimir, she did a picture of me, kneeling by a stone sarcophagus covered with white roses, with black draperies round me, my face hidden in my arms. Nobody would ever know who it was, the Grand Duchess said, but she had faithfully portrayed the colour of my hair, and I think a good many people guessed the identity of her model and commented, sometimes rather critically, on the inadequate black chiffon scarves.

That was a happy summer at Tsarskoe. There were dinners and dances, given by the Grand Duchess Vladimir and the Grand Duchess Cyril; picnics and excursions to Peterhof and Krassnoe; drives in the woods surrounding the Palace of Pavlovsk, which had once belonged to the Emperor Paul. There were visits to the big white Palace of Catherine the Great, with its bright-green roof, and endless succession of rooms and galleries; walks in the park, and in the Chinese garden with its swan-pond and little canals, and bridges of imitation coral, where quaint carved figures held open parasols. I enjoyed the mornings spent as a model in the Grand Duchess's studio, listening, as I knelt in the rather uncomfortable position, to her conversation with my mother, memories of her former unhappiness, occasional outbursts against what she called "the stuffiness" of her English relations, and of the Queen who had kept her so long in misery during her first marriage. "When we were young," I one day heard her say, "Missy and I adored Grandmama Queen. We used to think it a great honour to be invited to go and see her. We loved her bullfinch and all the photographs in her room, but we thought her spaniel was too fat. And, oh, how solemn her Court was. How tired I got of the talk of 'Grandpapa in Heaven', and of the constant mourning. And how I later resented the lectures she was always giving me."

Golden, lazy days, passed in a sense of unchanging security that was so soon to be shattered, for only twelve months later the First World War broke out, and the threatening clouds of havoc and devastation gathered on the horizon, growing darker, more full of menace, as the years went by.

The Grand Duchess Cyril had her own ambulance-train during the war. She travelled continually backwards and forwards to the Front, returning sometimes looking worn and harassed, her eyes heavy with lack of sleep and overpowering weariness. She was acutely aware of the lack of organization in the conduct of the war; she had seen the appalling shortage of ammunition, the scarcity of supplies and red-cross material. When the Emperor took command at Headquarters, and Stürmer and Protopopoff were given posts in the Government, she became more than ever opposed to the Empress, blaming her for the mismanagement in the administration in the country. There had never been any sympathy between them, but now her dislike flared into open hostility, and when she went to see her former sister-in-law, begging her to influence the Emperor into granting concessions, and was told that she was interfering in matters which were not her concern, she returned seething with exasperation, saying that she had been treated like an ignorant schoolgirl.

After the death of Rasputin, several members of the Imperial family, including the Grand Duke and Grand Duchess Cyril, wrote to the Emperor begging him to pardon the Grand Duke Dimitri for his part in the conspiracy. They received a curt reply, written across the corner of the envelope. "It is given to no one," the pencilled words read, "to occupy himself with murder. I know that the conscience of many gives them no rest, for it is not only Dimitri Pavlovitch who is implicated. I am astonished that you should address yourself to me." The Grand Duchess, showing this to my mother, had tears of anger and frustration in her eyes. This, she said, showed how misguided the Emperor was, it was yet another proof of his ignorance of what was going on. He had always said that Russia was not ready for a democratic government, but now was the time to act; he must be forced to see his folly, forced to go to the Duma, and bring in the necessary reforms.

It was believed at the time that the Grand Duke Cyril and his wife were at the head of a palace conspiracy to overthrow the Emperor and place the Tsarevitch on the throne, but so many rumours were current in those days that it is impossible to know the truth. It was said also, that they had asked Sandro to lead his Cossack regiment against the Government. But if he was approached, he certainly refused; it was he, who, after the Revolution of March, 1917, came to the Embassy to warn my father of the rising tide of anarchy and the danger to the Emperor. He begged him to do whatever was possible to get him out of Russia. The Grand Duke Cyril, on the other hand, was the first to surrender and swear allegiance to the Provisional Government, a fact that was never forgotten by many of his relations.

On his first interview with M. Miliukoff, the newly appointed Minister of Foreign Affairs, my father was told to have no further communication with the Imperial family; to this he replied that he would certainly not drop old friends who had been kind to him, and added that if there was trouble, he would offer the protection of the Embassy to the Grand Duchess Cyril, as she was a British Princess and entitled to any help he could give her, a statement that Miliukoff received with cold displeasure.

When my mother continued to visit the Grand Duchess, and took her out in the Embassy carriage to visit her English nurse, who was ill in hospital, M. Miliukoff sent for my father again, and told him sternly that he could not allow this intercourse to continue. In certain quarters, he said, people believed that the British Ambassador was plotting a counter-revolution with members of the Imperial family, and he would have to ask for my father's recall, as he could not be responsible should an angry crowd attack the Embassy.

It was a hard decision to take, but my father had to consider not only his personal safety, but the fact that the Embassy was British property, and that Britain had officially recognized the new Provisional Government in Russia. After a long discussion, my mother wrote to the Grand Duchess, and told her what had happened. She was somewhat comforted by the following reply: "Dear Lady Georgie, I quite understand, and thank you both for all your niceness. Of course you must not think of coming to see me, if it can be misinterpreted. It is hard to be accused of being 'vieux régime' when all one's sufferings are due to mismanagement. Fondest love, and I hope we will meet again in happier days."

Those who have not lived through a revolution may not, perhaps, realize how helpless one felt, or know how fundamentally one's daily life was affected when living in a town where sudden outbursts of shooting were an almost hourly occurrence, or where one was liable to be stopped by some workman, and ordered none too gently to show an official pass. We were not allowed to see our friends, but were forced to receive those now in control, who had, possibly with the best intentions, brought about the fall of the Empire, and were unable to restrain the violence they had let loose, or stem the growing power of the extremists.

Somebody once told me that revolution was always picturesque; but when I looked at the gradual disintegration, the rot that spread like a dark miasma over the town, the unswept streets, the broken windows which nobody repaired, the walls riddled with bullets, the bands of soldiers who had deserted from the Front, I could see nothing picturesque, but only something ugly, sinister and terrifying.

My father's position became more difficult with every day. Distrusted by Lloyd George, who saw in him the personification of a diplomat of the old school and consequently disliked him, accused on the one side of being a reactionary, and on the other of having instigated the Revolution, he was blamed by all, and especially by those who had themselves failed in their loyalty to the Emperor. Even the Grand Duchess Cyril, who had denounced the old régime, and written such an understanding letter, now turned against him, and told her sister the Queen of Roumania that my father had deserted her in the hour of trouble, and had refused to help her.

In the summer of 1917, she, with her husband and children, escaped to Finland, and it was there that her son, the Grand Duke Vladimir, was born in September. Only able to take the bare necessaries with them, they lived, almost in penury, in a small wooden house, lacking any comforts or amenities. Hearing of her desperate plight my mother sent her a case of red-cross stores, clothes for the children, tinned milk and butter, cereals and jam. But the only thanks she received was a letter from the English nurse, coldly acknowledging the arrival of the gift, and with tears in her eyes my mother sought in vain for a message from the woman who had been her friend for so many years. A little later the Grand Duke Cyril, giving an interview to members of the Press, told them that my father and my mother had turned their backs on them after the Revolution, "which", he added, "was not very nice, nor very brave".

How right Queen Marie of Roumania was, when she said of her sister, "Ducky was the most unforgiving of us all". With her own upright honesty, her unbending pride and integrity, she could visualize only one course of action; she could find no excuses for what she regarded as a failure to live up to her own high ideals, nor take into account the force of circumstances. But in judging her one must remember the hardness of her lot. After years of unhappiness she had married the man she loved, and, having at last got all she wanted, saw it destroyed, and herself faced a future of despair and bitterness, an exile in poverty and humiliation.

It was only after they had left Finland, and had settled down at St. Briac, near Dinard, that she learnt to adapt herself to circumstances; but even then she was never quite able to resign herself to the loss of power and position. The proclamation issued by her husband declaring himself to be the rightful guardian of the vacant throne of Russia, voiced her own inflexible hopes that one day she would be able to return there.

Their house at St. Briac was unpretentious, but with her gift for colour and decoration the Grand Duchess made it individual and charming, turning a wilderness into a beautiful garden, doing all the work herself. She was now able to make use of her talent for painting, for she illuminated old books and Bibles, and sold some of her lovely pictures of flowers, the money she made enabling her to keep the household going, and to pay for the education of her children. She lived in constant dread that her son, in whom she saw the heir to the Imperial crown, would be kidnapped by their enemies. She hardly allowed him out of her sight, would not send him to school but engaged a private tutor for him, would not let him learn a trade or profession, but brought him up as if he was to inherit the wealth of his ancestors.

There was a large English colony in Dinard, and in the summer cosmopolitan visitors brought gaiety and entertainment. The Grand Duke played golf every day, he and his wife joined in picnics and excursions, and became part of the social life of the community, going out to play bridge, getting up theatricals and *tableaux vivants*. One summer, when Queen Marie of Roumania was staying there, they gave a performance of *Fire Bird* in an empty barn.

They visited America, where they were welcomed with royal honours, being received as if they were indeed Emperor and Empress. The Grand Duchess may have been happy for a time, but the years passed by without her dreams being realized, and when she died, in 1936, her sisters, who were with her, could only lay the lilies and flowers she had loved around her, and mourn the passing of a bitter, disappointed woman, whose brilliant personality had been warped by failure and frustration.

The Grand Duke Cyril did not survive her many years. On his death, his son issued a proclamation, asserting his claim to be the rightful Emperor of Russia. As a boy he had been very good-looking, and was very like the Prince of Wales, but, as he once said laughingly, "Un edition de luxe." He has now grown stout, and is said to bear a strong resemblance to his great-grandfather, the Emperor Alexander III. He married a former Princess Bagration, who inherited a considerable fortune from her first husband, and they live mostly in the South of France, only paying occasional visits to the house at St. Briac. His sister, Princess Kyra, married Prince Louis Ferdinand of Hohenzollern, and lives at Lübeck with her numerous lovely children. His other sister, Princess Marie, married a Prince Leiningen, a descendant of Queen Victoria's half-sister, Theodora, and died at an early age a few years ago.

Old Russia, with all its sinfulness, its glamour and mysticism, has passed away for ever, the house at St. Briac stands empty. When I think of the Grand Duchess Cyril it is not there that I see her, but only as I saw her that day in the Winter Palace in St. Petersburg, with the fire of that magnificent tiara crowning her head, and the sweep of her blue-and-silver train adding to the regal dignity of her figure. She was born to be royal, to be surrounded with pageantry, to walk in procession through the rooms of Imperial Palaces, across gleaming parquet floors, under the light of crystal chandeliers. But fate decreed that she was to live in exile, in a strange country, to dig in a garden, to sell her paintings, to die with none of her dreams fulfilled.

# The Grand Duchess Olga Nicholaievna

IN the autumn of 1896 the young Emperor and Empress of Russia paid a visit to Balmoral, taking with them their daughter, who was barely twelve months old. "Dear baby Olga, so big and beautiful," the Queen said, sitting in her pony carriage with her great-granddaughter on her knee.

As Princess Alix of Hesse the Empress had been the Queen's favourite granddaughter, this visit had been eagerly looked forward to. She looked very handsome, dressed all in white, when she arrived at the castle, but when the Queen drew back in courtesy to allow her to precede her, the young Empress had, without a word of acknowledgement, sailed into the drawing-room in front of her grandmother, who had followed with a little flush of annoyance on her cheek. She had not expected that her gesture would be accepted, she was afraid "gentle little simple Alicky" had changed. She had lost some of the dewy freshness of youth which had so enhanced her beauty, her complexion had become a little florid; her mouth, when it was in repose, was set in a hard, thin line; and there was a stiffness and formality in her manner that had not been there before.

As her grandmother the Queen thought she had the right to admonish her gently, and advise her to be a little more amiable; but the reproof was not well received, and the Empress had become, if anything, even more restrained and withdrawn. Nevertheless the visit passed off well, there were drives and picnics on the moors, in her conversations with the Emperor the Queen was relieved by his assurance that Russia did not intend to side with France, over the matter of Egypt, nor to conclude an alliance hostile to England. On October 3, Mr. Downey came to take the first moving pictures of the royal family, and the Queen thought it very extraordinary when she was photographed walking on the terrace, or holding on her lap baby Olga, who was jumping up and down.

The Queen was sorry when the visit was over, and the Emperor and Empress left to go to Paris. "I am so fond of them both," she said sadly, for Russia seemed very far away. She kissed little Olga's pink cheeks and wondered when she would see her again. It was a pity the first child had not been a boy, but there was no doubt a brilliant future in store for this little girl whose father and mother ruled over such a vast country. The Queen hoped that Nicky would govern that country with prudence and far-sighted discernment, that he would be firm but benevolent, and that he would grant some of the concessions that had been planned by his grandfather, Alexander II.

It was after their visit to Paris that the Emperor and Empress came to stay in Darmstadt, and watching the official reception, the mounted troops, the State carriages, I wondered what had brought that look of cold aloofness to the face of the woman I had known as Princess Alix of Hesse. That night there was a torchlight procession in front of the old Schloss; the next day I went to tea in the New Palace, and saw the Grand Duchess Olga on the knee of her English nurse, Miss Orchard. "Is she not a beautiful baby?" Miss Wilson, Princess Elizabeth's nurse, asked me. I was too overcome with awe to do anything but agree in an almost inaudible whisper.

It was many years before I saw the Grand Duchess Olga again and during that time her life was not really very different from that of any other child whose parents had large country estates, except that in her case those estates were widely apart. There was the Alexander Palace at Tsarskoe Selo, not far from St. Petersburg, a big, low-built, white house on the shore of an artificial lake, surrounded by a beautiful park and gardens. There was the Alexandrai Dashka (or cottage), at Peterhof, almost hidden in the woods, near the big palace built by Peter the Great, overlooking the Gulf of Finland. There was the lovely white palace of Livadia in the Crimea, with terraces and gardens sloping down to the shores of the Black Sea. And lastly there were the hunting-palaces of Belovej and Spala, surrounded by vast, almost primeval forests.

Wherever they might be, the apartments shared by the Emperor's daughters were simple almost to the point of austerity, and the lives they led were unostentatious, and governed by routine. They spent their days studying under various tutors and governesses, they shared the midday meal with their father, their mother not always being present. They rode and went for drives and walks in the grounds of their various palaces, they played games and went out in boats, they hardly ever quarrelled, they were happy and united, but they had no young companions and seldom even saw any of their numerous cousins. Perhaps they sometimes wondered why their mother always seemed so anxious and distressed, and why the little brother, who had been born in 1904, was so often ill. He could not play games with them, or take part in violent exercise, the slightest blow or fall bringing on bleeding, fever, and agonizing pains. The Grand Duchess Olga was the eldest and most intelligent of all the sisters. She was strong and healthy, full of vitality, intensely patriotic, and it must have sometimes filled her with regret that she had not been born a boy, that she could not succeed her father on the throne and rule over Russia like her ancestress, Catherine the Great.

To the Empress the fact that her only son suffered from haemophilia was a continual, torturing anxiety. She knew that her younger brother, Prince Frederick William, one of her uncles, a cousin, and a nephew had all suffered from the same disease. Passed on only from mother to son, she realized that it was through her that the heir to the throne had inherited this incurable disease. She tried to hide it from the world, she hoped against hope that a cure might be found, and when doctors and surgeons appeared unable to find a remedy, she turned in prayer for a miracle to the man of God who had been introduced to her by the Archimandrite Theophane in 1905, with the assurance that this simple peasant from the village of Pokrovskoie, in the Government of Tobolsk, had been endowed with holy powers.

Rasputin, the name he had been given in his village, and which comes from the word "Raspoutnik" (debaucher) was not a true monk or priest; he had led a dissolute life, but had spent some time in a monastery, and when he returned to his village he seemed changed. He cured the sick, and had come to be regarded as a man who could work miracles, and his reputation spread through the country until eventually it reached St. Petersburg. There he had been introduced to various people in society, and finally to the Empress.

There can be no doubt that he possessed a certain magnetic power, for when he talked to the Tsarevitch, either in person or by telephone, there appeared to be an immediate improvement in his condition. The Empress became more and more convinced that in him lay the only hope for her son. What this power was, it is impossible to say. Was he merely a charlatan, trading on his ability to hoodwink those who believed in him? Or had he a supernatural gift of healing and of prophecy? How can one explain his repeated warnings that if anything happened to him the Russian Empire would fall? Or that it was imperative to avert war, as it would bring ruin and disaster? Or those solemn words to the Empress, "Remember my death means your death"?

The infamous libels at one time spread, concerning his relationship with the Empress and her daughters, have been entirely refuted by responsible witnesses. In his book, *The Tragic Destiny of Nicholas II*, M. Gilliard, tutor to the Grand Duchesses and the Tsarevitch for many years, has categorically stated that Rasputin never came near the children's private apartments, that he only entered the Palace when the Tsarevitch was ill, and that the little boy regarded him merely as a curious, amusing man who told him stories, and often seemed able to ease the pains from which he suffered so continuously. The young Grand Duchesses rarely saw him, or if they did, only in the presence of their parents, and the Empress herself kept in touch with him chiefly through Madame Wyroubova, to whom she had given a small house in the grounds, befriending her because of her unhappy marriage. Madame Wyroubova, foolish, gullible, credulous, believed in Rasputin, and was used by him as a tool to maintain his influence over the Empress.

The Grand Duchess Olga Nicholaievna was only fifteen when we arrived in St. Petersburg, in 1910. I first saw her in 1912, at a ball given in the Hall of the Nobles in honour of the Tercentenary Celebrations of the Romanoff Dynasty. That evening, the only time she appeared at a big public ball, she wore a pale-pink chiffon dress of almost classical simplicity, a silver ribbon was bound round her golden hair, which was parted in the middle, and her only jewels were a string of pearls round her slender neck. She had not the regular features, the almost mystical beauty of her sister, Tatiana Nicholaievna, but with her rather tip-tilted nose, her wide laughing mouth, her sparkling blue eyes, she had a charm, a freshness, an enchanting exuberance that made her irresistible.

In a dress of blue-and-silver brocade, crowned with a magnificent tiara of diamonds, the Empress opened the ball with her husband in the old traditional polonaise, to Chopin's beautiful music. She passed close to where I was standing; she was very pale, her eyes lowered, her mouth unsmiling. Then she vanished, leaving her husband and her daughter to continue the evening without her. She sat for a while in the Imperial box at the gala performance at the Marinsky Theatre, the diamonds, which covered the front of her bodice, shooting iridescent fire as her breast rose and fell with her quick, convulsive breathing, her hands trembling so violently that she seemed hardly able to hold her fan of white eagle's feathers.

Some stress of emotion, some physical torment, seemed to possess her, and before the performance was over she had retired to the back of the box, and had not reappeared.

Accustomed to the genial charm and ease of manners of the Romanoffs, society grumbled and complained. People recalled that other Hessian Princess, the Empress Marie, who had also suffered from ill health, who had also been cold and distant, and had seldom appeared in public. Some people compared the Empress Alexandra to her grandmother Queen Victoria, who had also withdrawn herself to nurse her sorrow at Windsor and Osborne.

In the winter of 1913-14 these murmurs and complaints grew in bitterness, for by then the Emperor's daughters Olga and Tatiana Nicholaievna were aged respectively eighteen and seventeen, and it was time, people said, that balls and entertainments should be given for them. Did the Empress think that contact with society would contaminate them? Were all the great families of Russia, the Kourakins, the Shouvaloffs, the Galitzins, the Cheremetieffs, the Orloffs, not good enough? Why were they kept sequestered at Tsarskoe? Why were they never seen, except at Te Deums, or Reviews, or on some State occasion?

But the Empress was already making her plans for entertainments to be given during the following season and was discussing with certain intimate friends the impossibility of including the whole of society at one big ball to which the members of the Duma and their wives would have to be invited. She was arranging to give several smaller balls, and concerts, and perhaps some informal dances as well. It was so easy to criticize and condemn her; few knew the inherent shyness which afflicted the Empress; she had never been able to overcome it, nor did they guess how she had suffered when she realized her own unpopularity. They did not see her by the bedside of her son, they did not know the anguish that was in her heart when she watched his sufferings. Over and over again, in their ignorance, people misjudged her, and more and more, realizing how prejudiced society was, she withdrew herself in proud and aloof disdain, happy only when she was alone in her family circle, and with the husband who was the centre of all her thoughts.

The Emperor's daughters accepted the life they led at Tsarskoe, the lack of gaiety, the hours of study, the various teachers of French, of English, of Russian, of history, geography, mathematics, of music and painting, who came and went. They seldom questioned the monotony of their days. Only the Grand Duchess Olga, with her discernment and her shrewdness, may have sometimes wondered why they lived so cut off from all contact with St. Petersburg.

We know little about this great-granddaughter of Queen Victoria. We have seen pictures of her sitting with her sisters, standing alone in Court dress, or on horseback in the uniform of her regiment. We have heard details of her life, of her devotion to her sisters, her parents, her little brother, but few know that her mentality, her intelligence, her gifts, would have made her a remarkable personality, had she lived.

The teacher from the Conservatoire of Music who gave her piano lessons once said that she possessed a talent that would have won her fame, had she been born in another sphere. She had only to hear an air once, to be able to play it by ear; she could transpose without hesitation any piece of music into another key; her touch and execution were remarkable. She read voraciously, studying the classics, the history of Russia, the lives of the peasants, the ancient traditions, the customs, the laws, the geography of her country. Her memory was extraordinary, and she never forgot anything that she had learnt, or that had once been told her. She took a keen interest in the lives, the problems, the difficulties of others, and the help she was able, so seldom, to give, was always practical rather than ostentatious. It was she, for example, who on her drives through the park at Tsarskoe, noticed a little crippled girl in one of the

[ 213 ]

keepers' cottages. She insisted on taking the matter up and arranged for the child to be sent to an orthopaedic hospital, and when she was asked who was going to pay for the treatment, replied, "Will you please find out what my allowance is, and deduct the necessary sum."

None of the Emperor's daughters touched the vast allowances set aside for them. They never bought their own clothes, or spent money on themselves, the small sum they received as pocket money always went in giving presents to their parents, or members of their household, and when that was expended they were without a penny. They had very little knowledge, or idea of the value of money, or of how far it went; the Grand Duchess Tatiana once asked a lady-in-waiting how much one could buy for a hundred roubles, and would it, for instance, pay for a pair of gloves. She was very surprised when told that even the most expensive gloves would not cost more than twenty-five roubles.

When, on rare occasions, the two elder Grand Duchesses appeared at services in the Kazan Cathedral, the eager interest they took in their surroundings was very apparent. The Grand Duchess Olga's alertness, her shrewd, mischievous eyes examining the women's dresses and hats, scrutinizing the faces round her, contrasted with the Grand Duchess Tatiana's reserve, her eyes discreetly lowered if she found anyone watching her. Tall and slender in their light dresses and big hats, I tried not to stare at them, but wondered what their thoughts were as they stood so motionless during those long services, while the voices of the choir rolled up to the roof of the great cathedral, and the blue incense drifted round us. Before the golden doors of the Ikonasatas the celebrant, in his jewelled mitre, raised his hands in prayer and intoned the hymn for the safety of the Emperor. What did the Imperial sisters say to one another, what remarks and observations did they make, when the service was over and they were alone? Had they noticed that the American Ambassador had copied my father's uniform, saying that he could no longer bear to be the only man in a frock-coat at these ceremonies? Had they seen the new, good-looking secretary at the Austrian Embassy? Had they noticed that the wife of one of the Italian diplomats had put more rouge on one cheek than on the other? Uneasily I felt that nothing much escaped them. I had seen the Grand Duchess Olga turn her head to whisper to her sister, had noticed the latter's dark amber eyes survey me with a secret amusement that made me wonder if my hat was on straight or my hair untidy; or had they, I asked myself in dismay, seen me blush when one of their cousins, standing close behind the Emperor, turned to smile at me?

During the winter of 1913–14 the engagement of the Grand Duchess Olga was frequently discussed in society, and several young men were mentioned as possible suitors. The Grand Duke Dimitri, Prince Arthur of Connaught, the Duke of Leuchtenberg, even at one moment the Prince of Wales. With the visit of the Crown Prince and Crown Princess of Roumania, accompanied by their eldest son, Prince Carol's name was on all lips, and everybody waited anxiously for news of an engagement. But although, with his parents, he stayed for several days at Tsarskoe, it was evident from the first that the young Grand Duchess was not attracted to him, and that there was no sympathy between them. Discussing the situation, the Empress and Princess Marie of Roumania agreed not to force matters, but to arrange further meetings in the hope that closer acquaintance might lead to mutual affection, or at least to a sympathetic understanding.

On June 11, therefore, the Emperor with his wife and daughters embarked on the *Standard*, the Imperial yacht which they often used for cruising in the Baltic and the Black Sea, and sailed to Constantza.

Olga Nicholaievna was too sharp-witted not to know the reason for this journey. She told M. Gilliard that she realized what people were saying and thinking, but that her father had promised her that she should not be forced into a distasteful marriage. She was, she said, averse to leaving her own country, and changing her nationality. "I am Russian, and I want to remain Russian," she concluded firmly. Had she known what lay ahead, would she have consented, in spite of her reluctance and want of sympathy? No one can tell, but those who knew her well believe that she would not have faltered in her decision.

That day at Constantza, during the Te Deum in the Cathedral, the lunch in Queen Elizabeth's pavilion on the shore, the tea on board the *Standard*, the dinner in the apartment which had been built for the occasion, she tried to appear unselfconscious, though she knew very well that her sisters were watching her with avid curiosity. Sitting next to Prince Carol at lunch and at dinner, she chatted with her usual spontaneity and natural gaiety; at dinner it was noticed that they seemed to be in earnest conversation, although what they said has not been recorded. But when the long day was over, and the Imperial family once again boarded the *Standard*, it was announced that there would be no engagement at present, although, it was added, all hope of a future *rapprochement* must not be abandoned.

Towards the end of June the First British Battle Squadron, under the command of Sir David Beatty, came on a visit to St. Petersburg and anchored off Kronstadt. On the last day of their stay the Emperor and Empress, with their daughters, lunched in H.M.S. *Lion*, and the Grand Duchesses spent the afternoon examining every corner of the ship, winning the hearts of every man and boy on board. The Naval officers I met at the ball, which took place on board that night, could talk of nothing but the Emperor's daughters, their beauty, their charm, their gaiety, the unaffected simplicity and ease of their manners. There was a wistful regret on many a face because the Empress had refused to allow them to remain for the ball. The girls had apparently accepted her decision without demur or argument, but they had looked a little crestfallen.

When the Grand Duchess Olga had followed her father and mother into the Imperial launch waiting to take them back to Peterhof, she looked back at the big grey ship, and waved her hand to the officers standing to attention on deck, but although she had smiled, there had been, it was declared, a hint of tears in her eyes.

After the British fleet had sailed came the French ships bringing the President, M. Poincaré, on a visit. There was a State dinner at Tsarskoe, a big review at Krassnoe, which was the summer camp of the Guard Regiments, near Peterhof, a gala performance at the Marinsky Theatre, a lunch on board the French cruiser. Hardly had the President sailed when war was declared with Germany.

At the review at Krassnoe I had seen the young Grand Duchesses smiling and gay, under their big flower-trimmed hats. On August 17 I saw them again in the Uspenky Cathedral in Moscow, when the Emperor, according to ancient usage, laid the plans of campaign at the feet of the wonder-working Ikon of Vladimir. That day they were all a little subdued and grave, their faces pale, their eyes lowered to hide the tears that were not very far away. At the head of a long procession the Emperor descended the famous Red Staircase leading from the Kremlin palace, and passed across the square to the open doors of the Cathedral, the crowds, kneeling on either side of the strip of red carpet, bending to kiss his shadow as he passed. When the ceremony was over and he came out again into the blazing sunshine of that cloudless summer day, everyone spontaneously burst into the National Anthem. That day he was to them not only the Emperor, as far away as the skies, but the Little Father, who held their fate in his hands and would deliver them from their enemies. Transported by emotion, their voices rose in a roar of applause, of praise and devotion that almost drowned the thunder of the bells clanging out from all the churches in the Kremlin. "This acclamation," the Emperor said, turning to my father and the French

Ambassador, M. Paléologue, "is not only for me; it is for you both, for England and France."

Twice, during those years of the war, I saw the two elder Grand Duchesses again; once when, with their mother, they visited the British Colony Hospital where I was working, and once when they came with the Dowager Empress, to the official opening of the big English hospital run by Lady Muriel Paget and Lady Sybil Grey. On both occasions they were dressed in red velvet gowns, with ermine stoles, and hats trimmed with ermine; they went round the wards talking to the wounded soldiers, the Grand Duchess Olga often making them laugh with her whimsical merriment, her sister talking to them gently, but with a greater reserve. How kind they were, the soldiers told me afterwards, how lovely they looked. Was it not wonderful that the daughters of the Emperor should come to talk to them? Some said that Olga Nicholaievna, with her frank simplicity and gaiety, was the more charming, others again declared that her younger sister, with her dark hair and golden eyes, was the more beautiful.

Immediately upon the declaration of war the Emperor's two elder daughters had started training as nurses, working with their mother in an auxiliary hospital at Tsarskoe. There was no question now of marriage, of suitors, of entertainment; all plans for Court balls had been put aside, their lives became more isolated, more monotonous. Nor was there any good news from the Front to cheer them with hopes of a speedy victory. The first successes had been transient; supplies, ammunition and transport were all breaking down; the Russian armies were suffering defeat after defeat; refugees from Silesia were streaming into St. Petersburg, or Petrograd as it was now called. Rumours of treachery and sabotage were rife, food was short, fuel was scarce, prices were soaring, despair, frustration and disillusion were taking the place of the earlier enthusiasm. Eventually, in 1915, the Emperor sent the Grand Duke Nicholas Nicholaievitch to the Caucasian front, and himself took command at Staff Headquarters at Mohileff—a decision which came as a complete surprise to Russia and caused general consternation.

The Emperor, however, regarded his action as a sacrifice demanded of him, and which he must accept as a sacred obligation. "In the moment of danger the duty of a Sovereign is to be with his army, and if need be perish with it," he told the Prime Minister M. Goremykin, when urged to reconsider his decision. In an audience he had with the Empress my father tried to warn her that it was laying on the Emperor the whole responsibility for a fresh disaster; that it was too heavy a burden for one man, to combine the duties of commander-in-chief with those of a ruler of a great Empire. She told him coldly that it had been a great mistake her husband not having taken command from the beginning. "I have no patience," she continued, "with Ministers who try to prevent him from doing his duty. The Emperor unfortunately is weak, but I am not."

Recovered from the injury inflicted on him by a woman in his own village, Rasputin was once more by the Empress's side, for in her distress and anxiety she had turned to him for comfort, believing in the potency of his prayers to save Russia from destruction. "All my trust", she wrote and told the Emperor, "lies in our Friend, who thinks only of you and Baby and Russia. Guided by him we shall win through."

By the end of 1916 the growing political unrest, and the skilful propaganda disseminated by German agents in Petrograd, fomented bitter hostility against the Empress. She was pro-German, people said; she was corresponding with her brother, the Grand Duke of Hesse; she was appointing men, known to be suspect, to high positions in the Government solely because they were friends of Rasputin, accusations which were wholly untrue, but they were believed by many who saw in her actions the confirmation of the lies so skilfully built up against her. In vain some of her relations tried to reason with her. Her sister

[ 219 ]

the Grand Duchess Elizabeth, the Dowager Empress, the Grand Duchess Vladimir, the Grand Duchess Cyril, the Grand Duke Paul, all warned her, but their appeals were received with the same determined assertion that she knew what was right for Russia, that a firm autocracy would preserve the Empire for her son. "We must give a strong country to Baby," she wrote and told her husband. "For his sake we dare not be weak."

Spending her days working in the hospital, knitting for the wounded, caring for her brother who had fallen ill again after a visit to Headquarters, the Grand Duchess Olga saw her mother daily more exhausted, more strained, more unhappy, and eventually overwhelmed with grief when Rasputin was murdered on December 16, 1917. She was keenly aware of the growing menace and dangers of the situation. "Why has the feeling in the country changed against my father?" she asked a lady-in-waiting, and then the latter replied that to explain that it would be necessary to go back to the reign of her grandfather who had countermanded all the progressive, constitutional plans of her great-grandfather Alexander II. She was silent and pensive, not entirely satisfied perhaps, wondering if there were not more ominous reasons for the unrest and ferment that she sensed rather than knew about, but which filled her with a growing anxiety.

Early in March 1917, the Tsarevitch fell ill with a severe attack of measles, and having helped to nurse him, the Grand Duchess Olga and her sisters, Tatiana and Anastasia Nicholaievna, caught the complaint, aggravated, as in the case of their brother, by an abnormally high temperature, and agonizing pains in the throat and ears.

Meanwhile riots had broken out in Petrograd, the Central Police Station was set on fire, the prisons stormed and the inmates set at liberty, the police butchered and a Provisional Government, under Rodzianko, President of the Duma, set up. Distracted over her children and especially over her son, whose condition gave rise to grave anxiety, the Empress received fresh reports of disorders every day, and on March 13 was told that the regiment in Tsarskoe had mutinied, and that a rabble of soldiers, workmen and deserters was advancing on the Palace. Throwing a fur coat over her white nurse's uniform, and accompanied by her daughter, the Grand Duchess Marie, she hurried out to the courtyard where the regiments guarding the Palace were preparing to resist the revolutionary troops. Her thin shoes soaked through with the snow that covered the ground, the Empress went up and down the line of soldiers, begging the officers to try and negotiate with the assailants, imploring them not to open fire, not to provoke bloodshed, until at last they promised to obey, and the battle which might have ensued, and could have ended only in one way, was averted.

By this time the electric light and the water had been cut off in the Palace; but all during that night with the mutineers camped outside the gates, and the possibility that, urged on by some hot-headed fanatic, they might launch an attack, the Empress remained calm, and collected, pacified the servants, visited her sick children, invented excuses for the failure of the light, not allowing them to know the extent of the danger.

Early the next morning the mutineers withdrew, but reports came from Petrograd of other regiments shooting their officers and to add to her trouble there had been no news of the Emperor for several days. It was known that he had left Headquarters on his way to the capital, but the train had not arrived and nobody could explain what had happened. On March 17 the Grand Duke Paul came to the Palace, and one look at his face warned the Empress that he brought bad news. He told her that the Emperor had abdicated in favour of his brother, not only for himself but for the Tsarevitch. She refused at first to believe it. At last, convinced that it was true, she accepted the fact with the courage that came to her in adversity, which remained with her all through the following months. "God grant that it may save Russia," she told Count Benckendorff. "That is the only thing that matters."

Her fourth daughter, the Grand Duchess Marie, had now also fallen ill with the measles; the Tsar was still absent. On March 21, General Korniloff came to tell her that the Grand Duke Michael had refused the throne, and that the Provisional Government had decided to hold her and her family prisoners at Tsarskoe. Whatever her feelings were she gave no sign of the despair in her heart, and there was no trace of her former arrogance, as she told him gently, "I am at your disposal. Do with me what you will."

Her children were still ignorant of what had happened, but now it was no longer possible to hide the truth from them. She asked M. Gilliard to break the news to the Tsarevitch, while she herself went up to her daughters. What words she found to tell them that they were now prisoners in their own palace, and that their father was no longer Emperor of Russia, we do not know. It is possible that with the exception of Olga Nicholaievna, who certainly realized the full import of what had happened, the young Grand Duchesses did not really take in the seriousness of their position. A fresh anxiety was occupying all their thoughts, for the Grand Duchess Marie, who had been sickening for measles when she went out with her mother to parley with the soldiers, had developed pneumonia, and was so dangerously ill that her recovery seemed doubtful.

On the Emperor's return to Tsarskoe, on March 22, he found the park and the Palace full of soldiers, who accosted him at every step, many of them insolent in their manners, untidy in their dress, slovenly in their bearing. "My God, what a difference," he noted in his diary, the words only a feeble and inadequate expression of what he must have felt.

He has been called weak, incompetent, obstinately stupid; by some he has been accused of treachery and disloyalty. But although he lacked decision and judgement, there can be no doubt of his incorruptible integrity and his determination to continue the war to the end. He had abdicated, hoping that by so doing he would avert civil war; he was unwilling to let blood be shed on his account, trusting that the men at the head of the Provisional Government would hold Russia together, and would fight the war to a successful finish. All who, like his mother, knew him well would have said with her, "Nicky is so pure in heart himself, that he cannot see evil in others."

In those early days few people understood the disintegration, the devastating upheaval of a revolution, but the prisoners at Tsarskoe must have realized the change in their position when Kerensky drove up to the Palace in one of the Emperor's former cars, driven by one of the Imperial chauffeurs. He came again a few days later, and gave orders that the Emperor and Empress were no longer to share the same apartments but were to meet only at meals, when an officer of the guard would always be present. The full comprehension of their helplessness and subjugation must have become abundantly clear.

The days passed, the Emperor's request to be moved to Livadia, which he and his family loved so dearly, had been refused and no news came of the projected departure to England. Neither the Emperor nor the Empress nor their eldest daughter wanted to leave Russia, but the thought of England brought the assurance of immunity from danger and humiliation, and before leaving Staff Headquarters at Mohileff the Emperor had told Sir John Hanbury Williams that if he was not permitted to go to Livadia he hoped to be able to go to England. On April 5 he wrote in his diary: "Worked for a little in the garden, then I went indoors. . . . I began to pack the belongings which I shall take with me if fate wills that I am to go to England."

In my book, *The Dissolution of an Empire*, I have given full details of my father's attempt to get the Imperial family safely out of Russia, his many interviews with M. Miliukoff, the newly appointed Minister for Foreign Affairs, his telegrams to the British Government, warning them of the growing power of the Soviet, and the weakness of the Provisional Government who, he said, would not be able to protect the Emperor if the Soviet demanded that he should be handed over to them, or, incited by extremists, attacked the Palace. His appeals for immediate action did not apparently fall on deaf ears, for on March 23 he received a telegram saying that a British cruiser would be sent to Port Romanoff to take the Imperial family to England, if arrangements could be made for their safe transport by the Murmansk railway. My father accordingly went again to see M. Miliukoff, who said that steps would be taken to protect the train as far as Port Romanoff. The Provisional Government, he added, would be very glad to get the Emperor safely out of Russia, though they would require a guarantee that if he reached England he would not leave again, so long as the war lasted. Through the intermediary of a neutral government, an undertaking was obtained from Germany not to molest the cruiser, and it only seemed necessary to wait till the Grand Duchess Marie, who was now out of danger, was well enough to travel.

But on April 10 came another telegram instructing my father to cancel all arrangements because the British Government feared that strikes would break out in the coal-mines and munition factories, the Labour Party having threatened to create industrial unrest if the Emperor was received in England. How violent this feeling was is shown by a speech made by a Labour Member of Parliament who came to Moscow in the spring of 1917, and, at a dinner given by the British colony, announced, "Now I am going to be diplomatic and tell you a secret. People are saying that the Tsar is going to England. Let me tell you at once, that this is not true. If he is not good enough for Russia, he is not good enough for us."

One can only hope that the Member of Parliament who made that speech had the grace to feel remorse and shame when he later heard the story of Ekaterinburg; but the responsibility for the tragedy rests to a certain degree with Mr.

Lloyd George, for it was he who predicted strikes and unrest, it was he who told the King that the danger to the Emperor had been grossly exaggerated, and who insinuated that the British Ambassador in Petrograd was an alarmist, completely under the influence of the old Court faction, and inclined to listen to all the fantastic, fabulous stories of scaremongers.

Meanwhile the prisoners at Tsarskoe were occupying the long days by making a new vegetable garden, taking walks within the prescribed limits, attending divine service, and, on warm days, bathing in the lake. The Grand Duchesses continued their studies with M. Gilliard, and although the Professor from the Conservatoire no longer came to give her lessons, Olga Nicholaievna spent hours at her piano. Now that so many of the former teachers were debarred from coming to Tsarskoe, the Emperor and Empress insisted on taking a part in their son's education, and the Emperor laughingly called M. Gilliard, "Mon cher collégue".

Nobody from the outside world was allowed to visit them, but they still received the papers, and the news they read was not consoling. Lenin and Trotsky, with their satellites, had arrived in Petrograd, having been given free passage through Germany in a guarded train. They were inciting the people to violence and revolt, and the Provisional Government seemed powerless to control the anarchy that was daily gaining ground. At the Front the soldiers were disobeying their officers, refusing to fight, and deserting in hundreds; powerless in his captivity, the Emperor watched the inglorious disintegration of his army.

Early in August the Imperial family were told that they were to be moved from Tsarskoe, news which at first filled them with elation, thinking that now at last they were to be taken to Livadia. Their hopes of the sunshine and warmth of the Crimea, however, were dashed when they received an order to take thick clothes with them. August 13 was the day fixed for their departure, and they were told to be ready to leave at midnight, for it was a cunning, diabolical habit invariably to fix any move or arrest during the hours of darkness.

With aching hearts the young Grand Duchesses visited their favourite haunts in the gardens, lingering sorrowfully on the little island in the lake that had been such a well-loved retreat, looking with wistful regret at the rows of vegetables they had planted, taking a last farewell of the two big bedrooms and the sitting-room they had shared, which held so many things they loved and could not take with them. For the last time, too, the Emperor and Empress walked slowly, hand in hand, through the rooms of the Palace in which they had lived so many years. In the sitting-room was a portrait of Marie Antoinette and her children, which the Empress had always loved: maybe she looked upon it now with dark foreboding. There were the big reception rooms with their parquet floors, their crystal chandeliers, the Emperor's study, where he had received so many foreign ambassadors, so many Ministers of State— would they ever return to this house, where every room, every picture, every table and chair, held memories of the past?

Sadly they said farewell to those remaining behind. Count and Countess Benckendorff, who had been with them for many years but now, on account of age and infirmity were unable to accompany them. Baroness Buxhoevenden, the Empress's lady-in-waiting, who was seriously ill. Mr. Gibbs, the English tutor who had not yet obtained permission to go with them. There were tears in many eyes, voices broken by sobs as they said good-bye; there were whispered blessings on those who were leaving for a far-away destination.

Among those to accompany the travellers were young Countess Hendrikoff, whom I remember looking radiant and lovely on the first day she had worn the ruby velvet dress of a *Demoiselle d'Honneur* attached to the Empress; Prince Dolgorouky, General Tatichtchef, M. Gilliard, Doctors Botkin and Derevenko, Mademoiselle Schneider, the Empress's secretary, her maid Mademoiselle Demidoff, the tall dark sailor Nagorny, who was so devoted to the Tsarevitch and always carried him when he was ill, some men servants, valets, maid, cooks and kitchenboys. This was the party that with their trunks and bags and coats, assembled at midnight in one of the big rooms of the Palace. Sitting on their boxes and suitcases, they were kept waiting for five long weary hours, while Government officials argued with workmen as to whether the train was to be allowed to leave.

Various reasons have been given for the action of the Provisional Government in sending the Emperor and his family to Tobolsk. Kerensky explains it by saying that he could not guarantee the safety of Tsarskoe if any serious riots broke out in the capital. Some people on the other hand declare that it was done in order to curry favour with the extremists, and that the Provisional Government thought they would win popularity by sending the Emperor, who in the past had banished people to Siberia, to Tobolsk. Others, again, say that the Soviet, hearing rumours of a rising in the army in favour of the Emperor, ordered the Provisional Government to remove him as far away as possible and that they were too weak and powerless to do otherwise.

The first months of their captivity at Tobolsk passed drearily, but in comparative peace. They inhabited the house of a former governor which had large rooms, and even a certain amount of comfort. They had sufficient food, were permitted occasionally to go under guard to a neighbouring church, and some members of their household were lodged near by, and were permitted to come and go without question. But they were watched continuously, there was only a small plot of garden in front of their house, only a courtyard where they could take a daily walk, a courtyard overlooked by the barracks, where soldiers were always leaning out of the windows. Feeling the lack of exercise acutely, the Emperor begged that he and his daughters might be allowed to saw logs of wood,

[ 227 ]

which would come in useful for heating in the winter months, and, permission having been obtained, this became their daily occupation.

They were now cut off completely, receiving only occasional letters, and no papers, except the local news-sheet. Watched and guarded by soldiers who were often surly and rude, the winter months passed in monotonous sameness. When the first frosts came the young Grand Duchesses, helped by M. Gilliard and Prince Dolgorouky, managed to erect an ice-hill in the courtyard, and sliding up and down this gave them for a time a certain amusement and pleasure. But it was soon destroyed by order of the Committee of Soldiers and they were left with the sole distraction of walking round and round the courtyard, or of sawing endless logs of wood.

There was no piano in the governor's house; deprived even of this comfort and joy, Olga Nicholaievna played games of cards in the evenings with her sisters, or, while the Emperor read aloud, made small gifts for her parents, and members of the household, or tried to alter and mend the few clothes she had been permitted to bring with her. How often, gazing out of the windows at the dreary, treeless road leading past the house, at the few people trudging along in the mud or snow, did her thoughts go back to the park at Tsarskoe, to the lovely white palace of Livadia with its flower-filled gardens, to journeys in the *Standard* along the coast of Finland, or to her rides in the woods of Peterhof. I remember seeing her there, reining in her horse at the edge of one of the small, willow-bordered canals, a young Diana on horseback, with the morning sun on her face, and the morning light in her eyes, which looked at me with a puzzled recognition, wondering what I was doing there.

In September the English tutor Mr. Gibbs obtained permission to join them, and his coming brought a little change into the dreary sameness of their days, for he had news of friends and happenings in Petrograd, though none were very encouraging. When Baroness Buxhoevenden, bravely risking the discomforts and perils of the journey, arrived in December, she was forbidden to enter the house, and had to find lodgings in the town. She could only wave to them from the road outside the windows, or send occasional messages through Countess Hendrikoff.

The Provisional Government fell in October 1917. Lenin and Trotsky were now in power, and new restrictions, new humiliations, were imposed on the prisoners in Tobolsk. The regiments that had at first guarded them, and been comparatively humane, were withdrawn, and were replaced by troops imbued with the Bolshevik doctrine. Orders were received that the prisoners were to be allowed only soldiers' rations, and the allowance they received to pay for these was so small that coffee and butter became prohibitive luxuries.

The winter days dragged on. News came that negotiations had been set on foot to conclude a separate peace with Germany, and the fact that his abdication had not saved Russia from ruin, had not inspired the army to continue the war, weighed heavily on the Emperor. Outwardly he remained resigned, showing no signs of his anxiety; neither he nor the Empress ever uttered a word of complaint, of discontent or vexation.

And then, on April 25, Yakovleff, the newly-appointed Commissar from Moscow, informed them that he had orders to take the Emperor away, intimating that he was to go to Moscow. The Tsarevitch had fallen gravely ill again, but, tortured though she was by anxiety, the Empress insisted upon accompanying her husband, and obtained permission to take her daughter the Grand Duchess Marie with her. It was the first time since their imprisonment that the family had been separated, and in his book M. Gilliard gives a description of that last evening at Tobolsk, and the despair and apprehensions that filled all their hearts.

Going up to the sitting-room after the evening meal, M. Gilliard found the Empress sitting on a sofa, with two of her daughters beside her, their faces swollen and blotched by crying. A sense of doom and foreboding oppressed them all, for nobody knew what fell purpose the new rulers of Russia had in their minds, or what their intentions were regarding the Emperor. All those present knew that he would never agree to put his signature to a treaty of peace with Germany, they realized the perils that confronted him, and the discomforts of the journey at that season, when the river was still covered by half-frozen ice, and it would be necessary to drive for miles along roads covered with snow and slush, instead of going by boat. However, none dared show their misgivings; the Emperor appeared serene and undaunted, the Empress showed no signs of fear, and seemed occupied only with anxiety for those who were being left behind.

It was not until she had gone to take farewell of her son that she lost her self-control, and her voice was broken by sobs when she begged M. Gilliard not to come outside to see them off, but to remain with the Tsarevitch.

It was again a midnight departure. In the bitter cold of the Siberian spring, the carriages waited—ordinary, open peasants' carts, with straw on the floor, only one of them boasting a hood. Seated by the side of the Tsarevitch, who was crying bitterly, M. Gilliard heard the noise of departure, the shouts of the guards and the drivers, the rattle of the wooden wheels, and a little later caught the sound of heavy, dragging footsteps on the stairs. Through the open door he saw the three Grand Duchesses, Olga, Tatiana and Anastasia Nicholaievna, pass along the passage, on their way to their room, clinging together, sobbing pitiably, forlorn and desolate in their desperate grief and fear.

On May 10 the soldiers who had accompanied the Emperor and Empress returned, and gave a description of that nightmare journey, of the bitter winds, the impassable roads, the arrival at Tioumen. Red Guards blocked their way there, refused to allow them to go on to Moscow and took them instead to

Ekaterinburg, where Prince Dolgorouky was thrown into prison. The Emperor and Empress and their daughter were taken to the house of a merchant named Ipatieff, together with Doctor Botkin and their three remaining servants.

The news was not consoling, but a few days later a company of Red Guards arrived, with orders to take everybody to Ekaterinburg. The three Grand Duchesses were overjoyed at the thought of rejoining their parents, and disregarded the warnings of both M. Gilliard and General Tatichtchef, who pleaded that the Tsarevitch was not yet well enough to travel, and tried to delay their departure. Nothing mattered, the Emperor's daughters said, so long as they were all together. Olga Nicholaievna certainly realized their terrible danger, for when on May 20 they started on their journey, she told Baroness Buxhoevenden whose repeated requests to be allowed to join them had now been granted that they were lucky to be still alive, and able to see their parents once more, whatever the future might bring.

M. Gilliard has described their arrival at Ekaterinburg. The train stopped some way outside the station, and from the window of the third-class carriage where he had been placed, he saw the sailor Nagorny pass, with the Tsarevitch in his arms, followed by the Emperor's three daughters, slipping ankle-deep in the mud that covered the road, staggering under the weight of their suitcases. The Grand Duchess Tatiana was further encumbered by her little dog, which she was holding in her arms. Nagorny turned back to try and help her, but he was brutally pushed forward by the guards who surrounded them, and when M. Gilliard attempted to get out of the train in order to go to her assistance, he found the door of his carriage locked, and was told by the soldiers to remain where he was.

Sitting there, imprisoned and helpless, he watched General Tatichtchef, Countess Hendrikoff, Mademoiselle Schneider, and several of the servants pass the window, passing hours in agonized anxiety and frustration waiting to be called out himself. At last, in the late afternoon, an officer of the guard opened the door of his carriage, and told him that he was free to go where he liked. He found Baroness Buxhoevenden, Mr. Gibbs, and Doctor Derevenko on the platform, having all of them, for some unknown reason, been set at liberty.

Why these four members of the household were spared whilst all the others were done to death has remained a mystery; but although they were free they were not permitted to enter the Ipatieff house. They could only pass it on the road, see the high palisade of wood surrounding it, which hid the windows from sight, could only dimly surmise how the family they had grown to love so deeply were faring within those walls, bereft of the loyal servants, who, of their own free will had followed them into captivity. Sverdlov, the valet, and Nagorny had been taken away and were shot a few days later; there remained only Dr. Botkin, Mademoiselle Demidoff, the Empress's maid, a cook, one or two menservants and a little kitchen-boy, aged fourteen.

Admiral Kolchak, supported by several Czech battalions, was meanwhile driving back the Red Armies in Siberia, and advancing on Ekaterinburg, filling the men who ruled Russia with anxiety lest their plans should after all miscarry; for the fate of the Imperial family had been determined in Moscow, although by cunning artifice it had been contrived that the blame should rest on the Ekaterinburg Soviet. There was one man in the Kremlin who was resolved that the plan should not miscarry, a man who held only a subordinate position, but of whom Lenin had said: "Stalin is infinitely more dangerous than Trotsky, his double-faced methods can only be measured by the intensity of his political frenzy, and the greatness of his ambition, which is unlimited." It was Stalin who said, "It is understood that Nicholas Romanoff must on no account be freed by the White Armies."

On June 23 Baroness Buxhoevenden, M. Gilliard, Doctor

Derevenko and Mr. Gibbs were ordered to leave Ekaterinburg. They were taken back to Tioumen, and kept prisoners there in the train until, on July 20, they were liberated by Admiral Kolchak's armies. When Ekaterinburg fell, a few days later, and communication was re-established, they made their way back there. Ignorant of what had happened, but desperate with anxiety, they hurried to the Ipatieff mansion. They found the doors open and an empty deserted house, rooms in a state of indescribable confusion, the stoves full of half-burnt clothing, heaps of ashes and cinders on the floors, in which were charred bits of hairbrushes, toothbrushes, buttons, safety-pins and hooks and eyes. With growing horror they continued their search, until at last they came to the basement, and to that room with the small barred window, where the walls were riddled with the marks of bullets, where the plaster was peeling off, and in one place there was a large gaping hole.

At first it was impossible to ascertain what had happened, or how many people had perished in that basement room. It was only many months later that the lawyer Sokoloff, instructed by Admiral Kolchak to make a searching requisition, was able to reconstruct the crime that had been committed on the night of July 16, the ghastly details of which need not be repeated. Bit by bit the evidences and depositions were pieced together, and at last, after endless search, the distant place in the forest was found where Yourovsky and his companions had burnt the bodies, having made their careful preparation for days beforehand, gradually carrying there three hundred litres of benzine and a hundred and seventy-five kilogrammes of sulphuric acid. "The world will never know what we have done with them," Voikoff, one of the murderers, boasted; telegraphing to Moscow, Beloborodoff, the Commissar at Ekaterinburg, declared with specious sophistry, "Officially the family will perish during evacuation."

The tragedy of Ekaterinburg has been told before, so much has happened since, and people's memories are short. But because the Grand Duchess Olga Nicholaievna was not known by many, and was loved by all the few who came in contact with her, I have outlined it again very briefly, in the hopes that those who read her story may perhaps remember with pity what was done to her. Not because she was the daughter of an Emperor, and the great-granddaughter of Queen Victoria, but because she was young and gay and gallant, and steadfast until the end.

Not quite twenty-two years had passed since Queen Victoria held "Dear Baby Olga, so big and beautiful", on her knees; but how far removed were those peaceful autumn days at Balmoral from that basement room in Ekaterinburg! What worlds apart for this young girl, who spent sixteen months of her short life as a prisoner, who, during the last weeks of her martyrdom had to sit at table with her drunken, brutal jailers, who was watched every hour of the day and night by men who gloated over her humiliation. This young girl was sacrificed to her father's indecision, to his vain attempt to save Russia from civil war, to her mother's mistaken policy, and to the besotted blindness of those who refused to recognize the danger which threatened her, and would not lift a finger to save her.

# Bibliography

*The Letters of Queen Victoria.*

*The Letters of the Empress Frederick.*

*The Letters of Princess Alice.*

*The Story of My Life*, Queen Marie of Roumania, 1934.

*The Downfall of Three Dynasties*, Count Egon Corti, 1934.

*A Biographer's Notebook*, Hector Bolitho, 1950.

*I Live Again*, Princess Ileana, 1952.

*Avant l'Exil*, Prince Yusupoff, 1952.

*Louis of Battenberg*, Sir Mark Kerr, 1934.

*My Fifty Years*, Prince Nicholas of Greece.

*Memoirs*, Prince Christopher of Greece, 1938.

*The Royal House of Greece*, Arthur Gould Lee, 1948.

*I Was to be Empress*, Princess Stephanie, 1937.

*Rudolf; the Tragedy of Mayerling*, Count Carl Lonyay, 1950.

*Embassies of Other Days*, Lady Paget, 1923.

*The Linings of Life*, Lady Paget, 1928.

*Aus dem Leben der Grafin Lonya*, Marie von Z . . . Z.

*H.I.H. Grand Duchess Elizabeth*, Countess Olsoufieff.

*Nicholas II*, Princess C. Radziwill, 1931.

*Royal Cavalcade*, Erica Beale.

*Ferdinand de Bulgarie Intime*, Alexandre Hep.

*Ferdinand of Bulgaria*, H. R. Madol, 1931.

*Old Diplomacy*, Lord Hardinge of Penshurst, 1947.

*Recollections of a Bulgarian Diplomat's Wife*, Madame Anna Stancioff, 1931.

*The Empress Frederick*, Princess Radziwill, 1934.

*She Caused World Chaos*, E. E. P. Tisdall, 1940.

*The Kaiser and English Relations*, E. F. Benson, 1936.

*Gross Herzog Ernst Ludwig*, Max Wauer.

*Le Tragique Destin de Nicholas II*, Pierre Gilliard, 1921.

*Memories of Forty Years*, Princess Radziwill.

*Queen Alexandra*, Sir George Arthur, 1934.

*Crown Prince Rudolf*, Baron von Mitis, 1928.

*Tragic Romance of Alexander II*, M. Paléologue, 1926.

*The Court of Russia*, E. Brayley Hodgetts, 1908.

*Intimate Life of the Last Tsarina*, Princess Radziwill, 1929.

*Life and Tragedy of the Empress Alexandra*, Baroness Buxheovenden, 1920.

*Index*

# Index

## A

ALBANY, DUKE OF, 9, 171
Albert, Prince Consort, 5, 6, 9, 47, 48, 54, 64, 69, 118, 135, 165, 167
Alexander II, Emperor of Russia, 63, 89, 90, 92, 93, 99, 112, 114–118 ; as Tsarevitch, 165–167, 170, 206
Alexander III of Russia, 96, 99, 100, 118, 140, 141, 146, 170, 206
Alexander, King of Greece, 185
Alexander, King of Serbia, 151
Alexander, Prince of Battenberg, 14, 16, 140, 142, 143, 144, 146, 170, 172
Alexander of Hesse, 49, 51, 52, 56, 58, 63, 89, 91, 167, 169, 170, 172
Alexandra, Princess of Wales (later Queen), 9, 51, 54, 59, 103, 134, 174, 175
Alexandra of Edinburgh, 114
Alfred of Edinburgh, 117, 127
Alice, Princess, Grand Duchess of Hesse, 13, 23, 24, 47–66, 88, 91, 114
Alix of Hesse (later Empress Alexandra), 25, 26, 29, 30, 31, 39, 42, 44, 58, 59, 64, 95, 96, 99, 100, 102, 103, 108, 109, 111, 168, 174, 175, 176, 185, 195, 207, 208, 210, 211, 212, 215, 219–225, 229, 230, 231
Anastasia, Grand Duchess of Mecklenburg Schwerin, 194
Anastasia Nicholaievna, Grand Duchess, 220, 230
Andrew, Prince of Greece, 174, 175, 177, 179, 182, 183, 184, 186, 188, 189
Angeli, 143
Arthur, Prince (later Duke of Connaught), 101
Arthur, Prince of Connaught, 215
Augusta, Empress of Germany (wife of William I), 13
Augusta Victoria of Schleswig-Holstein (wife of William II), 13
August, Prince of Coburg, 73, 139

## B

BADEN, GRAND DUKE OF, 62, 63
Bagration, Princess, 206

Battenberg, Princess, 168, 169
Battenberg Family. See Prince Louis, etc.
Bavaria, King of, 52
Beatrice, Princess (daughter of Queen Victoria), 171, 172
Beatrice of Edinburgh, 117
Beattie, Sir David, 216
Beloborodoff, 233
Benckendorff, Count and Countess, 222, 226
Berchtold, Count, 160
Bevan, Aneurin, 190
Bismarck, 4, 8, 9, 11, 13, 14, 16, 17, 53, 54, 62, 63, 140, 169, 170
Boehm, 66
Bombelles, 85
Boris, Prince (later King of Bulgaria), 146, 147, 157, 159, 163
Boris, Grand Duke, 127
Botkin, Dr., 226, 232
Bourbolon, Count de, 142
Brown, John, 64
Buchanan, Sir George, 19, 25, 31, 34, 35, 40, 121, 128, 129, 149, 150, 153, 157, 158, 193, 196, 202–204, 223, 225
Buchanan, Lady Georgina, 19, 26, 30, 35, 38, 39, 67, 80, 83, 225
Buxhoevenden, 226, 228, 232

## C

CAROL, KING OF ROUMANIA, 120, 121–123, 126, 127, 130
Carol, Prince (later King of Roumania), 122, 128, 129, 130, 132, 134, 135, 215, 216
Catherine the Great, 155, 209
Cecilia, Princess, Grand Duchesse of Hess, 45, 189
Charlotte, Princess, 69
Christian, King of Denmark, 52, 54, 56
Christopher, Prince of Greece, 176, 187
Churchill, Sir Winston, 190
Clarence, Duke of, 121
Clementine of Orleans, Princess of Coburg, 139, 140, 142, 145, 146, 149, 156, 159

[ 239 ]

Constantine, Grand Duke, 111
Constantine, King of Greece, 179, 180–206. *See also* Duke of Sparta
Cromie, Captain, 68
Cyril, Grand Duke, 33, 127, 193–206, 220
Cyril, Grand Duchess, 132, 135, 193–206, 220. *See also* Princess Victoria of Edinburgh
Cyril, Prince of Bulgaria, 146, 163

**D**

DEMIDOFF, MADEMOISELLE, 227, 232
Derevenko, Dr., 226
Dimitri, Grand Duke, 201, 202, 215
Dino, Duchesse de, 69
Disraeli, 4
Dobbrovitch, M., 151, 153
Dolgorouky, Catherine, 90, 93
Dolgorouky, Prince, 226, 228, 231
Downes, Mr., 207

**E**

EDINBURGH, PRINCE ALFRED DUKE OF, 30, 52, 56, 91, 99, 114, 115, 119, 120, 121, 127
Edinburgh, Grand Duchess Marie, Duchess of, 56, 91, 114–117, 119–121, 125, 131
Edward VII, 41, 149, 150, 152. *See also* Prince of Wales
Egerton, Lady, 178
Eleanor Reuss Köstritz, Queen of Bulgaria, 156, 160
Elizabeth, Queen of Roumania (Carmen Sylva), 126, 130, 216
Elizabeth, Empress of Austria, 75, 78, 85
Elizabeth, Princess of Hesse (later Grand Duchess Serge), 13, 39, 44, 59, 88, 92, 94, 98, 100, 102–112, 176, 185, 193, 220
Elizabeth, Princess of Roumania, 122
Elizabeth, Princess (daughter of Ernst Ludwig), 3, 4, 33, 36, 37, 40, 41–43
Ella. *See* Princess Elizabeth of Hesse
Ernst Ludwig, Grand Duke of Hesse, 3, 23, 24, 25, 27–30, 32–36, 37, 38, 39, 40, 42–46, 58, 61, 64, 99, 103, 122, 127, 174, 176, 219
Eudoxia, Princess of Bulgaria, 164

**F**

FERDINAND, PRINCE OF COBURG, KING OF BULGARIA, 73, 103, 139–164
Ferdinand, Crown Prince (later King of Roumania), 120, 121, 123, 132, 133, 134
Ferdinand, Prince Coburg Kohary, King of Portugal, 69, 139
Ferdinand, Prince of Coburg, 139
Franz Joseph, Emperor of Austria, 52, 81, 82, 83, 145, 147
Franz Joseph, Prince of Battenberg, 26
Fraser, Admiral, 189
Frederica, Queen of Greece, 191
Frederick, King of Denmark, 54
Frederick William, Prince of Hesse (Fritty), 24, 58, 59, 61, 209
Frederick William, Prince of Prussia (later Emperor Frederick), 5, 6, 7, 9, 10, 12, 14–17, 63
Frederick, Empress, 16–22, 146, 174, 180. *See also* Victoria, Princess Royal

**G**

GEDDES, SIR AUCKLAND, 45
George, Prince (later King George V), 119, 130, 132, 225
George Donatius of Hesse, 45
George of Hesse, 45
George, Grand Duke of Russia, 120
George, Prince Battenberg, 173
George IV, 69
George, King of Greece, 174, 178, 179
George II, King of Greece, 187, 189, 190, 191
George, Prince of Greece, 176, 181
Gethin, 162
Gibbs, Mr., 226, 228, 232, 233
Giers, M. de, 142
Giovanna, Princess of Italy, Queen of Bulgaria, 161, 163
Goethe, 24, 174
Goremykin, M., 219
Gosford, Lord, 175
Grancy, Fräulein von, 36
Grenaud, Comte de, 142, 162
Grey, Sir Edward, 181
Grey, Lady Sybil, 218

**H**

HARDINGE, LORD, 142
Hauk, Julia von, 168
Helena, Princess, 56
Helen of Greece, 134

Helen, Grand Duchess. *See* Princess Nicholas of Greece
Henrikoff, Countess, 226, 229, 231
Henry, Prince of Prussia, 12, 13, 16
Herder, 24
Hesse Darmstadt, Grand Duke of, 49, 50, 51, 54, 56
Hesse Darmstadt, 49, 50, 63, 65, 88
Hesse Darmstadt, Landgraf Louis, 24
Hitler, Adolf, 113
Hohenzollern, Prince Leopold, 11
Hoyos, Count, 84

I

IHNE, HERR, 18
Ileana, Princess, 135, 137
Irene, Princess of Hesse, 16, 55, 95

J

JENNER, SIR WILLIAM, 64
Joanna of Hesse, 45
Jonnard, M., 184

K

KALNOCKY, COUNT, 140
Kasper Mitzi, 73, 75
Kaulbach, 29
Kent, Duke of, 190
Kent, Victoria, Princess of Leiningen, Duchess of, 48, 69
Kerensky, 223, 227
Kohary, Count, 139
Korniloff, General, 222
Kyra, Princess, 199, 206

L

LAMBRINO, ZIZI, 132, 134
Lascelles, Sir Frank, 2
Leiningen, Prince of, 206
Lenin, 225, 229
Leopold of Coburg, King of the Belgians, 47, 69, 70, 72, 165
Leopold II, King of the Belgians, 69, 70, 71, 72, 74, 85
Leopold, Prince (later Duke of Albany), 9
Leuchtenberg, Duke of, 215
Lloyd George, David, 186, 225
Lonya, Count, 86
Louis, Prince of Hesse (later Grand Duke), 10, 47, 48, 50, 51, 57, 61, 63, 64, 95, 168, 171

Louis, present Grand Duke of Hesse, 45, 46
Louis, Prince of Battenberg, 169, 171, 172. *See also* Milford Haven
Louis Philippe, King of France, 139
Louis Ferdinand of Prussia, 206
Louise, Princess of Belgium, 39, 71, 73, 77, 86
Louise, Princess of Battenberg, 107, 172, 174, 185
Louise, Marie, of Orleans, 69
Louise, Queen of Prussia, 89
Lupesco, Helen, 134

M

MACKENZIE, MOREL, 15, 16, 17
Malinoff, M., 159
Margaret of Prussia, Princess Frederick Charles of Hesse, 19
Maria de Gloria, Queen of Portugal, 69, 139
Marie of Edinburgh, Crown Princess and Queen of Roumania, 28, 32, 36, 39, 96, 97, 112, 114, 117, 119–138, 174, 193, 204, 205, 215
Marie of Hesse, Empress of Russia, 24, 49, 51, 52, 88–95, 112, 166, 167, 168, 170, 212
Marie Feodorovna, Dowager Empress (widow of Alexander III), 94, 102, 118, 197, 218, 220
Marie Henriette, Queen of the Belgians, 69, 70, 71, 72, 74, 85
Marie of Hesse (daughter of Princess Alice), 24, 58, 64
Marie Bonaparte, Princess of Greece, 181
Marie, Princess (daughter of Grand Duchess Cyril), 199, 206
Marie Louise of Bourbon Parma, 145, 146, 147, 149
Marie Nicholaievna (daughter of Nicholas II), 221, 222, 224, 229
Marina, Princess, 179, 190
Markoff, General, 154
Melbourne, Lord, 166
Metternich, Princess Pauline, 140, 142
Michael Alexandrovitch, Grand Duke (brother of Nicholas II), 222
Michael Micholaievitch, Grand Duke, 194
Milford Haven, Lord and Lady, 92, 107, 112, 119, 170, 171, 173, 188. *See also* Louis of Battenberg

Mircea, Prince, 131, 132
Muir, Lady, 162

**N**

NADEJDA, PRINCESS OF BULGARIA,
DUCHESS OF WÜRTTEMBERG, 164
Nagorny, 227, 231, 232
Napoleon I, 69
Napoleon II, 11, 55, 59
Nicholas I, Emperor of Russia, 89, 90,
165, 167
Nicholas II, Emperor of Russia, 31, 33,
39, 42, 99, 100, 101, 107, 108, 109,
111, 122, 123, 130, 147, 176, 183,
185, 195, 196, 198, 201, 202, 207,
208, 210, 215, 217–219, 221–232
Nicholas, Prince of Greece, 38, 176,
179, 181–184, 187
Nicholas, Princess of Greece, 177, 179,
181, 187, 189
Nicholas, Prince of Roumania, 132
Nicholas Nicholaievitch, Grand Duke,
218

**O**

O'CONNOR, SIR NICHOLAS, 101, 102
Olga Nicholaievna, Grand Duchess, 39,
128, 207–218, 220, 222, 225, 228,
230, 231, 234
Olga, Grand Duchess, Princess of
Württemberg, 167
Olga, Queen of Greece, 178, 185, 187

**P**

PAGET, LADY MURIEL, 218
Paget, Walburga, Lady, 79, 141
Paléologue, M., 218
Paley, Prince, 111
Palmerston, Lord, 53, 166
Paris, Comte de, 99
Parma, Duke of, 145, 146
Paul, Grand Duke, 24, 91, 106, 111,
220, 221
Paul of Yugoslavia, 190
Paul, King of Greece, 191
Peter, King of Serbia, 151
Philip, Prince, 188, 189
Philip, Prince of Coburg, 73, 84, 86
Philip, Count of Flanders, 71
Poincaré, M., 217
Ponsonby, Sir Frederick, 22
Protopopoff, 201

**R**

RADZIWILL, PRINCESS, 102, 107

Rasputin, 201, 210
Rodzianko, 220
Rudolf, Crown Prince of Austria, 69,
73–79, 80–86, 141

**S**

SALISBURY, LORD, 144, 146
Sanderson, Lord, 33
Saxe Coburg Gotha, Duke Ernst of,
25, 49
Saxe Coburg Saalfeld, Duchess of, 139
Saxe Weimar, Princess of, 132
Schleswig-Holstein, Prince Albert of,
124
Schleswig-Holstein, Prince Frederick
of, 53
Schneider, Mlle, 226, 231
Schratt, Catherine, 86
Serge, Grand Duke, 24, 39, 91, 92, 93,
96–98, 102, 103, 105, 118, 135
Serge, Grand Duchess, 13, 39, 44, 59,
88, 92, 94, 98, 100, 102–112, 176,
185, 193, 220. See also Elizabeth,
Princess of Hesse
Sigismund, Prince, 10
Solms Hohensolms, Eleanor, 43
Sophie, Arch Duchess, 78
Sophie, Queen of Greece, 12, 18, 180,
181, 182, 183, 184
Sparta, Duke of, 18, 39
Stalin, 232
Stambuloff, 143, 145, 146
Stancioff, Dimitri, 142, 161
Stephanie, Crown Princess of Austria,
68, 71–87
Stürmer, 201
Sverdlov, 232

**T**

TALBOT, CAPTAIN GERALD, 187
Tatiana Nicholaievna, Grand Duchess,
211, 214, 220, 231
Taticheff, General, 226, 231
Tcharikoff, M., 147
Texter, Fräulein, 174
Theophane, Archimandrite, 210
Toerring, Count, 190
Trotzky, 225, 229
Tsarevitch, 210, 220, 221, 227, 229–231

**V**

VARVARA, SISTER, 111, 112
Venizelos, 186
Vetsera, Mary, 82, 83, 84

## INDEX

Victoire, Duchesse de Nemours, 139
Victoria, Princess Royal, Crown Princess of Prussia, 5, 6, 7, 8, 9–15. *See also* Empress Frederick
Victoria, Princess of Hesse, 24, 27, 51, 59, 63, 92, 171, 173. *See also* Milford Haven
Victoria Melita of Edinburgh, Grand Duchess of Hesse, 3, 30–36, 38–43, 99, 103, 114, 119, 122, 124, 174, 193, 194. *See also* Grand Duchess Cyril.
Vladimir Alexandrovitch, Grand Duke, 118, 123, 193, 195
Vladimir, Grand Duchess, 156, 177, 185
Vladimir, Grand Duke (son of Grand Duke Cyril), 204, 205, 206
Voekoff, 233

**W**

WALDEMAR, PRINCE, 13
Wales, Prince of, 9, 10, 12, 35, 39, 51, 52, 53, 59, 60, 65, 103, 117, 169, 172, 174. *See also* Edward VII

Wales, Prince Edward of, 206, 215
Wauer, Max, 25
William, King of Prussia (later Emperor of Germany), 9, 11, 15, 54, 62, 169, 170, 183
William, Prince of Prussia (later Emperor William II), 11, 12, 13, 14, 16, 17, 18, 21, 29, 39, 44, 62, 79, 83, 94, 95, 103, 110, 127, 144, 180, 183
Wilson, Miss, 37, 208
Winterhalter, 143
Württemberg, Duchess of, 176
Wyroubova, 211

**Y**

YAKOVLEFF, 229
Yourovsky, 233
Yusupoff, Princess, 122
Yusupoff, Prince Felix, 123

**X**

ZWEIBRUCKEN BIRKENFELD, CAROLINE, 24

This book is to be returned on or before
the last date stamped below.